Conrad's Trojan Horses

Tom Henthorne

Foreword by Andrea White

Conrad's Trojan Horses

Imperialism, Hybridity, & the Postcolonial Aesthetic

Texas Tech
University Press

This book is typeset in Adobe Caslon. The paper used in this book meets the minimum requirements of ANSI/NISO Z39.48–1992 (R1997). ♾

Designed by Lindsay Starr

LIBRARY OF CONGRESS CATALOGING-IN-PUBLICATION DATA
Henthorne, Tom.
Conrad's Trojan horses : imperialism, hybridity, and the postcolonial aesthetic / Tom Henthorne ; foreword by Andrea White.
p. cm.
Summary: "Examines Conrad's efforts to cloak his political leanings with a Trojan horse strategy and other postcolonial techniques, in order to satisfy conservative publishers and ensure himself a larger imperial audience. Analyzes both major and early works, as well as Conrad's influence on modernist and postcolonial writers"—Provided by publisher.
Includes bibliographical references (p.) and index.
ISBN-13: 978-0-89672-633-8 (hardcover: alk. paper)
ISBN-10: 0-89672-633-9 (hardcover: alk. paper)
1. Conrad, Joseph, 1857-1924—Criticism and interpretation. 2. Conrad, Joseph, 1857-1924—Political and social views. 3. Imperialism in literature. 4. Postcolonialism in literature. 5. Postmodernism (Literature)—Great Britain. 6. Modernism (Literature)—Great Britain. I. Title.
PR6005.O4Z7434 2008
823'.912—dc22

2008000839

Printed in the United States of America
08 09 10 11 12 13 14 15 16 / 9 8 7 6 5 4 3 2 1

TEXAS TECH UNIVERSITY PRESS
Box 41037, Lubbock, Texas 79409–1037 USA
800.832.4042 | ttup@ttu.edu | www.ttup.ttu.edu

Contents

Foreword

As readers and students of literary texts, we are familiar with the hidden, the concealed, and the repressed as concerns central to psychoanalytic inquiry. We have learned to read texts as analysts, suspecting the Freudian iceberg whose silences are made manifest only in occasional, flickering glimpses. We have learned to suspect the text itself of unconsciously concealing its secrets, which are only unwittingly revealed through verbal slips and apparent strangenesses. And as readers of Joseph Conrad, we have become familiar with the concerns in his novels and stories with secret selves, secret sharers, and uncanny doppelgängers whose mysteries are rarely made entirely manifest.

It is something of a puzzle, then, to recall Conrad's own pronouncements about the function and responsibility of the artist, which were—as he famously declared in his preface to *The Nigger of the "Narcissus"*—to make us see. The artist, he writes, "speaks to our capacity for delight and wonder, to the sense of mystery surrounding our lives"; at the same time, as he goes on to say, the artist's task is "by the power of the written word to make you hear, to make you feel—it is, before all, to make you *see.*" The aim of art, he continues a few paragraphs later, like life itself, is "obscured by mists," and is, apparently, only definable in privatives: it is "not in the clear logic of a triumphant conclusion; it is not in the unveiling of one of those heartless secrets which are called the Laws of Nature" (xv–xvi). To make us see that which remains veiled, to make us understand the mystery of a visible universe obscured by mists: the artist's task is a difficult one indeed, and the Conradian reader/critic has been accordingly challenged as well. Most have noticed, either with delight and wonder, or with dismissive confusion, that Conrad's prose conceals as it reveals.

As early as 1924, only days before Conrad's death, "The Art of Conrad" was published in *La Nouvelle Revue Française.* In it the French critic Ramon Fernandez wrote that

> few writers have more knowingly hidden their universe from the grasp of the intelligence. By this very skill in projecting the mystery . . . Conrad sets himself off from his fellow Slavs. For them the world is in fact incomprehensible and sometimes, yes sometimes, in spite of themselves; with Conrad on the other hand the precise intelligence of man as observer comes to terms with the emotion of man as actor, but the intelligence instead of interpreting the experience, calls up through creation of an atmospheric picture, the obscure coming into being of the event. A thoughtful mastery of things beyond the grasp of thought, such is the impression which his best books leave on us. (Stallman 8)

And, he adds, the "tentative quality of the commentary throws the weight of the narrative on to the acuteness of the reader's intuition" (12).

Fernandez understood Conrad's interest in representing, rather than explaining, the mysterious nature of experience as well as the collaborative nature of reading Conrad, the kind of dialogue that had to take place between reader and text so one could experience "the obscure coming into being of the event" while living within the mystery, one might even say the paradox, of trusting to the writer's "thoughtful mastery of things beyond the grasp of thought." From the beginning, metaphors of concealment and revelation informed critical commentary on Conrad's texts. As early as 1902, Edward Garnett spoke of *Heart of Darkness* as an unblurring, a revelation of that which had been formerly concealed; he saw it as "a page torn from the life of the Dark Continent—a page which has been hitherto carefully blurred and kept away from European eyes" (Sherry 133). More recently, Edward Said described *Nostromo* as "the great novel of empire and imperial arrogance" that "illuminates what had been, in the press and in the world, kept under wraps." What was concealed, Said continued, "which Conrad brings out with ruthless tenacity, was that these schemes [by missionaries for the "improvement" of the natives] were also for the benefit of the people creating the schemes" (Kaplan 291).

Tom Henthorne also finds the quality of hiddenness central to Conrad's texts. But rather than attributing that quality to psychoanalytic repression or the text's unconscious or poststructural undecidability, Henthorne—preferring Bakhtin to Bhabha—argues that it is a case of intentional hybridity, conscious political subversion, a smuggling into an otherwise compliant-seeming text of radical countertexts that put in question ruling paradigms. His Trojan Horse theory, that Conrad's writing is of necessity double, accounts for the direction Conrad's texts took, becoming more, not less, politically conservative between the writing of *Outcast of the Islands* (1896) and *Nostromo* (1904). It was as he began that novel, in the flush of *Youth*'s success, that he had begun to feel more confident and thus less inclined to conceal his rather unpopular condemnation of imperialism from his conservative publishers and the reading public generally, whose approbation he depended on in the early days of his writing career. During those years, however, Conrad worked to smuggle in his more resistant thoughts through irony, silences, subterfuges, multiple points of view, and misdirection. Through his heteroglossia, he "mastered the art of revealing through concealment," Henthorne argues here.

Henthorne's theory makes productive use of Bakhtin's ideas about "intentional hybridity," in which alternative perspectives are set against one another dialogically. Conrad, Henthorne claims, "concealed radical critiques of imperialism in seemingly innocuous tales set in exotic places" (9), and he did so through various narrative strategies, such as multiple narration, *style indirect libre,* and dramatic irony, that allowed him the subterfuge and misdirection necessary to his task of simultaneously veiling and unveiling. Henthorne's Trojan horse framework explains the somewhat surprising direction Conrad's texts followed, becoming less openly anti-imperialistic after his second novel and the hard-to-place "Outpost of Progress," rather than more pronounced; it also leads him to the assertion that Conrad was not only not a proponent of imperialism but rather a postcolonial writer himself, whose modernist techniques actually spearheaded postcolonial heteroglossia. Of course it was these very qualities that led many to fault Conrad's texts for their evasiveness, obfuscation, and mistiness, but rather than attributing these features to "modernist difficulty," Henthorne argues that these difficulties of tone and intention are the very features of a postcolonial aesthetic. The duplicity of Conrad's double-voiced texts, inherently antiauthoritarian hybrids that seemingly reinforce while actually challenging the hegemonic order, is a feature of postcolonial texts as well. Conrad's texts actually helped "establish the postcolonial novel as a viable genre" (277), Henthorne convincingly argues here.

In part, the veiling comes from silences of our own rather than in the text, a concern that initially prompted Henthorne's thoughts, as his introduction explains. In fact, this study takes up that question—What has prevented readers until this time from reading Conrad as postcolonial?—as a real, rather than a rhetorical, one and goes on to demonstrate the hiddenness of that which exceeds the limits of our horizons of expectations. For example, Henthorne points out that *Almayer's Folly* wasn't read as a subversion because readers couldn't see Nina as a protagonist. Not only was she female but the child of a Dutch father and a Malaysian mother, and as such, she was invisible to contemporary readers as an agent crucial to the novel's actions and its anticolonialist insurgency, so complete was her otherness.

In fact, after Conrad's reemergence on the critical scene in the 1940s—after something of a decline in the 1920s and 1930s—the political engagement of his writing remained invisible as well. Formalist studies emphasized his modernist aesthetic, others his psychological depths. Albert Guérard wrote *Conrad the Novelist* in 1958 in part as a correction to his earlier 1947 monograph. In that earlier work, he admitted, he hadn't "given Conrad his political due" (ix): "I undervalued Conrad [in the political area] because I found so few concrete references to the specific issues and conflicts of his time. It has taken the full aftermath of the Second World War to make me recognize [his] political insights" (xi). Eloise Hay's *The Political Novels of Joseph Conrad* (1963) and Avrom Fleishman's *Conrad's Politics: Community and Anarchy in the Fiction of Joseph Conrad* (1967), among others, followed Guérard's study, opening Conradian texts to more political understandings that, as it turned out, had been hidden in plain sight all along.

Henthorne's careful scrutiny of Conrad's early novels and stories helps us hear the tangle of voices in Conrad's texts, the irreconcilable antagonisms, the opacities and circumspections, and the negotiating and countering that the many voices accomplish; it makes us *see* and understand them anew. His study contributes to an unblurring of its own, bringing light to a particularly vexed aspect of modernist and Conrad studies.

Andrea White

Carson, California, 2008

Works Cited

Conrad, Joseph. *The Nigger of the "Narcissus."* Garden City, N.J.: Doubleday, Page & Company, 1923.

Fleishman, Avrom. *Conrad's Politics: Community and Anarchy in the Fiction of Joseph Conrad.* Baltimore: Johns Hopkins University Press, 1967.

Guérard, Albert. *Conrad the Novelist.* Cambridge, Mass.: Harvard University Press, 1962.

Hay, Eloise Knapp. *The Political Novels of Joseph Conrad: A Critical Study.* Chicago: University of Chicago Press, 1963.

Kaplan, Carola, Peter Mallios, and Andrea White, eds. *Conrad in the Twenty-First Century: Contemporary Approaches and Perspectives.* New York: Routledge, 2005.

Sherry, Norman. *Joseph Conrad: The Critical Heritage.* London: Routledge & Kegan Paul, 1973.

Stallman, R.W., ed. *Joseph Conrad: A Critical Symposium.* East Lansing: Michigan State University Press, 1960.

Acknowledgments

This book would not have been possible without Juliet, Zane, and Paul Way-Henthorne, all of whom were helping even when they didn't know it. I would also like to thank my Pace colleagues Jeannie Chiu, Kristen di Gennaro, Martha Driver, Amy Foerster, Karla Jay, Bill Offutt, Trisha Pender, Nancy Reagin, Jonathan Silverman, and Catherine Zimmer for their patience and support. Sid Ray deserves special thanks for reading the entire manuscript in bits and pieces over and over again, helping me to figure out what I was trying to say and how to say it. Paul Hernadi, Shirley Geok-lin, Wally Chafe, Kerry Kaneshiro, and Tracy Tennenhouse also helped me formulate my ideas, as did Eloise Hay and Frank McConnell, both of whom are missed now more than ever. And, of course, there are all the Conradians who have guided me over the years: Bruce Harkness, Carola Kaplan, John Peters, and Andrea White to name a few. I'd also like to acknowledge gratefully the staff of Pace University's Birnbaum Library, particularly Elisabeth Birnbaum, Amermel Denton, Chloe Pimera, and Madeleine Rizzo, and the staff at the Rosenbach and Huntington libraries, all of whom are wonderful. Critical funding was provided by Pace University's Scholarly Research Committee and Dyson College. Finally, I'd like to thank Misty Gonzales, Lindsey Lee, Richard Nardi, Mike Pierry, Sue Smith, Joe Sudano, and Lee Transue.

I don't know how to thank Patricia Way, my partner, for everything over the years, including her belief that this project was worth pursuing while we were struggling to do so many other things. And thanking the Scaleras—Holly, Tomm, Ruby, and Jack—is difficult too, because thanks are not enough for the people who do the most. Finally, I have to thank my parents, particularly my mother, for teaching me how to argue; Nancy and Susan, for being good friends and good sisters; and my brother, Bill, who forced his way through Conrad novels because he cared about what I was doing.

Conrad's Trojan Horses

Introduction

> But I will confess to you under seal of secrecy that *I don't believe* I am such as I appear to mediocre minds.
>
> JOSEPH CONRAD in a letter to Arthur Symons, August 29, 1908 (*Letters* 4:114)

At a 2002 Modern Language Association panel entitled "The Postcolonial Conrad," the respondent Andrea White asked the panelists why, if Conrad's works could indeed be understood as postcolonial, no one had recognized them as such before. The answer, of course, is that they had been, at least by a number of postcolonial writers. Although some, including Chinua Achebe, consider Conrad to be a proponent of imperialism, many others, including Jorge Luis Borges, V. S. Naipaul, and Gabriel García Márquez, acknowledge him as an important influence (Moore 231, 234). Even Ngugi wa Thiong'o, who argues that Conrad was "unable to condemn British imperialism or rid himself of the very racism he correctly saw as inherent in colonialism," seems to recognize Conrad's postcoloniality, writing, "The African writer and Joseph Conrad share the same world and that is why Conrad's work is so familiar. Both have lived in a world dominated by imperialism" (Thiong'o 72). Peter Nazareth goes even further, identifying Conrad as a "Third-World Writer" and claiming that he and a number of other postcolonial writers, including Tayeb Salih, Lloyd Fernando, and Wilson Harris, are his "descendents."[1]

Whether Conrad can be classified as "postcolonial" depends, of course, on how one defines the term. Certainly, Conrad is not postcolonial if one uses the term only to describe the period of decolonization that immediately followed World War II since he died in 1924.[2] If, however, following Bill Ashcroft, Gareth Griffiths, and Helen Tiffin, one employs the term "to cover all the culture affected by the imperial process from the moment of colonization to the present day," then Conrad can be understood as postcolonial since he addressed imperialism directly in most of his work (2). Such a definition has obvious uses, if only because it recognizes that writers such as Achebe, who began writing while their nations were still colonies, did not suddenly become postcolonial the moment their nations attained political independence. The definition is so broad, however, that using it, one might consider Rudyard Kipling to be postcolonial, or Katherine Mansfield, or even Paul Scott.

In "The Postcolonization of the (Latin) American Experience," Jorge de Alva offers a more discriminating definition, suggesting "that postcoloniality can best be thought of as a form of contestatory/oppositional consciousness, emerging from either preexisting imperial, colonial, or ongoing subaltern conditions, which fosters processes aimed at revising the norms and practices of antecedent or still vital forms of domination" (245). This definition has a distinct advantage over the one offered by Ashcroft et al. since its focus is on oppositional subjectivity, and thus it has the potential at least to distinguish "colonialist" writers such as Rider Haggard and Isak Dinesen from "colonial" ones such as Olive Schreiner and Bessie Head.[3] If one were to apply de Alva's definition to Conrad, then it would be difficult to argue that Conrad was not postcolonial, at least early in his career, since he challenged imperialist ideology directly in works such as *Almayer's Folly, An Outcast of the Islands,* and "An Outpost of Progress." And if one were to follow Peter Hulme in using the term *postcolonial* in a "descriptive" rather than "evaluative" way to refer to "a process of disengagement from the whole colonial syndrome, which takes many forms and is probably inescapable for all those whose worlds have been marked by that set of phenomena," then one would have to accept Conrad and all of his work as postcolonial (120).

Despite the fact that, according even to more narrow definitions, Conrad could be considered postcolonial, he is rarely if ever identified as such by literary critics and theorists. Indeed, even those who offer the broadest definitions identify Conrad as either a colonialist or an imperialist writer rather than a postcolonial one. In *The Empire Writes Back,* for example, one of the most influential works on postcolonial literature and theory, Ashcroft et al. classify Conrad as an imperialist, focusing on what they see as primitivism in *Heart of Darkness* rather than on his attitudes toward imperialism or his own colonial subjectivity (158). Similarly, in *Colonialism/Postcolonialism,* Ania Loomba identifies *Heart of Darkness* as an example of "colonialist fiction" (136) and in *Colonial and Postcolonial Literature,* Elleke Boehmer does the same, even though according to her own definition, it would seem that Conrad's work was "colonial" rather than "colonialist" (2).[4]

To an extent, the fact that Conrad is most often identified as an imperialist or colonialist writer can be attributed to the prominent position his work has been given in the Western literary canon. Ever since F. R. Leavis declared Conrad to be a major English novelist of the "Great Tradition," it has become commonplace to regard Conrad as an English writer who happened to be born in Poland.[5] Not surprisingly, perhaps, those who consider Conrad essentially English ascribe to him stereotypically English points of view, particularly with regard to imperialism, ignoring the fact that Conrad frequently asserted his Polish identity and maintained an active interest in Polish affairs throughout his life (Moser 52; Schwarz 52).[6] Thomas Moser, for example, identifies "Conrad's moral code" with "the code of the British Merchant Marine," and Terry Eagleton relates Conrad's views on imperialism to those of "the traditionalist English conservative" (Moser 12; Eagleton 135). Such critics tend to ignore Conrad's direct criticism of British imperialism in his letters, particularly during the Boer War, and his unflattering portrayals of British imperialists in his fiction.[7]

That Conrad is frequently labeled a modernist has also led critics to overlook Conrad's postcoloniality since his work is most often discussed in terms of aesthetics rather than politics.[8] Instead of considering Conrad's texts in their original cultural context, many critics focus on Conrad's style, identifying him as a modernist, as does *The Oxford Companion to English Literature,* since his novels "constantly experiment with abrupt temporal and spatial shifts in the presentation of narrative information, with many long gaps in exposition or seeming digressions," among other things (682–83). Even Fredric Jameson, who charges critics to "Always historicize!" focuses on Conrad's supposed "will to style," all but ignoring the specific cultural context of the works he analyzes in *The Political Unconscious* (3, 225).[9] Critics like Jameson who associate Conrad with a literary movement that emerged in Western Europe only after Conrad had completed his major works tend to miss Conrad's postcolonial subjectivity and thus the political implications of his work.

The racial politics that pervade postcolonial criticism also prevent many critics from accepting Conrad as postcolonial since he was a white European. Even critics like Geoffrey Harpham, who concede that Conrad was himself a colonial subject, judge his subjectivity to be qualitatively different from that of those who were born and raised in overseas colonies since he was never subjected to the racial prejudices that were such an important component of imperialist domination (Harpham 50).[10] It should be remembered, though, that Conrad lived during a time when racial distinctions between various types of Europeans were widely recognized by Europeans themselves and that such distinctions were used to justify various types of domination.[11] As a Pole, Conrad was treated as a racial "other" not only by the Russians occupying Poland but also by the English once he settled in Great Britain, as evidenced by the fact that many of his acquaintances and friends remarked on his dark complexion and foreign features. Just after meeting him, John Galsworthy, for example, described him as "a capital chap, though queer to look at," and Ford Madox Ford calls attention to Conrad's alterity in the opening of his biography on him by noting that he was "dark in complexion with black hair and a clipped black beard" (Najder 1983, 157; Ford 3). Others, such as H. G. Wells and Henry John Newbold, comment on Conrad's "Oriental" appearance, and Edwin Pugh describes him as "simian" (Wells 109; Newbold 115; Pugh 96). Such responses to Conrad's alterity may explain why he was mistaken for a "bomb-carrying anarchist" when in Rouen in 1894: his "Eastern" appearance may have made him seem suspect to Western Europeans (Najder 1983, 161).[12] Accordingly, although it would be difficult to argue that the prejudices Conrad faced in England or even Poland were anything like those Africans and Asians faced in European colonies, it would be a mistake to ignore them entirely since they clearly affected not only his sense of his own identity but the behavior of others toward him.[13] Certainly, the fact that Conrad's own colonial subjectivity was different from that of people from overseas colonies does not make the prejudices he faced any less real. At the very least, one could argue that Conrad is as postcolonial as Irish writers such as W. B. Yeats and Eavan Bolan.

Finally, critics may not have recognized Conrad's postcoloniality because of his cultural identity. Even if, as I suggest, Conrad was treated as a racial "other" by Russians when he was a child and by the English and other Western Europeans as an adult, one could argue that as a Pole his views were by definition "Western" and therefore not postcolonial. Edward Said makes just such an argument, asserting, "Conrad writes as a man in whom a Western view of the non-Western world is so deeply ingrained that it blinds him to other histories, other cultures, other aspirations" (Said 1988, 70). If Said's assessment of Conrad is correct, then it would be reasonable to argue that Conrad was, in fact, a colonialist writer, however much he recognized and condemned the immorality of imperialism, since he was unwilling or unable to posit an alternative to it. As I shall demonstrate, however, in *Lord Jim* and *Nostromo,* at least, Conrad does imagine an end to imperialism and the formation of postcolonial states and therefore can be regarded as postcolonial in even the strictest sense of the term.[14]

Nowadays, of course, it is fashionable to label everything postcolonial, from Chaucer to the contemporary urban classroom, even though doing so tends to make the category overly general and therefore less useful.[15] When classifying something as postcolonial leads to new insights, such classification has a legitimate purpose, however. In *The Subaltern Ulysses,* for example, Enda Duffy demonstrates just how valuable radically reclassifying an author or text can be by analyzing *Ulysses* as a postcolonial novel.[16] As Michael Hart notes, Duffy not only "provides a model for further research on the relation of *Ulysses* to the social history of its time" but "provides new approaches to the study of modernism and its relation to history" (183). Since Duffy's book appeared in 1994, it has become commonplace to regard Joyce and other Irish writers as postcolonial, in part because of Duffy's suggestive work.[17]

On the surface, my own project may seem even more ambitious than ones like Duffy's since, in arguing that Conrad is postcolonial, I directly contradict received opinion that Conrad was, in fact, a colonialist writer. I am not suggesting that Conrad can only be read as postcolonial, however. To say that Conrad was a complex man who led a complex life would be an understatement, a fact that helps explain the number and variety of Conrad studies that have been published in the last fifty years. The English Conrad, of course, has been studied in detail, as have the Polish and Continental ones. Considerable attention has also been paid to Conrad the mariner, the man of letters, the modernist, the misogynist, and the reactionary. The Conrad who recognized the various imperialisms he encountered as parts of a larger system of exploitation has not received much notice, however, and the Conrad who acted to subvert this system has been largely ignored. It is my hope that examining this Conrad—the postcolonial one—will lead to a better understanding of Conrad's texts and the influence he had on later postcolonial writers.

Reconsidering the work of a major author like Conrad is, of course, difficult, since so much has already been written. In completing this study, I have done my best to avoid repeating what has already been said while at the same time providing complete readings of pivotal texts. In general, I incorporate interpretations that are consistent with my own into my argument and use notes to indicate where readers may find further discussion. I also use notes to acknowledge alternative interpretations of important passages. Since this study is intended not only for Conradians but also for those more generally interested in twentieth-century literature and culture, I summarize lesser-known stories before analyzing them and provide close readings of key passages. For better-known works such as *Heart of Darkness, Lord Jim,* and *Nostromo,* I dispense with summaries and provide close readings only when making major points.

Adopting a postcolonial approach has also proven difficult, not only because so much postcolonial theory is based on outdated poststructuralist theory, but also because it is often needlessly opaque.[18] Since I do not agree with most of the premises of postcolonial criticism, I am reluctant to employ it, even though I recognize its rigor and even its value in the analysis of certain texts. Accordingly, although I frequently refer to the work of poststructuralist, postcolonial critics such as Said, Homi Bhabha, and Benita Parry, I do so either to make local points or to demonstrate how their approaches may lead to conclusions different from my own. This study is decidedly not poststructuralist. The Trojan horse theory I develop in this study to explain the changes in Conrad's narrative technique as he began writing for a larger, more conservative readership is based on M. M. Bakhtin's theory of "intentional hybridity" rather than Bhabha's theory of "colonial hybridity" and influenced more by the work of cultural critics such as Raymond Williams and Alan Sinfield than poststructuralists such as Jacques Derrida and Jacques Lacan.

Chapter 1 provides a theoretical framework for the rest of the study by discussing Conrad's narrative technique in terms of Bakhtin's theories of language and the novel. Like other early postcolonial writers publishing in English, including S. K. Ghosh and Solomon Plaatje, Conrad had to contend with a fiction market that for the most part demanded monologic affirmations of Britain's "civilizing" mission. Because Conrad's earliest work was overtly anti-imperialist, he failed to acquire a popular audience in Great Britain even though his work was widely reviewed and acclaimed by critics. To expand his readership, Conrad developed a Trojan horse strategy, creating "intentional hybrids," to borrow Bakhtin's phrase, that is, texts in which alternative perspectives are set against one another dialogically. Like Ghosh and Plaatje, Conrad concealed radical critiques of imperialism in seemingly innocuous tales set in exotic places, a strategy he continued using until he established himself professionally and had a stable readership.

Chapter 2 focuses on Conrad's first two novels, *Almayer's Folly* and *An Outcast of the Islands,* radically anti-imperialist texts published by T. Fisher Unwin, a well-known liberal critic of British expansion. In *Almayer's Folly,* Conrad challenges imperialist ideology directly through his representation of Sambir, a fictional, remote community in the Dutch-controlled Malay Archipelago. In addition to presenting the title character, Kaspar Almayer, as a foolish man who, like Dravot in Rudyard Kipling's "The Man Who Would Be King," tries to exploit his racial prestige as a white man, Conrad develops alternative perspectives on imperialism through his Sulu, Balinese, and Malay characters. Although the text presents itself as an adventure novel and as an exotic romance, it defies the conventions of both genres by endlessly deferring Kaspar's upriver adventure and by developing his "half-caste" daughter, Nina, as a protagonist.[19] Instead of accepting her role as a colonial subject, Nina declares herself a Malay and joins an indigenous insurgency against the Dutch. Ultimately, I argue that Nina's developing consciousness parallels Conrad's own. *Almayer's Folly* did not begin as a postcolonial novel when Conrad started it in 1889; it became one, however, as Conrad's own postcoloniality emerged over the course of the next five years.

An Outcast of the Islands, a novel Conrad began in 1894, is in some ways even more radical than *Almayer's Folly* since, in addition to presenting alternative perspectives on imperialism, it attacks British imperialism directly through its representation of Thomas Lingard, the English colonist who controls Sambir, as a deluded man who cannot understand why the subjects of his private "Arcadia" resent him. Eventually, a "great revolution" occurs and the paternalistic Lingard's rule ends, suggesting that even the most self-consciously benevolent forms of imperialism cannot last, since they, too, rely on force to govern colonial subjects. *An Outcast of the Islands* is also more radical than *Almayer's Folly* in its representation of subalterns. By according characters such as Aïssa and the "Bajow vagabonds" agency, Conrad suggests that the subaltern cannot only speak but act, to borrow Gayatri Spivak's formulation, and that therefore they represent a threat to the colonial system that exploits them. Given its overt anti-imperialism, it should not be surprising that *An Outcast of the Islands* was no more popular than Conrad's first novel: there simply was no market for postcolonial novels in Great Britain during the 1890s. Like *Almayer's Folly, An Outcast of the Islands* was well received by critics, however, who responded to the novel's complexity and power, giving Conrad the confidence to give up the sea permanently and pursue a career as a professional writer.

Chapter 3 addresses Conrad's initial efforts to make a living as a writer through the short-fiction market, focusing on the three short stories he wrote immediately after *An Outcast of the Islands*—"The Idiots," "An Outpost of Progress," and "The Lagoon." In these stories Conrad continues to challenge imperialism directly, suggesting that despite their claims of bringing "light" to the "dark places of the earth," European imperialists are, in fact, morally inferior to their colonial subjects since they refuse to take responsibility for their actions. Ultimately, this chapter argues that Conrad's early style is consistent with his radical, anti-imperialist content: as in *Almayer's Folly* and *An Outcast of the Islands,* Conrad uses irony, free indirect discourse, and other techniques to develop alternative perspectives on imperialism, ones that question not only its excesses but its underlying ideology. Of the three stories discussed in this chapter, it is only in "The Lagoon" that Conrad makes a significant concession to the expectations of imperialist readers by employing some of the conventions of the exotic romance, and even these are undercut by the story's dialogism and unconventional ending. Because he was largely uncompromising in expressing his attitudes toward imperialism in his early fiction, Conrad had difficulty placing these stories despite his literary reputation. Like novels, British short stories were expected to affirm the legitimacy of Great Britain's imperial mission.

The fourth chapter focuses on changes Conrad made in his narrative strategy as he tried to acquire a larger market for his fiction. In particular, this chapter examines the narrative techniques Conrad developed to cloak his radical, anti-imperialist politics. In *The Nigger of the "Narcissus,"* a novel first serialized in a conservative monthly, *The New Review,* he uses misdirection, presenting a story that explores racial prejudice and colonial subjectivity as a paean to the British Merchant Service. By setting the story at sea, Conrad distances himself from his earlier anti-imperialist fiction, and by employing a narrator whose perspective shifts as the story proceeds, Conrad is able to insulate himself from the novel's more radical implications. In "Karain," which appeared in *Blackwood's Edinburgh Magazine,* another conservative monthly, Conrad uses subterfuge to conceal his radical politics. Rather than misdirect his readers by setting the story at sea, Conrad returns to a colonial setting, telling the story of a Malay leader who is haunted by the ghost of his friend. Superficially, the story resembles his earlier story, "The Lagoon": both feature Malay characters who betray trust and then try to make amends for their actions, proving themselves superior to their European counterparts who act only for profit. In "Karain," however, the title character is an insurgent whose war against European imperialists is represented as being just, since he has experienced the horrors of imperialism firsthand. To distance himself from the story's message about the legitimacy of indigenous insurrections and the immorality of white adventurers and profiteers, Conrad relates Karain's story through a character-narrator who rejects its radical implications. The story thus functions as an intentional hybrid to the extent that two differing perspectives are set against each other dialogically and unmask one another.

In "Youth," the first of Conrad's stories written expressly for *Blackwood's,* Conrad employs both misdirection and subterfuge. By setting the story primarily at sea, Conrad avoids being directly critical of imperialism: like *The Nigger of the "Narcissus,"* "Youth" appears to be a tribute to the courage and perseverance of English seamen as Marlow and the all-English crew survive a shipwreck and make it to the Dutch East Indies in open boats. Once the character-narrator, Marlow lands in Java, however, the story shifts its focus to imperialism, albeit briefly, as Marlow is subjected first to the abuse normally reserved for colonial subjects, and then to the gaze of colonial subjects, who see Marlow and his companions for what they are—masters of an Empire that cannot forever be controlled. As in "Karain," the anti-imperialist implications of this story are ultimately rejected by the narrator, who refuses to see that the tale is anything but a treatise on youth. "Youth," too, is thus an intentional hybrid, one that criticizes imperialism only to reject its own critique.

Chapter 5 focuses on *Heart of Darkness,* the story in which the Trojan horse strategy Conrad experimented with in stories such as "Karain" and "Youth" fully emerges. In this story Conrad develops dual critiques of imperialism, one liberal and the other radical. The liberal critique comes from Marlow, who challenges the excesses of imperialism but not imperialism itself. Rather than question the notion of bringing "light" to the "dark places of the earth," Marlow criticizes the Continental powers for refusing to shoulder the "White Man's Burden" as the British do. By reducing complex social and moral issues into black-and-white terms, Marlow helps perpetuate European imperialism even as he criticizes certain imperialist practices. In contrast, the narrator who frames Marlow's tale offers a radical critique of imperialist ideology by subverting the light/dark opposition that imperialist ideology relies on. By concealing a radical critique of imperialism within a liberal one, Conrad constructs a Trojan horse, as it were: a story whose deceptive surface enables it to reach readers who would reject overtly anti-imperialist works.

The sixth chapter argues that in *Lord Jim,* Conrad again adopts a Trojan horse strategy as he represents the development of a revolutionary consciousness on the part of the peoples living in Jim's model colony of Patusan. Like *Heart of Darkness,* this novel was first serialized in *Blackwood's,* and therefore Conrad felt compelled to obfuscate his radical, anti-imperialist politics by presenting the novel as an imperial romance. The novel's character-narrator, Marlow, represents the title character as a romantic hero of sorts—a man who sacrifices his life for the benefit of those he rules. *Lord Jim* proves to be more than just the story of a noble white colonist, however, since the frame narrator undercuts Marlow's credibility by representing him as deluded, hypocritical, and obtuse. By highlighting Marlow's limitations as a narrator, the frame narrator opens up an alternative interpretive possibility—one in which Jim figures as a fool rather than a hero, a man who, like Lingard in *An Outcast of the Islands,* fails to realize that no matter how benevolent he tries to be, as a colonist, he participates in a system of oppression and exploitation that will eventually be overthrown. Marlow's limitations also prevent him from recognizing the political significance of events in Patusan: he fails to realize that the colony undergoes a revolution and that Jim's death marks the beginning of the postcolonial period. As he himself concedes, he does "not know" what the uprising "really meant" (245).

Chapter 7 discusses *Nostromo,* a book Conrad began after he had established himself professionally and acquired a literary agent to market his fiction. No longer writing primarily for conservative readers, Conrad discards the Trojan horse strategy he had developed for *Blackwood's* and resumes his direct attacks on imperialism, employing an ironic tone similar to the one he used in his earliest work. Set in the imaginary nation of Costaguana, this novel addresses the difficulties a postcolonial state has in establishing itself in a world dominated economically by Europe and the United States. Although the nation is nominally free, outsiders still control the people and resources of Costaguana. Ultimately, Conrad suggests that the end of empire does not necessarily mean the end of colonialist exploitation: this will only happen when a fully realized postcolonial consciousness emerges and once-colonized peoples establish a new social order based on their unique histories and cultures. By ironizing every character and the positions they represent, Conrad demonstrates the futility of individual action, thereby challenging history itself, at least as it is told by humanists: individuals may have agency in *Nostromo,* but only in a limited sense. It is "material interests" that determine how people live, and these interests can be contested only by creating a new kind of society, one that prioritizes justice rather than profits.

The book ends with a brief discussion of Conrad's aesthetic in the context of later postcolonial writers ranging from R. K. Narayan to Salman Rushdie. Such writers truly are Conrad's descendents, to again borrow Nazareth's phrase, in the sense that they create linguistic hybrids, that is, texts that operate on two levels at once. The postcolonial aesthetic, I argue, is a duplicitous one, one that Conrad not only pioneered but also mastered.

CHAPTER ONE

Imperialism, Hybridity, and Conrad's Postcolonial Aesthetic

Conrad's is one of the most remarkable stories in literary history. Born Josef Teodor Konrad Nalecz Korzeniowski in a Polish town under Russian rule, Conrad's first career was as a merchant seaman. In 1895, at the age of 38 and after 23 years at sea, he began his literary career in England. He became one of the premier prose stylists in English, his adopted language, which he did not begin to learn until age 20.

DANIEL BURT, *The Literary 100*

Luckily for us historians of literature, most writers, including those of the first rank, fit more or less neatly into some general pattern of artistic and intellectual life of their time. Even when "exceptional", "outstanding" and "breaking new ground" they allow themselves to be arranged in groups and sequences. . . . Occasionally, however, we encounter figures so peculiar, so aberrant, that it is virtually impossible to fit them into the general formula of their time. *Conrad seems to be a good candidate for the first place among these freaks.*

ZDZISLAW NAJDER, *Conrad in Perspective* (emphasis added)

As the above passages suggest, Joseph Conrad is widely regarded as a "freak" of sorts, a timeless genius whose work transcends both place and history.[1] Even outstanding critics such as Zdzislaw Najder—critics who themselves recognize the importance of considering a text in its cultural context—are susceptible to the Conrad mystique, presenting him as a master of English prose who, though he chose to write in English, could just as easily have written in Polish or French. Writing in a language and publishing in it are two very different things, of course, a fact that such critics frequently overlook. Although Conrad certainly could have written in Polish or French, he would have had difficulty publishing regularly in any language other than English once he settled in England permanently, since he had direct access only to the British literary market.[2] As his letters of the mid-1890s reveal, establishing himself as a professional writer involved not only writing fiction but marketing it—and himself. From the very beginning of his career, Conrad met tirelessly with editors, publishers, and other writers to promote himself and his work.[3]

Succeeding in the British market proved to be difficult for Conrad, however, not only because his knowledge of English language and culture was still developing but because as a former colonial subject, he was unwilling to celebrate imperialism in his work. Born in the Russian-occupied Polish Ukraine in 1857, Conrad had good reason to loathe imperialism.[4] His parents, Ewa Bobrowska and Apollo Korzeniowski, both active Polish nationalists, were exiled in 1861 to the Russian province of Vologada because of their political activities.[5] As Najder indicates, Conrad's parents were "reds," anti-Russian activists who "linked the struggle for national independence with a programme of broad social reforms, beginning with the liberation of the peasantry" (1997, 29). Although Korzeniowski took a more public role than Bobrowska in the insurrection of 1861—which occurred when Conrad was just four years old—both were sentenced in 1862 "to exile, under police supervision," on the basis of the letters Bobrowska wrote to Korzeniowski during the period (Najder 1997, 24).[6] Conrad accompanied his parents to Vologada, where the harsh climate aggravated their tuberculosis, and although they were permitted to move south to the northeast Ukraine, both parents were dead by 1869 (Najder 1997, 31). Facing compulsory service in the Russian military because of his parents' political activities, Conrad left Poland at age seventeen for Western Europe where he began a career as a seaman (Najder 1964, 12–13). Although he went on to serve in the British Merchant Service for twenty years, becoming a British subject in 1886, he spent very little time in England until he settled there permanently in 1894.

Conrad's Anti-Imperialism

When Conrad began publishing fiction in the mid-1890s, he identified strongly with subject peoples and was sharply critical of imperialism and imperialists in his fiction. In *Almayer's Folly,* for example, his first novel, the title character is a weak, deluded Dutch colonist who marries a Sulu woman to advance his material interests. As the novel proceeds, it becomes increasingly clear that it is not Almayer but his "half-caste" daughter who is the protagonist of the novel. Despite her father's efforts to "make her white," Nina Almayer rejects him and his dream of taking her to Europe, instead marrying a Balinese prince and joining an anticolonial insurgency against the Dutch (25). Ultimately, the novel affirms that she makes the correct choice by contrasting her success to her father's continuing failure: whereas Nina Almayer becomes a Rani, her father dies miserable and alone, an opium addict who is, in the end, led around by a monkey (152). As I shall argue in chapter 2, as a novel with a half-caste protagonist, *Almayer's Folly* was something entirely new to British fiction: although a few other European writers, including Robert Louis Stevenson, had depicted indigenous peoples and those of mixed identities sympathetically, Conrad challenges imperialist ideology by developing alternative frames of reference through his protagonist and other non-European characters, thus exploiting the dialogic possibilities of the novel.[7]

Not surprisingly, perhaps, Conrad's early, overtly anti-imperialist works had "a very limited public," as his publisher, T. Fisher Unwin, reminded him (*Letters* 1:180). At a time when the British were telling themselves that their rule, in the words of Secretary of State for the Colonies Joseph Chamberlain, "brought security and peace and comparative prosperity to countries that never knew these blessings before," Conrad suggested that the British and other European colonists were anything but benevolent (Chamberlain 3). At first, poor sales did not seem to concern Conrad, since he still planned to earn his living as a mariner: his letters of the period suggest that he was pleased simply to be published and widely reviewed.[8] It was only after he married in 1896 and became fully committed to writing as a profession that he began to cloak his anti-imperialist politics in an effort to acquire a larger audience, developing narrative techniques that allowed him to distance himself from the radical content of his work. As I shall argue, even though later critics identified these techniques with modernism, they were, in fact, part of Conrad's postcolonial aesthetic, and as such, would have considerable influence on later postcolonial writers who wrote for imperial audiences.

Hybridity and Colonial/Postcolonial Discourse

To better understand Conrad's narrative technique, we must first consider his works as hybrid constructs, that is, as texts that operate on two levels at once. Hybridity, of course, emerged as a key concept in post-structuralist, postcolonial theory as critics began to address the question of whether the "subaltern can speak," to borrow the phrase popularized by Gayatri Spivak. Like Ranajit Guha and the other members of the Subaltern Studies group, Spivak distinguishes "subalterns" from an "indigenous elite," noting that the voices of the former have not been recorded in colonial histories. It is not possible to recover subaltern voices, Spivak argues, because they have "no history and cannot speak," at least "in the context of colonial production" (Spivak 1996, 289; Spivak 1994, 82–83): in her view, those who are not subjected to and conditioned by colonial institutions are by definition "objects" rather than "subjects" and therefore effectively silenced or "effaced" (Spivak 1994, 82).[9]

Unlike Spivak, who differentiates the "subaltern" from the "indigenous elite"—or what I term the "colonial subject"—to explore the silencing effect of colonial institutions, Homi Bhabha focuses more broadly on the "colonized" as he explores the ways in which subject peoples did and do speak through colonial discourse.[10] In *The Location of Culture,* he identifies "hybridity" as "the name for the strategic reversal of the process of domination through disavowal." He continues:

> Hybridity is the revaluation of the assumption of colonial identity through the repetition of discriminatory identity effects. It displays the necessary deformation and displacement of all sites

> of discrimination and domination. It unsettles the mimetic or narcissistic demands of colonial power but reimplicates its identifications in strategies of subversion that turn the gaze of the discriminated back upon the eye of power. For the colonial hybrid is the articulation of the ambivalent space where the rite of power is enacted on the site of desire, making its objects at once disciplinary and disseminatory. (Bhabha 1994, 112)

As the passage suggests, for Bhabha, the authority of colonial discourse is never absolute since it reproduces traces of that which it attempts to contain, thereby putting the colonizer under the colonized's "gaze." He goes on to argue that this "ambivalence" "enables a form of subversion, founded on the undecidability that turns the discursive conditions of dominance into the grounds of intervention" (112).

To the extent that he identifies a space of and for resistance within colonial discourse, Bhabha seems to accord subject peoples agency: to him the subaltern can speak, at least in theory.[11] As Rey Chow indicates in "Where Have All the Natives Gone?" however, since for Bhabha the subaltern voice is already contained within colonial discourse, what the subaltern has—or had—to say is of little importance. Chow writes:

> The colonial text's "hybridity," to use Bhabha's word, means that the subaltern has spoken. But what kind of an argument is it to say that the subaltern's "voice" can be found in the *ambivalence* of the imperialist's speech? It is an argument which ultimately makes it unnecessary to come to terms with the subaltern since she has already "spoken," as it were, in the system's gaps. All we would need to do would be to continue to study—to deconstruct—the rich and ambivalent language of the imperialist! (127–28)

Chow goes on to argue that the poststructuralist approach to hybridity as represented by Bhabha is a limited one since, like liberal humanism, it inscribes indigenous voices within colonialist discourse, effectively theorizing them away (128). As a result, Chow suggests, Bhabha's subaltern cannot speak any more than Spivak's can.

One does not have to be a poststructuralist to apply the concept of hybridity to colonial/postcolonial discourse, of course, as Robert J. C. Young demonstrates in *Colonial Desire: Hybridity in Theory, Culture and Race.* Indeed, as Young notes, in 1890 the *Oxford English Dictionary* recognized that the word *hybridity* was used to relate linguistic difference to "racial intermixture" (6). Following Young, in this study, I want to return to the concept of hybridity developed by M. M. Bakhtin.[12] According to Bakhtin, linguistic hybridization involves the "mixture of two social languages within the limits of a single utterance, an encounter within the arena of an utterance, between two different linguistic consciousnesses, separated from one another by an epoch, by social differentiation or by some other factor" (358). As Young suggests, such "double-voiced" discourse is a product of "language's fundamental ability to be simultaneously the same but different" (20). He continues:

> This insight, often identified with Romantic irony, is central to the contemporary work of Derrida and de Man, who point to it as a general characteristic of language, an undecidable oscillation in which it becomes impossible to tell which is the primary meaning. Bakhtin's irony is more dramatic: he uses hybridization to describe the ability of one voice to ironize and unmask the other within the same utterance. (20)

Bakhtin identifies this conscious use of one voice to unmask another as "intentional hybridity," contrasting it to the "unintentional, unconscious hybridization" that occurs whenever language is used, since language use always involves the "mixing of various 'languages' co-existing within the boundaries of a single dialect, a single national language, a single branch, a single group of different branches, in the historical as well as paleontological past of languages" (358–59). The essential difference between intentional and unintentional hybridity is that in the former, "two points of view are not mixed but set against each other dialogically" (360). Intentional hybridity, then, has an ideological function, one that is potentially subversive, since such discourse can be constructed so as to contest dominating ideologies even as it gives them voice. When this subversive potential is developed—when a seemingly subordinate or partially concealed voice emerges and becomes dominant—the discourse takes on a Trojan horse function in the sense that a particular voice and the point of view it represents is advanced through misdirection and subterfuge.[13] For example, Gandhi's concept of *satyagraha,* or "passive resistance," functioned as a Trojan horse since, as an oxymoron, its precise meaning and implications could not be determined by British authorities, and therefore, Gandhi was able to disseminate his anticolonial message widely in colonial India.[14] Certainly, Gandhi would have faced more restrictions had he called for "active resistance," and he may even have been held incommunicado by British authorities. Because he generally employed terms that, on the surface at least, seemed to reject the use of revolutionary violence, however, he was able to organize a broad-based resistance movement that allowed for such violence even though it did not promote it directly.[15]

Intentional Hybridity and the Postcolonial Novel

Bakhtin's theory of intentional hybridity is particularly useful in the study of postcolonial novels that were published in the British Empire in the late nineteenth and early twentieth centuries since it provides a means for identifying the textual dynamics that made it possible for them to be published in the first place. In India, for example, one of the first of the overseas British colonies to develop a nationalist literature, Indian writers publishing in English created intentional hybrids to challenge British imperialism even as they appeared to support it.[16] As Meenakshi Mukherjee indicates in *The Perishable Empire: Essays on Indian Writing in English,* British efforts to establish English as the official language of higher education in India created a small but growing market for novels written in English by Indians (12–15). The first of these novels were anything but subversive, something that should not be too surprising since the British controlled the publishing industry both in England and India and certainly would not allow anything to appear that openly challenged the legitimacy of their empire: those writing in English had to be "careful not to antagonize their imagined [English] addressee through overtones of sedition" (Mukherjee 2000, 15). This of course does not mean that every novel published in English by an Indian during the period promoted imperialism. As Makarand Paranjape points out in the afterword to the recent Oxford edition of Shevantibai Nikambe's 1895 novel, *Ratanbai,* "just as collaboration with imperialism comes in various garbs, resistance too wears many guises" (67). In these early novels the guises are often difficult to penetrate, since, as is the case with *Ratanbai,* these texts were also forced to present themselves as imperialist propaganda tracts (Lokugé xiii–xv, Paranjape 67).[17]

As the Indian nationalist movement gained strength near the turn of the century, however, Anglophone writers were able to be more critical of imperialist practices, though they still had to affirm imperialist ideology, at least on the surface, if they were to have any hope of success in Great Britain. In *The Prince of Destiny or the New Krishna* (1909), for instance, S. K. Ghosh employs a Trojan horse strategy, writing what appears to be a conventional imperial romance, complete with unruly heathens, unspeakable rites, comic natives who ape their English betters, a white virgin, a sagacious British official who knows natives but does not "go native," and a happy ending in which the empire is preserved so that the British can carry on their good work.[18] The novel's protagonist, Barath, the crown prince of Barathpur and a potential anti-imperialist insurgent, develops a love for England after studying mathematics in Cambridge and ultimately becomes a defender of British imperial authority in India. Refusing to participate in a widespread rebellion that has the potential to end British rule not only in Barathpur but also in all of India, he becomes a leader in name only, effectively abdicating his throne to become "a New Buddha . . . one who will teach all earth anew the doctrine of peace" (629). The "revolution at Barathpur" fails "because of Barath's love of England" (621).

To the extent that it seems to legitimate British control of India, Ghosh's novel resembles works such as S. M. Mitra's *Hindupore* (1909).[19] Ghosh goes to great lengths, however, to make his protagonist a ridiculous figure, one whom Indian readers would immediately recognize as a caricature of Indians who try to be more British than the British, something that becomes apparent when Barath admits to "wearing secretly an English cricketing shirt under . . . [his] Indian choga" (515). Because he is so comic, it is hard to take Barath and his views seriously. Indeed, it is difficult not to read his failure to support the uprising against the British as a betrayal of his own people, a betrayal that results from his ridiculous efforts to be "ultra-English" (515).

Ghosh's suggestion that the novel's pro-English protagonist is both foolish and treacherous is not the novel's only subversive element. He also develops an ironic authorial voice, one that mocks British readers, addressing them as "my brother" and "my masters" even as he celebrates what he terms "the lesson of Adowah"—the defeat of the Italian imperialists by the Ethiopians—and warns the British that "Europe itself will become a vassal of Asia" unless it enters into a partnership with India rather than trying to subjugate it (150). British reviewers, apparently, did not realize that the British were being mocked. Rather, they interpreted the novel as a well-intentioned warning from a loyal colonial subject. The *Cork Constitution* called it "a tremendous sermon," for example, and the *Observer* wrote, "As a serious warning, a sympathetic and dignified rebuke, its passionate sincerity makes of it a voice that should be heard."[20] Colonial reviewers responded in a similar way. The *Colonial Bookseller,* for instance, states: "A great and absorbing work. . . . It needed such a genius as the author possesses to show the beauty and the need of both the mysticism of the East and materialism of the West to give India her place as the brightest jewel in the British Crown." Such responses indicate just how successful the novel was as an intentional hybrid. By creating a text that on one level at least seemed to affirm imperialist ideology, Ghosh was able to disseminate ideas that on another level challenged it.

Intentional hybrids developed in a similar manner in other British colonies such as South Africa, where colonial administrations attempted to establish English as an official language. In *Mhudi: An Epic of South African Native Life a Hundred Years Ago,* for example, the first novel written by a black African to be published in English, the Rolong writer Solomon Plaatje celebrates the Boer-Rolong alliance that formed a century earlier in response to Zulu aggression even as he suggests that the

Rolong may have been better off had they allied themselves with the Zulu against the Boers. He does this in part by making his Rolong protagonist who champions the Boer-Rolong alliance a poltroon who is dominated by his shrewish wife and by employing a naïve narrator fittingly named "Half-a-Crown" who is unable to properly interpret the story he himself tells.[21] Although, as its subtitle indicates, the novel presents itself as an epic, it is also comic, since the protagonist, narrator, and title character prove themselves fools. The novel thus operates on two levels at once, challenging the very ideas it seems to promote through what amounts to burlesque.

Although Plaatje completed the novel in 1920, he was unable to find a British publisher for *Mhudi* despite his efforts to cloak its radical content, in part because the British were unwilling to alienate their Boer subjects for fear of losing control of the resource-rich Union of South Africa.[22] In 1930, however, ten years after Plaatje completed the manuscript, the Lovedale Press accepted it for publication, and it appeared later that year. Even though Lovedale was a small, South African missionary press that specialized in religious and educational texts, *Mhudi* received a number of reviews, both in Africa and in Great Britain. Like *The Prince of Destiny,* it was generally praised, albeit less lavishly and with even more condescension. The East London *Daily Dispatch,* for example, noted that "the style is wonderfully good for a native," and the *South African Outlook* called it "thrilling" and "well-written" (Willan 361–62). The *Times Literary Supplement* declared that the novel was "definitely memorable" but suggested that it would have been even more impressive if Plaatje had written like a "Native" rather than emulated English writers (Willan 363). The fact that none of these reviewers noted anything objectionable in the novel suggests that as an intentional hybrid, at least, it was successful: by concealing his attack on the Boers within a seemingly innocuous story about a domineering woman and her weak-willed husband, Plaatje was eventually able to publish a work that otherwise would have been deemed unacceptable.[23]

Not every early postcolonial novel is an intentional hybrid, of course. In general, writers like the Caribbean novelist A. R. F. Webber, who published through small, local presses, were able to be more direct in challenging imperialism: in *Those That Be in Bondage,* for example, a novel published by the *Daily Chronicle* in Demerara in 1917, Webber ridicules British colonists, attacks the plantation system, and decries racial discrimination. Not surprisingly, perhaps, novels like *Those That Be in Bondage* that overtly contested imperialist practices and beliefs were limited to small press runs and distributed only locally; indeed, Selwyn R. Cudjoe reports that only two original copies of Webber's first novel remain in existence (viii). Early postcolonial writers who wanted a wider readership, however, were forced to obfuscate their radical politics through misdirection, subterfuge, and various forms of irony, including the hybridized forms Bakhtin describes. The early postcolonial aesthetic is thus largely a duplicitous one, as writers ranging from Lal Behari Day to Amos Tutuola developed new techniques for subverting the established social order.[24]

Conrad and Hybridity

Even though Conrad began writing well before Ghosh, Plaatje, and even Nikambe, he faced many of the same challenges they did in getting work published and establishing an audience for it. Like Ghosh and Plaatje, he was a colonial subject for whom English was a foreign language, writing stories that were in many respects critical of empire. Conrad had certain advantages over writers like Ghosh and Plaatje, of course: as a "minor aristocrat" with a European education, he had opportunities that were unavailable to writers from British overseas colonies (Simmons 2004, 10).[25] Moreover, as Conrad's correspondence reveals, both critics and publishers treated him with respect and rarely disparaged his work, even when they were criticizing or rejecting it.[26] His privileged status also helped him to establish contacts with influential British writers, including H. G. Wells, George Bernard Shaw, and Arnold Bennett, who generally were impressed by the Polish gentleman-turned-seaman who wrote so well in English.

Although Conrad enjoyed certain advantages that distinguished him from writers such as Ghosh and Plaatje, he faced certain disadvantages as well, not the least of which was the fact that he began his career as a writer at a time when imperialism was becoming increasingly popular with the British public. There simply was not much of a market in Great Britain for texts that were critical of imperialism in the 1890s. The market for Conrad's work was also limited geographically. Whereas Ghosh and Plaatje could count on sales in both Great Britain and their respective homelands, there was no market for Conrad's work in Poland since there were very few English speakers there.

As I suggested earlier, the limited market for his work did not concern Conrad at first, since writing was not his livelihood. Even though T. Fisher Unwin offered Conrad only twenty pounds for *Almayer's Folly,* a novel that took him four years to complete, he accepted, telling Marguerite Poradowska that "the mere fact of publication is of great importance" and that it is "truly difficult to get oneself in print" (*Letters* 1:178). In the same letter he tells her that he has stopped working on what was to become *An Outcast of the Islands* because he was "too busy chasing ships." Until the mid-1890s, it seems, Conrad still considered himself primarily a seaman. Upon committing himself to writing as a profession two years later, he began to alter both the style and content of his work in hopes of increasing his readership.[27] In particular, he began to create texts that operated on at least two levels: as exotic tales of empire that appeared to affirm imperialist ideology and as subversive tales that challenged its legitimacy. By concealing the latter within tales that seemed to legitimate empire, Conrad was able to expand his readership without compromising his ideals. More important, perhaps, Conrad's Trojan horse strategy enabled him to better advance his ideals, since it allowed him to reach imperialist readers who normally would not read anti-imperialist texts. It also enabled him to reach colonial readers who normally would not be permitted to read subversive texts. As Peter Nazareth observes in "Out of the Darkness: Conrad and Other Third World Writers," "There was censorship in the colonial world: no Marx or Lenin":

> But there was Conrad, sneaking through as a member of Leavis's Great Tradition, actually undermining that tradition. Jane Austen's characters in *Mansfield Park* could live a luxurious life while

> the patriarch left for the colonies; Conrad actually takes us to the colonies to show us what happened there when the patriarch and his agents arrived and how his wealth at home came from brutal colonial action. Conrad was therefore a mental liberator: not only for those blinded at home but also for those who were to come later, the colonized elite wearing the eyes of Europe. (178)

Nazareth's insight into the complex ideological functions of Conrad's texts represents a starting place for this study. Rather than focus on Conrad's influence on postcolonial writers, however, this book considers Conrad's early work in the context of late nineteenth-century discourse on imperialism in order to determine its ideological effect. Like other early postcolonial writers who adopted Trojan horse strategies to challenge imperialist ideology, Conrad uses literature to attempt an "intervention," to borrow Alan Sinfield's term (35–37): in other words, he writes in a particular way to change the way people think and act.

Conrad and His Critics

To argue that Conrad was postcolonial is, of course, to challenge the received view of him as an imperialist, first introduced in Chinua Achebe's 1977 essay, "An Image of Africa: Racism in Conrad's *Heart of Darkness,*" and popularized by other postcolonial critics. In his essay, which was revised in 1987, Achebe writes that Conrad was a "purveyor of comforting myths" that helped legitimize European imperialism in Africa (253). Although he concedes that to some extent, Conrad insulates himself from Marlow and his opinions by filtering Marlow's narrative through an anonymous narrator, Achebe asserts that Conrad was a "thoroughgoing racist" since "he neglects to hint, clearly or adequately, at an alternative frame of reference by which we may judge the opinions and actions of his characters" (256–57). Conrad, he concludes, "had a problem with niggers" (258); he does not provide an alternative frame of reference because he could not—he could not imagine an Africa populated by human beings.

Twenty years later, in *Culture and Imperialism,* Edward Said tells us more about Conrad's limitations, arguing that Achebe's criticism "does not go far enough" (165). According to him, Conrad "writes as a man whose *Western* view of the non-Western world is so ingrained as to blind him to other histories, other cultures, other aspirations": "All Conrad can see is a world dominated by the Atlantic West. . . . He could not understand that India, Africa, and South America also had lives and cultures with integrities not totally controlled by the gringo imperialists and reformers of the world" (xviii). Said goes on to say that "Conrad does not give us the sense that he could imagine a fully realized alternative to imperialism: the natives he wrote about in Africa, Asia, or America were incapable of independence, and because he seemed to imagine that European tutelage was a given, he could not foresee what would take place when it came to an end" (25).

Since the appearance of Achebe's and Said's critiques, it has been increasingly popular to regard Conrad as a racist and imperialist, at least among postcolonial critics. Indeed, as Marianna Torgovnick notes, many such critics consider Conrad a "Western demon," arguing that "the only value in reading Conrad is to expose the rotten Western attitudes he articulates" (142–43).[28] Not surprisingly, given Conrad's canonical status, such views have prompted a variety of strong responses from more traditional literary critics.[29] Some, like Patrick Brantlinger, argue that Conrad was a racist but not an imperialist. Others, like Cedric Watts, assert that Conrad was neither racist nor imperialist. Others still insist that Conrad was antiracist and anti-imperialist. In *Kipling and Conrad: The Colonial Fiction,* for example, John McClure identifies Conrad's efforts to subvert racist stereotypes of subject peoples as the "often disguised social project of Conrad's serious colonial fiction" (100). He argues, among other things, that in *Almayer's Folly,* Conrad's treatment of Dain Maroola suggests "that the Malays' traditional precolonial culture was superior in important respects to that of modern Western civilization" (103), and that by "acknowledging the influence of social forces on human character, Conrad implicitly rejects the racist theories of inherent differences and inferiority supported by many imperialists" (107).

Even though McClure rejects Achebe's assertion that Conrad was a racist, his position on whether Conrad's Africans are capable of achieving independence is not inconsistent with that of Said, albeit for different reasons. In his discussion of *Lord Jim,* for example, McClure argues that the Patusanis "have lost their self-reliance," that "they have projected all their powers, all their faith, onto an alien master [Jim]" (129). Although ultimately, McClure concludes that Conrad was an anti-imperialist, he finds the ending of *Lord Jim* "deeply pessimistic," since in his view, Doramin, the Bugis leader, emerges as "the vengeful representative of a shattered tradition" rather than as the leader of a postcolonial nation (130). Unlike Said, however, who attributes this supposed pessimism to Conrad's imperialist prejudices, McClure interprets the ending of *Lord Jim* as an indictment of imperialism's destructiveness.

Like McClure, Eloise Knapp Hay believes that Conrad was antiracist and anti-imperialist; she argues, however, that Conrad's natives are not only capable of independence, but that revolution is inevitable. In "Cities like Whited Sepulchres," an essay that focuses on *Heart of Darkness,* Hay challenges Achebe's "great misreading" of Conrad, arguing that the "'alternative frame of reference' is plainly an Africa that Conrad visualizes as ready to be liberated from the 'fantastic invasion' of whites":

> The British had already learned a lesson from the heroic Zulus, who had defeated and massacred a large contingent of British forces in 1878, just before the more celebrated British victory at Rorke's Drift. This retaliating Africa Marlow only dimly infers from the black helmsman's dying look, a "brooding and menacing expression," "as though in response to some sign we could not see, to some whisper that we could not hear." (Hay 1992, 131)

Hay's interpretation is valuable not only because she identifies Conrad's representation of Africa as an "alternative frame of reference" but because she finds in the "silence" of Conrad's African characters "unshaped resolves in their incipient forms" (134). Even though the Africans have been temporarily quieted by "pain," "death," and "overwhelming force," Hay argues that there will come a "turn of tide"—a time when it will be the European imperialists, including Marlow, who are silenced (134). In

Hay's view, although Conrad's Africans have not yet developed a revolutionary consciousness—that is, the resolve to change the social order—*Heart of Darkness* suggests that such consciousness will emerge, and that "the people of Africa *will* eventually strike back" (132).

Hay's reading of Conrad's early work is clearly at odds with those of Achebe and Said. She argues, like McClure, not only that Conrad develops alternative frames of reference through "native" characters, but that he foresees an end to imperialism, a time when once-subject peoples will be free from European domination. She also suggests that in *Heart of Darkness,* at least, Conrad represents the "incipient resolves" that will lead to revolution (Hay 1992, 134). She even hints that such a resolve can be found in both "Youth"—"when Marlow hears an English captain cursing 'Eastern' natives and reflects that a 'stealthy Nemesis' lies in wait for the arrogance of conquering nations"—and in the Patusan chapters of *Lord Jim* (Hay 1992, 127). She stops short, though, of arguing that revolutionary consciousness fully emerges in Conrad's early texts. According to her, this occurs only in *Nostromo,* the first of Conrad's novels to address "revolution and its consequences in a post-colonial world" (Hay 1996, 81).

Although *Nostromo* is, indeed, a novel about revolution, it is not Conrad's first: Conrad addresses revolution in virtually all of his early colonial novels. As Hunt Hawkins notes, most non-European characters in Conrad's early novels "transcend whatever dependency they may have on Europeans and enter into active revolt. Mrs. Almayer, Nina, Lakamba, Babalatchi, Abdulla, Dain Maroola, Omar, Aïssa, Gobila, Rajah Allang, Doramin, and Jewel all end up hating Europeans, and most have as their primary goal in life the expulsion of the colonialists from their land" (86–87). Ultimately, Hawkins argues, Conrad's representation of colonial subjectivity anticipates that of Frantz Fanon: like Fanon, Conrad focuses on the "psychological mechanisms" that lead to revolt (86).

In arguing that Conrad can be understood as postcolonial since he not only challenges imperialist ideology but imagines imperialism's end and the formation of postcolonial states, I am, of course, building on the work of the critics mentioned so far and others as well—including Byron Caminero-Santangelo, Terry Collits, Linda Dryden, Avrom Fleishman,

Christopher GoGwilt, Robert Hampson, and Andrea White—critics who have considered Conrad's work in the context of empire and identified anti-imperialist elements in it. None of these critics, so far as I know, identifies Conrad as postcolonial and analyzes his works as such or regards his stylistic innovations as anything but part of his modernist aesthetic. As I shall demonstrate, however, analyzing Conrad's stylistic innovations in relation to his ever-changing relationships with British publishers leads to new insights into how Conrad's aesthetic developed out of pragmatic concerns as well as writerly ones. Like other early postcolonial writers, Conrad was forced to obfuscate his radical politics to succeed professionally.

CHAPTER TWO

"There Will Be Fighting": Insurgency & Postcoloniality in *Almayer's Folly* & *An Outcast of the Islands*

Almayer's Folly

In the novelty of its local color, in the daring originality of its dramatic force, in the fresh disclosure of new scenes and characters, in the noble and imaginative handling of life's greatness and littleness, *Almayer's Folly* has no place in the prevalent fiction of the hour, which, like a flooded stream, sweeps past us into oblivion. It leaps at once to a place of its own—a place which ought to rank its author high among novelists worthy of the name in its best sense

UNSIGNED REVIEW of *Almayer's Folly* in *Literary News*, September 1895

[*Almayer's Folly*] departs altogether from the conventional happy ending, as well as from many other conventions of the novelist's art. But it is distinctly powerful, and not less distinctly original.

UNSIGNED REVIEW of *Almayer's Folly*, *Speaker*, June 1895

As these two reviews suggest, many of Conrad's earliest critics recognized that his first novel, *Almayer's Folly*, was "remarkable" and even "unique," even though it was marketed by T. Fisher Unwin and Company as popular exotic fiction (Sherry 1973, 48; Watt 1994, xli–xlv). Unlike the works of writers such as Pierre Loti and Carlton Dawes, however—books that sold well but were largely ignored by literary critics—Conrad's first novel was, as H. G. Wells puts it, "praised . . . rather more than it was read" (Sherry 1973, 73). Writing many years later, Edward Garnett, Conrad's first editor and lifelong friend, seems to confirm Wells's observation, noting that the first printing of the novel "rested for years on the booksellers' shelves" and the "title *Almayer's Folly* long remained a jest in 'the trade'" because they were unable to sell it (Garnett 1956, 16). That *Almayer's Folly* did not sell well despite positive reviews can be explained in part by the fact that the book violated genre conventions.[1] In a sense, *Almayer's Folly* is an adventure book without an adventure. Although the title character contemplates a gold expedition into the interior of Borneo that will result in "wealth and power" for himself and his daughter, no such expedition takes place (5). Indeed, by the end of the first chapter, it becomes clear that Kaspar Almayer is a dreamer and a fool and therefore no adventurer at all: he is a man of mediocre abilities whose only outstanding characteristic is his white skin.

Almayer's Folly is not without a hero, however, for as the novel proceeds, Nina Almayer, Kaspar's "half-caste" daughter, emerges as the protagonist, albeit an unconventional one, of a romance (15). Through her, Conrad depicts not only an alternative perspective on imperialism but also the formation of national consciousness as she comes to reject her European heritage and declare herself Malay. By presenting her as heroic, Conrad suggests that Nina is correct in preferring Malay culture to European culture, thereby radically challenging European presumptions of superiority. Conrad also challenges imperialist ideology by representing alternative points of view and histories through his Sulu, Balinese, and Malay characters and by employing a seemingly omniscient narrator whose sympathies appear to shift from the colonizers to the colonized as the novel proceeds. Such features distinguish Conrad's first novel from others published in Great Britain in the 1890s: rather than monologically affirming Britain's civilizing mission as most British fiction of the period does, *Almayer's Folly* contests imperialist ideology and ongoing forms of oppression from colonized perspectives, perspectives Conrad was better able to represent after his own postcoloniality began to emerge in the early 1890s.[2]

Almayer's Folly and Conrad's Emerging Postcoloniality

In terms of sensibilities at least, the man who completed *Almayer's Folly* in 1894 was not the same person who carried drafts of the early chapters with him to Africa in 1890. Conrad himself told his friend Garnett that until he went up the Congo, he had "not a thought in his head," that he "was a perfect animal" (Garnett 1956, 8). Recalling the conversation, Garnett comments, "The sinister voice of the Congo with its murmuring undertone of human fatuity, baseness and greed had swept away the generous illusions of his youth, and had left him gazing into the heart of an immense darkness" (8). As Garnett suggests, the horrors Conrad witnessed in Africa forced him to rethink not only his attitudes toward imperialism and imperialist ideology but also his own complicity in what he describes in "Geography and Some Explorers" as "the vilest scramble for loot that ever disfigured the history of human conscience" (25).[3] One could argue, of course, that Conrad's change in consciousness is similar to the political one George Orwell underwent as a result of his experiences in colonial Burma: both Conrad and Orwell were European-educated white men who reacted against British imperialism only after participating in it.[4] Orwell was neither a colonial subject nor an ethnic "other" to the British, however, and therefore could only imagine, in texts such as *Burmese Days,* what it was like to be a subject person. Conrad, in contrast, knew from his childhood in Russian-occupied Ukraine what it was to be "othered," even though during his long career as a merchant sailor, he had occupied many other positions in the colonial social hierarchy. As a result of his own particular subjectivity, Conrad's change in consciousness was more than just a political one: he became "postcolonial" in the sense that his experiences as a colonial subject coupled with his experiences in Africa led him to develop the sort of "contestatory/oppositional consciousness" that de Alva and others identify with postcoloniality (245). In this regard, at least, Conrad's change in consciousness resembles Gandhi's, whose postcoloniality emerged only after he had lived in both Great Britain and South Africa and developed a broader perspective on imperialism.[5]

Such an account of Conrad's changing sensibilities is necessarily speculative, at least from a biographical point of view, since little of Conrad's correspondence from the period survives, and his autobiographical writings are notoriously unreliable.[6] Indeed, the best record we have of Conrad's emerging postcoloniality is the manuscript of *Almayer's Folly*, since Conrad's changing sensibilities are reflected in it. That fact that he carried the manuscript with him as he traveled back and forth between Europe, Africa, and Australia during this critical period of his life explains at least in part why Conrad treats the manuscript itself "as if it were a sort of hero in an adventure story" in *A Personal Record* (GoGwilt 1995, 112): it becomes a metonym for his own developing consciousness. As we shall see, Conrad's "puzzled wonder as to the meaning of all [he] saw" in Africa in 1890 led him not only to revise the chapters he had written the previous fall but to reconceptualize the entire novel, beginning with its title character (*Letters* 1:294).

The Man Who Would Be White: Kaspar Almayer and the Folly of Racism

Kaspar Almayer certainly lacks the outstanding qualities generally associated with adventure heroes (White 5; Dryden 52, 106–7): he is not brave, smart, or intrepid. He does, however, share one important characteristic with the typical adventure hero: his white skin. Although most critics focus little attention on his racial identity, Kaspar seems to regard his whiteness as his greatest asset, and, like Daniel Dravot in Kipling's "The Man Who Would Be King," he tries to use it to his advantage. Kaspar lacks the initiative, charisma, and drive of Dravot, however, and therefore is unable to exploit his "quality" as a "white man" (31): he is a pathetic figure rather than a vainglorious one, a man who considers himself European even though he has never been there, holding himself above the "savages" around him.

Raised in Java by a father who "grumbled all day" about the "stupidity" of the natives and a mother who "bewailed the lost glories of Amsterdam" from her easy chair, Kaspar demonstrates no propensity for greatness (6). He does, however, learn English and arithmetic well and so manages to find work as a clerk with a successful trader in Macassar and then with Tom Lingard, an English adventurer who has acquired a lucrative trade monopoly in Sambir, a river settlement in Eastern Borneo (6). Kaspar, who left "the poisonous shores of Java" in order "to conquer the world" soon finds what he believes is an opportunity to make his fortune (6): Lingard, it seems, has informally adopted a Sulu girl he had captured in a battle with "pirates," and he has "sworn a mighty oath to marry her to a white man" (8). Kaspar agrees to be that white man, thinking that once Lingard is gone, it would be "easy enough to dispose of a Malay woman, a slave after all, to his eastern mind" (10).[7]

Almayer's decision to advance his material interests by exploiting his racial identity rather than his abilities quickly proves to be a mistake. Immediately following the wedding, Lingard builds the couple "a pretty little house" in Sambir, where Kaspar becomes Lingard's exclusive agent (20). Kaspar thus begins his life as the only white settler on the east coast of Borneo, "eager and full of hope," thinking that "the world was his" (20). The Almayers' marriage quickly fails, however, and his trading success is limited, in part because Mrs. Almayer provides Lakamba—her lover and one of Kaspar's business rivals—with "secret" information about his financial affairs (20). Eventually, with the help of Mrs. Almayer and Syed Abdullah, an Arab trader who has established a post in Sambir, Lakamba rises to power and shuts Kaspar out of the local trade entirely. Kaspar's troubles are compounded when Lingard loses his fortune, for it soon becomes apparent even to Kaspar that the "great piles of shining guilders" that he expected in exchange for marrying Lingard's adopted daughter will never materialize and that his decision to marry a Sulu woman was a tremendous folly: it becomes the "greatest regret" of his life (32).

As Kaspar's hopes for an easy fortune fade, his relations with his wife and the Malay community deteriorate further. Although Mrs. Almayer's intimate relationship with Lakamba ends once he becomes the local Rajah, she treats her husband with "savage contempt expressed by sulky silence, only occasionally varied by a flood of savage invective," and Kaspar, in turn, contemplates murdering her (21). With Lingard appearing in Sambir only infrequently, Kaspar lives in what he regards as isolation, since to him, Malays are not fit "company for a white man" (92).

His only companionship comes from his daughter, Nina, who seems to prefer him to her mother (21). He does not want her to grow up in a "savage" environment, however, so he sends her to Singapore to live with a white family so she can receive "Christian teaching, social education, and a good glimpse of civilized life" (34). Despite his efforts to ensure that Nina is "taught properly" (22), Kaspar cannot "make her white," as his friend, Captain Ford, reminds him (25). In fact, he cannot even make her wish to be white. On the contrary, after returning to her parents' home following "an outburst of contempt from white people for her mixed blood" (34), Nina becomes "gradually more indifferent, more contemptuous of the white side of her descent represented by a feeble and traditionless father" (35).

Not surprisingly, perhaps, given his racial arrogance, Kaspar is oblivious to his daughter's change in attitude: it is unthinkable to him that she would want anything but to live as a white woman. Until the very end, he believes that Nina shares his dreams of leaving Borneo for Europe, where no one "would think of her mixed blood in the presence of her great beauty and of his immense wealth" (5).[8] Accordingly, when he learns of the establishment of the British Borneo Company, he builds a large "new house for the use of the future engineers, agents or settlers of the new Company" in the hopes of making his fortune (26). Once again Kaspar tries to profit from his white skin, fully expecting that business from the European company will come to him rather than to his Malay and Arab rivals. His plans come to nothing, however, when the British give up their claim to Sambir, leaving it "under the nominal power of Holland" (28). Soon afterward, visiting Dutch naval officers dub the unfinished house "Almayer's Folly" since Kaspar wasted "every available guilder" on it (30).

Kaspar makes one last effort to exploit his "quality" as a "white man" after finding Lingard's notes on gold expeditions he made in the Bornean interior (48): in particular, Kaspar hopes that his racial prestige will allow him to succeed "with the up-river tribes" that control "Gunong Mas—the mountain of gold" (31, 63). To make such an expedition, however, he needs laborers, and he is unwilling to trust either Lakamba or Abdullah, the only men who can provide them. When Dain Maroola appears in Sambir hoping to procure gunpowder to use in his fight against the Dutch, Kaspar's labor problem appears to be solved. He agrees to help the desperate insurgent acquire gunpowder if Maroola and half his men will accompany him on a gold expedition upriver once Maroola's brig and the other half of his men get underway with their cargo.

Kaspar Almayer's illicit dealings with Dain Maroola eventually lead to disaster, not only financially but personally, since Nina, whom he hoped to "make" white, elopes with Maroola to become a Rani. It is at this point in the novel that Kaspar's race consciousness surfaces a final time. Although he briefly considers setting aside his prejudices and leaving Sambir with Nina, ultimately, Kaspar does what he considers "his duty to himself—to his race—to his respectable connections" and disowns his daughter. "I will never forgive you, Nina," he tells her: "And tomorrow I shall forget you" (144). He spends what remains of his life trying to forget, an effort that the narrator calls "the undying folly of his heart" (151). Indeed, he goes so far as to erase "carefully with his hand all traces of Nina's footsteps" from the beach after she leaves, making himself ridiculous before his servant, Ali, who looks on with "great dismay" (147).

As the scene on the beach suggests, Kaspar becomes increasingly ridiculous as the novel proceeds, a process that culminates with him being led around by his pet monkey, who "seemed to have taken complete charge of his master" (152). That Kaspar, who consistently held himself above those who are not European, ultimately subordinates himself to an animal is significant: he undergoes a reversal so extreme that he becomes a subject of comic irony. Equally important is the fact that he becomes a comic figure under the gaze of subject peoples: by the end of the novel, Almayer is a caricature of sorts, an object of fun. In effect, Conrad reverses the colonialist gaze so prominent in novels such as Kipling's *Kim* and Joyce Cary's *Mr. Johnson,* subjecting white colonists to a form of irony that has become a part of the postcolonial aesthetic as evidenced by characters ranging from "Big Jim" Walton in A. R. F Webber's *Those That Be in Bondage,* a drunken white colonist named after his mule, to Mr. Winterbottom in Chinua Achebe's *Arrow of God,* a man who tries to impress fellow Europeans with his knowledge of a language he does not even speak. In this sense, at least, Conrad's representation of Almayer seems to become increasingly postcolonial as the novel proceeds.

Nina Almayer: The Half-Caste Hero of an Unconventional Romance

Conrad's negative depiction of Kaspar Almayer has led a number of critics, including Ian Watt, to conclude that Kaspar is an antihero and that, therefore, Conrad can be considered a modernist since, as Malcolm Bradbury and James McFarlane put it, in Conrad's "nihilistic," fictional worlds, the "central figures are men on the point of test, threatened by a secret or alternative self, or a void at the center of their values" (616). Such a description could only be applied accurately to *Almayer's Folly* if Kaspar were the novel's only protagonist.[9] As Ruth Nadelhaft suggests, however, Kaspar is one of several central figures in the novel. Indeed, she argues that Nina Almayer and her mother "carry the weight of the novel in a number of ways, not least by their presence in so many scenes that the first quarter of the novel must be said to be about them" (1991, 20). If Nadelhaft is correct, then *Almayer's Folly* cannot be categorized as nihilistic unless all of the central characters are devoid of values, something that is certainly not true of Nina. As we shall see, far from being an antihero, by the end of the novel, Nina emerges as a powerful, independent character whose decision to be Malay rather than European is represented as being correct.

Nina's emergence as a protagonist is significant not only because she provides Conrad with a means of representing postcolonial consciousness but because, like the narrative's increasingly ironic treatment of Almayer, it illuminates Conrad's own developing postcoloniality. In the initial draft of chapter 1, Nina does not appear at all: she is introduced in what was originally chapter 2 as a seemingly minor character. When Conrad revised his early draft following his return from the Congo, however, he not only restructured the opening chapters so that Nina is introduced in the first chapter but also mentions her on the very first page. He also provides more detail about Nina's experiences in Singapore in what is now the third chapter and adds Captain Ford's comment cited earlier about Kaspar's efforts to "make her white." Taken as a whole, the changes Conrad made to his initial drafts of the opening chapters suggest that he did not conceive of Nina as a protagonist until after his experiences in Africa: what began as a study of a failed adventurer becomes an unconventional romance about a colonial subject who develops a postcolonial consciousness. In this reconceived version of the novel, Nina becomes so important that Conrad considered titling the Polish translation "Almayer's Daughter" (McLauchlan 81).[10]

Predictably, perhaps, most nineteenth-century reviews of the novel did not recognize Nina's significance as a character.[11] The *World,* for example, reports that *Almayer's Folly* is simply the "dreary record of the still more dreary existence of a solitary Dutchman doomed to vegetate in a small village in Borneo" (Sherry 1973, 51), and *Athenaeum* identifies Kaspar Almayer as the "central figure," listing Nina and Mrs. Almayer with "an old servant, Ali, and sundry other retainers" as supporting characters (Sherry 1973, 52). As Nadelhaft suggests, the failure of such readers to recognize Nina's significance can be explained in part by gender prejudice: "Although from his earliest novels Conrad created and developed powerful and credible images of women, male friends, colleagues, and critics disregarded those images and focused instead on images of men" (Nadelhaft 1991, 2). To many of Conrad's readers, a female protagonist was simply unthinkable. Nina's status as a "half-caste" also seems to have contributed to the inability of many of Conrad's original reviewers and critics to recognize Nina's role as hero. This, too, perhaps, should not be surprising, since the heroes of nineteenth-century European novels were almost exclusively white. Indeed, *Almayer's Folly* may be the first novel published in Great Britain to feature a "half-caste" as a protagonist.[12] What is surprising is the fact that a number of reviewers failed to assign Nina any significance at all. The reviewer for *Academy,* for example, apparently groups Nina with "the wily, half-savage Malays" that surround Almayer (Sherry 1973, 54), and *Nation* places her in "a mob of raging heathen" (Sherry 1973, 60). The latter review adds, "Borneo is a fine field for the study of monkeys, not men." Apparently, non-European heroes were as unimaginable to Conrad's original readers as female ones.

Although most of the novel's reviewers seem to have missed it, Nina's role as a hero is signaled in the opening chapter in her encounter with her father after he has learned that Dain Maroola has returned to

Sambir, presumably to accompany him on his gold expedition. To Nina, whose "dreamy eyes" signal her "impatient expectancy," Maroola's reappearance has a different significance—her lover has returned. The narrator's description of Nina makes it clear from the very beginning that the novel is a hybrid of sorts and can be read in at least two different ways: as an adventure story and as an exotic romance.[13] As if to underscore this, in the very next passage Conrad represents her in terms characteristic of the latter genre—she is at once what Linda Dryden identifies as the "oriental *femme fatale*" and a vulnerable European woman in need of rescue (94):[14]

> She was tall for a half-caste with the correct profile of the father modified and strengthened by the squareness of the lower part of the face inherited from her maternal ancestors—the Sulu pirates. Her firm mouth with the lips slightly parted and disclosing a gleam of white teeth put a vague suggestion of ferocity into the impatient expression of her features. And yet her dark and perfect eyes had all the tender softness of expression common to Malay women, but with a gleam of superior intelligence. (15)

If on one level Conrad suggests that *Almayer's Folly* can be read as an exotic romance by including an "oriental *femme fatale*" and a vulnerable European woman, on another level he indicates that the novel is anything but conventional by conflating the two in Nina: her hybrid identity makes it clear that the novel is more than just formulaic entertainment and that Nina is more than just a stock character. Indeed, the description just quoted helps establish Nina as a potential hero since it suggests that she has the best features of both her father and her mother. It also highlights Kaspar's deficiencies, particularly his weak chin: Almayer may be a central character, but as a hero he shows little promise. Nina, in contrast, has all the attributes one might expect of the lead female character in a romance, which suggests that her story is the dominant one.

The conversation that ensues between father and daughter seems to confirm that her story is at least as important as his. Kaspar, who seems oblivious to the fact that his daughter is now grown, repeatedly calling her "little girl," expresses his hope that the success of the gold expedition will allow him to take his daughter to Europe where they can live a "glorious life" (15, 16). Nina, however, is "unmoved" by her father's fantasies of wealth (16). As her father prattles on about his coming triumphs, she gazes into the night, thinking about Maroola. The chapter ends by contrasting Nina directly to her father: "Undisturbed by the nightly event of the rainy monsoon, the father slept quietly, oblivious alike of his hopes, his misfortunes, his friend and his enemies;—and the daughter stood motionless, at each flash of lightning, eagerly scanning the broad river with a steady and anxious gaze" (17). That the first chapter ends by juxtaposing Nina's alertness with her father's lethargy is important since it suggests that the two are essentially different: Nina is an active, independent woman, while her father is a foolish, self-indulgent dreamer. Nina's evident anxiety is also significant: the reader knows why Kaspar is ebullient upon Maroola's return, but the reason for Nina's nervousness is not explained immediately, generating a tension that makes Nina's mysterious response one of the main focuses of the first part of the novel.

Nina's importance in the narrative remains evident in the chapters that immediately follow as the narrator begins to tell Nina's story, beginning with her childhood. We learn that she was born two years into the Almayers' failing marriage, that as a child she had an "evident preference" for her father (21), and that her father sent her to Singapore to "be brought up decently" (22). When she returns unexpectedly to Sambir ten years later, she has become "a woman, black haired, olive skinned, tall and beautiful, with great sad eyes, where the startled expression common to Malay womankind was modified by a thoughtful tinge inherited from her European ancestry" (24). Nina, we are told, "was never happy over there," in part because she was "slighted" by the European women (25). Eventually, her hosts force her to leave their household, because, as Captain Ford explains to Kaspar, having a beautiful young "half-caste girl in the house" is "deucedly awkward" (25). Although Captain Ford offers her a place in his own household, Nina decides to return to Sambir unannounced, apparently tired of being treated with contempt by whites.

In the chapter that follows, the narrator describes how Nina's relationships with her mother and father change after her return to Sambir.

Although she still has great affection for her father, her experiences in Singapore taught her to despise not only colonial society but whites in general, something that becomes most clear in chapter 9 when she tells a Dutch naval officer, "I hate the sight of your white faces," and then, "touching lightly her father's cheek," adds, "I hoped to live here without seeing any other white face but this" (106). It is her relationship with her mother that changes the most, however. At first, Nina approaches her mother "curiously, guarding her skirts from the betel juice" her mother had spit on the floor (33). Eventually, her mother's descriptions of her own childhood, "the glories of the Sultan of Sulu," and the "fear which benumbed the hearts of white men at the sight of his swift piratical praus" make a strong impression upon Nina:

> And listening to the recital of those savage glories, those barbarous fights and savage feasting, to the story of deeds valorous, albeit somewhat bloodthirsty, where men of her mother's race shone far above the Orang Blanda, she felt herself irresistibly fascinated, and saw with vague surprise the narrow mantle of civilized morality, in which good-meaning people had wrapped her young soul, fall away and leave her shivering and helpless as if on the edge of some deep and unknown abyss. Strangest of all, this abyss did not frighten her when she was under the influence of the witch-like being she called her mother. (33)

The more Nina reflects on her experiences in Singapore, particularly the final "outburst of contempt from white people for her mixed blood" that led to her departure, the more she falls "under the influence of her mother" (34, 35). Eventually, she decides that "the savage and uncompromising sincerity of purpose of her Malay kinsmen" is preferable to the "sleek hypocrisy, . . . the polite disguises, [and] to the virtuous pretenses of such white people as she had the misfortune to come into contact with" (43).

Because of the influence of her mother's stories, Nina is predisposed to admire Dain Maroola when he first appears in Sambir, an event the narrator describes in chapter 4. When Maroola first looks at her with "an uncontrolled expression of admiration and desire," Nina feels "a hitherto unknown feeling of shyness mixed with alarm and some delight, enter and penetrate her being" (43). Their mutual attraction soon leads to romance, one that they and Mrs. Almayer are careful to hide from Kaspar and everyone else in Sambir. To Nina, Dain Maroola is "the ideal Malay chief of her Mother's tradition," and her relationship with him allows her to escape her humiliating life as a "half-caste":

> She recognized with a thrill of delicious fear the mysterious consciousness of her identity with that being.—Listening to his words it seemed to her she was born only then to a knowledge of a new existence, that her life was complete only when near him, and she abandoned herself with a feeling of dreamy happiness, while with half veiled face and in silence—as became a Malay girl—she listened to Dain's words giving up to her the whole treasure of love and passion his nature was capable of with all the unrestrained enthusiasm of a man totally untrammeled by any influence of civilized self-discipline. (50)

As the passage suggests, Nina is attracted to Maroola in part because he makes her feel as if she were "a Malay." Her relationship with him helps her to forget her earlier existence as a "half-caste" among whites. It is for this reason that when, toward the end of the novel, circumstances force her to decide whether to continue life with her parents in Sambir or leave with Maroola for Bali, she chooses the latter, telling her father, "I am not of your race. Between your people and mine there is . . . a barrier nothing can remove" (134). As John McClure notes, Conrad casts Nina "in the role of judge," and she "chooses Malay culture over European" (105).[15]

Nina Almayer and the Malay Insurgency

Many critics, including Thomas Moser and D. C. R. A. Goonetilleke, dismiss Nina's decision to join Dain Maroola as "romantic."[16] To do so is to ignore the political context of her decision. Dain Maroola is not a trader or a pirate but a prince who has come to procure gunpowder to fight encroaching Dutch imperialists. That he does so "at a time when the hostilities between Dutch and Malay threaten to spread from Sumatra over the whole archipelago" is even more significant (62): as we shall see, he is part of a larger revolutionary struggle to drive Europeans from the archipelago. Nina, it seems, wants to be part of the insurgency as well. When she learns from a naval officer that Dain Maroola has killed two white men by exploding his boat when Dutch sailors are near, she exclaims, "Two only!" as if disappointed that more had not died as Maroola had hoped (105). Leaving Sambir with Dain Maroola affords Nina the opportunity to participate in the insurgency. Although she feels that, as a woman, she cannot "slay the white men" herself, she can "give him [Maroola] his kriss" and "bid him go" as her mother suggests (115). That she intends to do just that becomes clear in her final conversation with her father when she says of Maroola, "He is brave; he will be powerful, and I hold his bravery and strength in my hand, and I shall make him great" (134).

Not surprisingly, given the pro-imperialist sentiment of the 1890s, Nina's rejection of her European heritage and her decision to join the insurgents bothered many of Conrad's late nineteenth-century British readers, implying as it did that Malay culture was, in some ways at least, superior to European culture and that resistance to European imperialism was legitimate. One early critic asserts that "Conrad, beyond all others has identified himself with the standpoint of the natives," and another complains that the "moral" of *Almayer's Folly* "seems to be that white Christians can be much worse than black pagans, and generally are, along the Straits of Macassar" (Sherry 1973, 119, 81). Despite their limitations and obvious prejudices, these early critics see what many contemporary critics miss: by contrasting Nina's undoubted happiness and success as a Malay to her father's continuing failure, Conrad affirms that Nina has made the right choice. Whereas Kaspar Almayer dies miserable and alone as an opium addict, Nina renounces her European identity, helps the fugitive, Dain Maroola, escape to Bali, and becomes Rani of a powerful, independent state.[17] Through Nina, then, Conrad provides his readers with an alternative perspective on imperialism. More important, perhaps, as Christopher GoGwilt argues, "Nina's rejection of the 'white side of her descent' shows Conrad imagining an alternative political and historical consciousness," one that will eventually provide a basis for a new national identity (GoGwilt 1995, 82). This becomes most clear when Nina tells her father, "I have been rejected with scorn by the white people, and now I am a Malay!" (134). Nina's formal assertion of Malay identity is significant since it anticipates the formation of a national identity for the many peoples of the Malay Archipelago.[18] She is not Dutch, Sulu, or a "half-caste" but Malay—part of an emerging nationality that will eventually challenge European hegemony in the archipelago.[19]

Other Ways of Seeing: Indigenous Perspectives and the Provincializing of Europe

Conrad's "half-caste" hero, Nina Almayer, is only one of the novel's radical features, for in addition to developing a critique of imperialism through Nina, Conrad develops alternative frames of reference through indigenous characters. By including such perspectives, Conrad not only recognizes that the peoples of the Malay Archipelago have distinct interests and points of view but also suggests that resistance to imperialism takes many forms and operates on many levels. Moreover, as we shall see, Conrad's dialogization of various perspectives on imperialism challenges the "master narrative" offered by European histories of the colonization of the archipelago, effectively provincializing them (Chakrabarty 43).

Set in the 1870s, *Almayer's Folly* offers an alternative to imperialist accounts of the pacification of the Sulu—accounts that deny the legitimacy of Sulu beliefs, values, and practices—through the thoughts, words, and actions of Sulu characters such as Mrs. Almayer.[20] Despite enduring years of indoctrination in colonial institutions following her capture by Lingard, Mrs. Almayer retains her sense of Sulu identity and continues to regard the world much as she did before she became a colonial subject, "concealing her hate and contempt" for her "new life" (19). Years later, after her daughter is grown, Mrs. Almayer still "glories" in her Sulu past, communicating the history of her people to Nina in a "monotonous recitative" (33). Ultimately, Mrs. Almayer makes the intent of her recitations clear, telling Nina, "When I hear of white men driven from the islands then I shall know that you are alive and that you remember my words" (115). As this passage suggests, Mrs. Almayer recognizes that maintaining a sense of cultural identity is essential to resisting domination on both a personal and a communal level.

Babalatchi, Lakamba's "prime minister, harbour master, financial advisor, and general factotum," another character "of Sulu origin," shares many of Mrs. Almayer's attitudes toward Europeans and their culture (31). Like her, he believes that whites are "stronger" but not "better" (113), and he hopes that the peoples of the archipelago will eventually rebel, telling Captain Ford "with energy" toward the end of the novel, "There will be fighting. There is a breath of war in the islands" (154). He realizes, however, that the peoples of the archipelago cannot resist European domination militarily and so "circumvent[s]" white colonists rather than fights them, commenting, "White men were strong but very foolish. It was undesirable to fight them, but deception was easy. They were like silly women; they did not know the use of reason and he [Babalatchi] was a match for any of them" (66, 64). Although the narrator indicates that Babalatchi's "confidence" in his ability to deceive Europeans is based on "deficient experience," Babalatchi successfully manipulates Europeans, not only engineering Dain Maroola's escape to Bali after he kills two Dutch sailors but also shielding the Rajah from the consequences (64). More important, perhaps, with Kaspar's demise, which Babalatchi is at least partially responsible for, Europeans no longer have a permanent resident in Sambir, thus diminishing their power there. Although Sambir is still nominally controlled by the Dutch, indigenous peoples can live there without fear of European interference in their day-to-day lives.

Conrad offers yet another perspective on European imperialism through Nina's lover, Dain Maroola, a Balinese prince who fights the Dutch because they threaten Balinese autonomy. As the subject of an independent state, Maroola's attitude toward imperialism is very different from that of subjects such as Mrs. Almayer and Babalatchi: he believes that the colonization effort can be effectively resisted through direct action. To Maroola, the struggle against the Dutch is not merely local, a point the novel reinforces by having Maroola's appearance in Sambir coincide with what it terms the "Acheen war"—a lengthy conflict in which the Aceh effectively resisted Dutch efforts to occupy parts of northern Sumatra for more than forty years (38).[21] The inability of the Dutch to defeat the Aceh outright diminished their military reputation, which, in turn, made their control of the archipelago all the more tenuous. This problem became particularly acute for the Dutch when the Aceh defeated the first expedition against them in 1873, and, as the narrator of *Almayer's Folly* notes, "the hostilities between the Dutch and Malays threatened to spread from Sumatra over the whole archipelago" (62). By introducing Maroola in such a context, the novel suggests that although Maroola acts primarily to preserve Balinese autonomy, he is also part of a larger struggle in which peoples throughout the archipelago resist the Dutch colonization effort. Maroola demonstrates his commitment to this broader insurgency when, pursued by a Dutch frigate far from Bali, he tries to kill the Dutch sailors rather than simply escape them (167).[22] Like Mrs. Almayer and Babalatchi, he wants to "see white men driven from the islands" (200). Rather than simply hope for such a struggle, however, he participates in it.

Until recently, Maroola has been generally dismissed by critics as a mere love interest.[23] He is more than just a convention of a popular romance, however, for it is through him that Conrad represents what it is to be an anticolonial insurgent. Certainly, the Indonesian novelist Pramoedya Ananta Toer recognizes this, recalling *Almayer's Folly* as a "story about a Balinese prince who is smuggling guns to organize resistance against Dutch colonial rule" (GoGwilt 1996, 156). To Toer, Maroola is the novel's central character. Toer goes on to comment that in the novel, "Conrad was writing about the history of armed struggle against colonialism not recorded in Dutch historiography" (156).

Toer is not the only one to credit Conrad with recording events ignored by European histories, of course: the Indonesian historian G. J. Resink also recognizes that Conrad's fictions provide useful supplements to official European historical accounts (GoGwilt 1995, 83). In effect, Conrad "provincializes" Europe, to borrow Dipesh Chakrabarty's term, recording "the ambivalences, contradictions, the use of force, and the tragedies and the ironies" that European histories ignore in constructing their own "master narrative" (27, 43). By directly representing the consciousness of characters such as Maroola, Mrs. Almayer, Nina, and even the "slave girl" Taminah (48), Conrad presents contact zones such as Sambir—spaces where peoples "geographically and historically separated come into contact with each other and establish ongoing relations, usually involving conditions of coercion, radical inequality, and intractable conflict"—in all their complexity (Pratt 6).[24] Like other early postcolonial novels set in contact zones, including Solomon Plaatje's *Mhudi* and A. R. F. Webber's *Those That Be in Bondage, Almayer's Folly* is dialogic in the sense that it sets various languages in relation to one another, making them "live," as Bakhtin might put it (361).

Narratorial Shifts, Dialogism, and Conrad's Postcoloniality

So far I have argued that *Almayer's Folly* exploits the dialogic possibilities inherent in the novel through its representation of the various social voices that exist in Sambir. Not every voice contained within a novel belongs to characters, however: it is important to consider the narrator's voice as well because it, too, represents a particular perspective. In the case of *Almayer's Folly,* ascertaining this perspective is difficult, since, as Allan Simmons notes, "the narratorial perception shifts" as the novel proceeds, gradually moving "from a colonising perspective to a colonised perspective" (Simmons 1997, 163). According to Simmons, this shift in narratorial perception is most evident in the treatment of Nina. Near the beginning of the novel, for example, the narrator describes Nina in a way that reinforces the opposition between Europeans and Malays, noting her "correct [European] forehead" and how her "eyes had all the tender softness of Malay women, but with a gleam of superior intelligence" (166). As Simmons notes, the narrator's description seems "to replicate, and hence endorse, the racial bias of Almayer"—and by extension, those of white imperialists in general (1997, 166). The binary opposition upon which such racism is based, however, is "deconstructed" as the narrative continues (167): the narrator later tells us, for example, that Nina loses "the power to discriminate" between Europeans and Malays and then goes on to suggest that there is, in fact, no significant difference between "the barbarian" and the "so-called civilized man" (Simmons 1997, 168). Moreover, as Simmons demonstrates, the narrator's speech is "gradually infiltrated by the voices of the colonised," and the text becomes "culturally polyphonic" (1997, 170). Finally, Simmons shows how the narrative voice that initially sympathizes with a European perspective "come[s] full circle" and "come[s] to reflect, to empathise with, and to champion the plight of the Orientals" (1997, 172).

The way in which the narratorial perspective shifts from a colonizing perspective to a colonized one clearly challenges British claims of superiority and righteousness. The shift does more than simply contest imperialist ideology, however: to the extent that the narrator's voice becomes "reified" as it enters a dialogic relationship with the other voices in the novel, that voice functions as a subject position within the text, one available to readers through the process of identification (Bakhtin 361). Accordingly, as this narratorial perspective moves from a colonizing perspective to a colonized one, it has the potential to move readers along with it. To put it another way, as the narratorial perspective shifts, it may induce certain readers to shift with it, potentially affecting their assumptions and attitudes.

Although the shift in narratorial perspective that Simmons identifies seems to have a political function, it appears to be as much a product of Conrad's emerging postcoloniality as it is of conscious design. As I indicated earlier, Conrad's attitude toward imperialism and imperialist ideology changed while writing *Almayer's Folly* as a result of his experiences in Congo, leading to an increasingly ironic treatment of Almayer, the development of Nina Almayer as a protagonist, and the dialogic representation of the various social voices present in Sambir. The shift in narratorial perspective appears to be a product of the same process, and *Almayer's Folly* can thus be read as a record of Conrad's developing consciousness: Conrad may not have begun it as a postcolonial novel—that is, as a text that contests imperialist ideology and ongoing forms of colonial domination through the consciousness of subject peoples—but it became one as Conrad's own postcoloniality developed (de Alva 245).

With all this in mind, it is no wonder that *Almayer's Folly* failed to acquire a popular audience: there simply was no market for a novel that not only features a "half-caste" hero but presents a number of alternative perspectives on imperialism through a variety of indigenous characters and even a narrator who ultimately sympathizes with the colonized. As Andrea White suggests, many readers found such "ventriloquism" unacceptably subversive since "the dialogic possibilities permitted by the discrepancies of multiple viewpoints begin to dislodge the authority of the white man's telling" (White 119, 127).[25] In addition, many readers may have been uncomfortable with the novel because it did not affirm their own racist beliefs. As Geoffrey Harpham notes, the novel was "alien" to many of its readers because of "the equality of treatment allotted to all characters, as though absolutely nothing were at stake in noting racial differences" (47). Readers may also have been disturbed by the novel's social and political implications. Even though *Almayer's Folly* closes with the Malay Archipelago still dominated politically, economically, and militarily by the Dutch, British, and Spanish, European hegemony ends as a national identity develops, the anti-imperialist insurgency grows, and an end to imperialism becomes imaginable. As a postcolonial novel published near the peak of British imperialist sentiment, *Almayer's Folly* relates a story most British readers did not want to hear.

An Outcast of the Islands

Conrad began his second novel, *An Outcast of the Islands,* just after submitting the typescript of *Almayer's Folly* to T. Fisher Unwin for publication in the summer of 1894. Superficially, this novel, which is set in Sambir some time before the action of *Almayer's Folly* takes place, resembles Conrad's first novel, if only because it features many of the same characters and addresses many of the same themes. In some ways, however, *An Outcast of the Islands* is even more radical than *Almayer's Folly,* since, in addition to depicting white colonists in a negative manner and representing the formation of a postcolonial consciousness, the novel focuses on subalterns, their subjectivity, and the threat they represent to colonial authority.[26] Whereas in *Almayer's Folly,* subalterns such as the "slave girl" Taminah are represented as having only limited agency, in *An Outcast of the Islands,* subalterns not only speak but act, in Aïssa's case killing the white colonist who betrays her. By depicting subalterns, including Aïssa, a Malay-Arab woman who is one of the novel's central characters, in such a manner, Conrad exposes an important contradiction within the colonial system: subalterns represent a threat to colonial power because they are ungovernable, and they are ungovernable because as subalterns they are excluded from the very institutions that are designed to contain potential insurgents. As a result, *An Outcast of the Islands* not only reinforces the critique of imperialism Conrad offers in *Almayer's Folly* through its representation of Nina and other characters but also supplements it: colonial subjects no longer represent the sole threat to the colonial system; they are joined by subalterns, since they are beyond the control of colonial institutions.

Fools, Thieves, and Megalomaniacs: White Men in the Colonies

Like Robert Louis Stevenson's *The Ebb-Tide* (1894), *An Outcast of the Islands* is, among other things, a study of imperialists at their worst (White 136; Dryden 77).[27] In it, Almayer is an indolent, ineffectual man hoping for an easy fortune just as he is in *Almayer's Folly.* In *An Outcast of the Islands,* he is more of a whiner than a dreamer, however, as evidenced by his long, complaining conversations with Lingard when the latter reappears after a lengthy absence from Sambir (181–96). Peter Willems, in contrast, a protégé of Lingard's who marries Joanna Da Souza, a Malay-Portuguese woman, to improve his fortune, is a talented, arrogant man who believes that scruples are for "the fools, the weak, the contemptible . . . Where there are scruples there can be no power" (8). For him, power is of the utmost importance. Accordingly, he supports his Malay-Portuguese in-laws even though he regards them as "lazy," because in exchange for his money, "he had their silent fear, their loquacious love, their noisy veneration" (4): as the narrator puts it, "It is a fine thing to be a providence, and to be told so on every day of one's life. It gives one a feeling of enormously remote superiority, and Willems revelled in it . . . They lived now by the grace of his will. This was power. Willems loved it" (5). Willems, it seems, is a megalomaniac of sorts, a man who enjoys nothing more than domineering those he considers his inferiors, including his "half-caste" wife, Joanna, and his "dark-skinned" brother-in-law, Leonard (25). His attitude towards Aïssa, the Malay-Arab woman who becomes his lover once his marriage fails, is similar: despite his overwhelming attraction to her, he considers her "a complete savage" and takes great pleasure in the idea of having her all to himself "to fashion—to mould" (80, 92). Unlike Almayer, who believes in his own racial superiority but seems to take no particular pleasure in asserting power for its own sake, Willems has been corrupted by the power the colonial system accords him as a white man, and he exercises that power at every opportunity.

Lingard, an Englishman, is very different from the two Dutch colonists, Almayer and Willems. Like them, he is primarily motivated by profit, but he is paternalistic toward Malays rather than contemptuous.[28] To him, Sambir is a private domain of sorts, one in which he controls the trade and rules indirectly through the local rajah, Patalolo (43). Even though he is the one who profits most from the trade, he boasts to Willems, "I brought prosperity to that place. I composed their quarrels, and saw them grow under my eyes. There's peace and happiness there" (45). Despite Lingard's confident assertion of the positive effects of his rule, as the narrative proceeds, it becomes increasingly clear that Sambir is anything but peaceful and happy and that Lingard maintains control by force, quelling rebellions with his "armed brig" (51).

Because Lingard is English—something emphasized repeatedly both in *Almayer's Folly* and *An Outcast of the Islands*—Conrad's ironic treatment of Lingard's self-satisfied paternalism toward Sambir functions as a critique of British paternalism toward its colonies. This critique becomes explicit in a conversation between Lingard and Babalatchi after the "great revolution" occurs and Lingard loses control of the colony (360). Lingard expresses disdain for Dutch imperialist practices and suggests to Babalatchi that he and his allies will regret seeking Dutch protection, telling him "with great earnestness" that in dominating Sambir, he acted "for the good of all" (225, 226).[29] Babalatchi, however, recognizes Lingard's statement as self-serving and hypocritical:

> "This is a white man's talk," exclaimed Babalatchi, with bitter exultation. "I know you. That is how you all talk while you load your guns and sharpen your swords; and when you are ready, then to those who are weak you say: 'Obey me and be happy, or die!' You are strange, you white men. You think it is only your wisdom and your virtue and your happiness that are true." (226)

Although Babalatchi addresses Lingard here, his words pertain to all imperialists who believed that they best knew what was good for others (200). For all their professed altruism, Babalatchi suggests, British imperialists are limited by their own ethnocentrism: they refuse to accept the possibility that what they consider to be "good" may very well be seen as "bad" by others.

Disparaging depictions of white colonists—even British ones—are not unusual, of course, even in the works of late nineteenth-century British colonialist writers. What differentiates Conrad from writers like Haggard and Kipling is that in Conrad's work, there are no good colonists: even well-meaning Englishmen like Lingard and, as we shall see, Jim of *Lord Jim,* are deluded, hypocritical, and self-serving. Another thing that distinguishes *An Outcast of the Islands* from colonialist novels of the same period is Conrad's pervasive use of irony in his treatment of his white colonists: the narrator even employs sarcasm at times, describing Almayer and Willems as "specimens of the superior race" even as they "glared at each other savagely" and describing Lingard as a "doer of justice" immediately after demonstrating that the actions Lingard contemplates are actually motivated by "revenge" (62–63). As I argued earlier, such use of irony has become part of the postcolonial aesthetic, a means of subjecting white colonists to the kind of ridicule to which colonialist writers subjected the colonized. To white colonists, there is nothing worse than "to be made a laughing-stock of before a parcel of savages," as Almayer puts it (207).

Colonial Subjectivity and Resistance

In addition to disparaging white colonists, *An Outcast of the Islands* explores in detail what it is to be a colonial subject. In *Almayer's Folly,* as we have seen, Conrad depicts the formation of a national consciousness through his representation of Nina, a "half-caste" living in "savage" surroundings who rejects her European heritage to join the rebellion against the Dutch in Bali. In *An Outcast of the Islands,* he focuses on the colonial subjectivity of Joanna and Leonard Da Souza, "half-castes" living in a colonial center who resent being subjugated by Europeans even though they depend on them financially.

As Robert J. C. Young demonstrates in *Colonial Desire: Hybridity in Theory, Culture and Race,* in the nineteenth century, the British generally regarded "half-castes" as racial inferiors, people whose white blood was essentially compromised or polluted. Despite this—or perhaps because of it—they were considered by some to be ideal colonists, particularly in tropical regions when the mortality of white colonists was high. Regarding Jamaicans of African/European descent, Anthony Trollope, for example, writes, "My theory—for I acknowledge to a theory—is this: that Providence has sent white men and black men to these regions in order that from them may spring a race fitted by intellect for civilization; and fitted also by physical organization for tropical labour" (75). In *Ten Years in Saráwak,* Charles Brooke made a similar argument for what Young calls "the breeding of a new strain of mixed-race colonials" in Asia, a belief that, according to Young, "would influence conditions in Sarawak right into the twentieth century" (143–44). To many imperialists, the economic advantages of employing "mixed-race colonials" seemed obvious: the dominant racial stereotypes of their time led them to believe that these half-castes would be hardier than the average European and more intelligent than the average native.[30] Such hybrids, they believed, would also be ideally suited to manage natives even as they themselves were managed by Europeans.[31] This scheme could only work, however, if natives accepted "half-castes" as their superiors, and in turn, half-castes accepted Europeans as theirs. In *An Outcast of the Islands,* Conrad suggests that neither is likely to happen since whites despise half-castes as inferiors, half-castes consider themselves to be white, and native inhabitants treat half-castes as outcasts.

That the whites living in the archipelago despise half-castes becomes evident very early in the novel, not only because of Willems's contempt for his wife but because, as a couple, they will not be accepted into white society because of her mixed blood (9).[32] One reason whites apparently dislike people of mixed race is because they do not accept the place in the colonial social hierarchy that Europeans have assigned them. Rather than assume a subordinate status, half-castes like Joanna and Leonard consider themselves white, something that becomes clear when, just before Willems assaults him, Leonard implores him not to be "brutal" since it would be "unbecoming" for "white men" to fight "with all those natives looking on" (29). As Leonard's words suggest, to half-castes, being white is more than just a matter of blood: acting white is just as important as being white. Indeed, Leonard comes to regard Willems as his inferior because of Willems's actions, at one point telling him that he is "a savage . . . Not at all like we whites" (28).

Conrad's half-castes are not docile, either, even though his white characters expect them to be. When, coming home late on his thirtieth birthday after a night of drinking, for example, Willems wakes Joanna so that he can boast to her of his various exploits and successes, expecting that "she would stand at the further end of the table, her hands resting on the edge, her frightened eyes watching his lips, without a sound, without a stir, hardly breathing, till he dismissed her with a contemptuous: 'Go to bed, dummy'" (9). The passage continues, "She would draw a long breath then and trail out of the room, relieved but unmoved. Nothing could startle her, make her scold or cry. She did not complain, she did not rebel." Much to Willems's "surprise," she does in fact rebel just two days later when she learns that he has embezzled money from her father, Hudig:

> As Willems was looking at Joanna her upper lip was drawn up on one side, giving her melancholy face a vicious expression altogether new to his experience. He stepped back in surprise.
>
> "Oh! You great man!" she said distinctly, but in a voice that was hardly above a whisper.

> Those words, and still more her tone, stunned him as if somebody had fired a gun close to his ear. He stared back at her stupidly . . .
>
> "Joanna!" exclaimed Willems.
>
> "Do not speak to me. I have heard what I have waited for all these years. You are less than dirt, you that have wiped your feet on me. I have waited for this. I am not afraid now. I do not want you; do not come near me." (27)

Just as Lingard finds it difficult to accept the fact that the people he dominated in Sambir were anything but grateful to him, Willems cannot believe that Joanna resents him, even though he has systematically abused her since they were first married: "Willems stared motionless, in dumb amazement at the mystery of anger and revolt in the head of his wife. . . . He felt terror at this hate that lived stealthily so near him for years" (27). That Joanna's hatred for Willems was hidden for so long is as significant as the fact that she finally revolts. Colonial subjects like Joanna may hide their hatred, but that does not mean it does not exist and that they will not revolt when they have the opportunity. As if to underscore this point, the narrator dramatizes Leonard Da Souza's rebellion in a similar manner. When Willems first meets him, Leonard is obsequious to the point of being ridiculous, even chalking Willems's "cues when playing billiards" (34). After years of being "patronize[d] loftily" by Willems, however, Leonard turns on Willems, helping to document his "irregularities" and reporting them to Hudig (3, 33). Willems is stunned when he learns from Lingard what Leonard has done:

> "Why, Captain Lingard," he [Willems] burst out, "the fellow licked my boots."
>
> "Yes, yes, yes," said Lingard testily, "we know that, and you did your best to cram your boot down his throat. No man likes that, my boy." (33)

Lingard's explanation as to why Leonard would ruin the man who supports him and his family seems plausible: people resent being abused even when they are dependent on their abusers. Ironically, Lingard fails to realize that the same dynamic is at work in Sambir: he forces the people there to lick his boots, so to speak, and they rise up against him at their first opportunity.

Governability and the Unspeaking Subaltern

If the narrator's description of Joanna and Leonard Da Souza's actions highlights the tenuousness of imperialist control over the seemingly docile subjects living in colonial centers such as Macassar, Willems's fear of the subaltern "Bajow vagabonds" whom Joanna hires to take her downriver highlights the challenges imperialist control faces on the periphery (309). Although these subalterns do not "speak" in Gayatri Spivak's sense of the term, they do function as "figures of colonial resistance," to borrow Jenny Sharpe's phrase, since their ungovernability exposes the limits of colonial power. As we shall see, Conrad's representation of the men from Bajow does more than just demonstrate that not all subject peoples can be governed. It also suggests that the "vast ideological machinery" of colonization "that silences the subaltern" is the very same machinery that will ultimately bring about the end of colonization, since, in excluding the subaltern, colonial institutions prevent them from being conditioned as subjects (Sharpe 143).

That the men from Bajow have never been subjected to colonial institutions is clear: they are "sea gypsies," to borrow Almayer's term, speaking neither English nor Dutch and knowing little of colonial practices (310, 312). As subalterns they are of no account, at least to white colonists and, as Almayer notes, "could disappear without attracting notice" (310). Even Almayer's servants hold them in contempt: to them, the men are "ill-behaved savages" who "should not be spoken to by white men" (316). Despite their low status—or, perhaps, because of it—they are of great use to white colonists like Almayer, because "they are ready for anything if you pay them" and unlikely to reveal any secrets because "nobody . . . would dream of seeking information of them" (312, 310).

Ironically, the unaccountability that makes subalterns valuable to colonists in some ways also makes them a threat. Because they are considered insignificant, at least as individuals, subalterns are never systematically conditioned to accept colonial beliefs and practices, and therefore they are more difficult to control. This becomes evident in the case of Mahmat Banjer, one of the Bajow boatmen, when Almayer threatens to evict him. Even though Banjer abases himself to Almayer, he "made up his mind that if the white man ever wanted to eject him from his hut, he would burn it and also as many of the white man's other buildings as he could safely get at" (318). Subalterns like Banjer are governed by force rather than consent and therefore cannot be expected to follow colonial law when they are not under direct supervision.

The threat that subalterns pose to colonial society becomes even more pronounced in Willems's encounter with the boatmen later in the novel. Like Almayer, Willems strongly believes in his own racial superiority and expects to be treated with deference by subject peoples even as he bullies them, sometimes with "profane violence" (19). At the same time, however, he refuses to travel unarmed with the subaltern boatmen, even though doing so may be his only means of escaping exile: "Couldn't think of trusting himself unarmed with those Bajow fellows," he tells himself (349). As if to emphasize the need for colonists to be armed while among colonial subjects when on the periphery of empire, the narrative reports Willems's desire for his gun three times: when he meets with Joanna upon her arrival (349), when the boatmen land the boat near him (350), and again when he sees Aïssa in the distance (352). Even though he has no particular reason to fear these subalterns, he also seems to know that he cannot rely on racial prestige to protect him from people who have not been conditioned to accept his authority; ultimately, he depends on force to control them.

The novel's climax strongly affirms this point. When Aïssa sees the subaltern boatmen, she arms herself with Willems's revolver to protect him from them. Once she realizes that Joanna has come to take Willems away, however, she becomes angry and refuses to give the gun to him when he demands it (354). Following a confrontation between Aïssa and Joanna in which Joanna slaps her and runs to the boat, Willems tries to reach the gun, which Aïssa has set down. Aïssa grabs it first, however, and puts it behind her back: "You shall not have it. Go after her. Go to meet danger . . . Go to meet death . . . Go unarmed . . . Go with empty hands and sweet words . . . as you came to me . . . Go helpless and lie to the forests, to the sea . . . to the death that awaits you . . ." (359, ellipses in original). As Aïssa's words indicate, she recognizes that Willems can only control the boatmen by force, that "sweet words" will not be enough to control subalterns who have not been conditioned by colonial institutions to accept white authority. The implications of this are important: if, as subalterns, they cannot speak, then they cannot be spoken to and thereby controlled. Their silence is, in a sense, their strength.

The Subaltern Shoots: *Aïssa and Willems*

If the subaltern boatmen represent a potential threat to Willems, Aïssa proves herself a very real one. It is not savagery that makes her dangerous to him, however, but her ungovernability, something that distinguishes her from subject peoples as they are represented in the colonialist fiction of writers such as Haggard, Kipling, and Cary.[33] Since she has had no contact with whites or colonial institutions until coming to Sambir, she does not realize at first that the racial hatred imperialist ideology fosters—the "contempt of a white man for that blood which is not his blood, for that race which is not his race"—makes a stable, long-term relationship with Willems impossible (152): she cannot comprehend why Willems despises her despite his attraction to her or why Willems comes to despise himself for having an adulterous relationship with someone he considers an "animal" (270). Once she realizes that she has been betrayed by Willems, who never told her he had a wife and child, she recognizes that he is a duplicitous white man who, like most of Conrad's other colonists, acts only in self-interest. Her reaction, as described by the narrator, makes it clear that she represents not just an injured lover but an injured class of people: "Hate filled the world . . . —the hate of race, the hate of hopeless diversity, the hate of blood; the hate against the man born in the land of lies and of evil from which nothing but misfortune comes to those who are not white. And as she stood, maddened, she heard a whisper near her, the whisper of the dead Omar's [her father's] voice saying in her ear: 'Kill! Kill!'" (359).[34] Despite her realization that she has been used by Willems, Aïssa resists her impulse to shoot him, cautioning him not to "come near" (360): unlike the stereotypical savage in an exotic romance, she is not governed by her passions but, rather, shows restraint. Willems, however, decides to risk charging the gun: "Willems pulled himself together for a struggle. He dared not go unarmed [with the boatmen]. He made a long stride and saw her raise the revolver. He noticed that she had not cocked it, and said to himself that, even if she did fire, she would surely miss. Go too high; it was a stiff trigger. He made a step nearer—saw the long barrel moving unsteadily at the end of her extended arm. He thought: this is my time" (360). Willems's final effort to get the gun underscores just how much he fears the men from Bajow: he would rather charge a gun than face them, a decision that costs him his life. That he is killed by a subaltern whom he has sexually exploited is also important, since the narrative holds him accountable for his actions. Although he appears to believe that as a native woman she would be "easy to dispose of," just as Almayer believes of his own wife in *Almayer's Folly,* Willems could not be more wrong (11): it is she, a subaltern, who disposes of him.

Even though Aïssa was originally conceived of by Conrad as a device to advance the stories of Willems and Babalatchi, ultimately she emerges as a fully rounded character through whom Conrad explores not only subaltern consciousness but agency.[35] As we have seen, she is anything but the subaltern who cannot speak or act: she not only shoots Willems but taunts Almayer after the "great revolution" and forces the usually indomitable Lingard to alter his plans through direct confrontation (255).[36] Ironically, despite the directness of her words and actions, white men find her incomprehensible: accordingly, the narrator describes her in paradoxical terms as at once "defiant yet shrinking" (244), "timorous and fearless" (245), "savage and tender" (249). She is unknowable even to her lover, Willems, who exclaims at one point, "How can I know what's in her? She may want to kill me next!" (270). In part, Willems fears her because she is a woman and therefore "inscrutable": "You can't believe any woman. Who can tell what's inside their heads? No one. You can know nothing" (268). He also fears her as a racial "other," however, as someone whose "motives, impulses, desires he had ignored, but that had lived in the breasts of despised men, close by his side" (149). As the reference to "despised men" suggests, to Willems, Aïssa has come to represent a whole indigenous underclass, a class of ungovernable subalterns: what "frightened him . . . was the horror of bewildered life where he could understand nothing and nobody round him; where he could guide, control, comprehend nothing and no one" (149). In what amounts to an epiphany, Willems briefly recognizes the threat that subalterns pose to colonial society and is overwhelmed by it.

Dialogism, Difficulty, and British Fiction Market

Taken as a whole, *An Outcast of the Islands* is even more radical than *Almayer's Folly,* something that should not be too surprising since Conrad began his second novel well after his postcolonial consciousness began to emerge. Like his first novel, *An Outcast of the Islands* exploits the heteroglot possibilities of the genre by dialogizing the various social languages present in Sambir and by depicting imperialism and imperialists in a negative manner. In *An Outcast of the Islands,* Conrad pushes his critique of imperialism further, however, targeting British imperialism through a detailed representation of Lingard's misguided paternalism and suggesting that European control of subject peoples is precarious, particularly on the periphery of empire, where subject peoples have not been conditioned by colonial institutions. Indeed, the novel's climax suggests that imperialism is bringing about the conditions of its own destruction: the more Europeans oppress and exploit subject peoples, the more these subjects are likely to rebel, as the "great revolution" in Sambir demonstrates. With all this in mind, it should not be surprising that the novel sold poorly: like *Almayer's Folly, An Outcast of the Islands* presented multiple perspectives on imperialism at a time when the British reading public was demanding monologic affirmations of its social mission.[37]

Ironically, the complex, dialogic representations of imperialism that limited the novel's popular success were at least partially responsible for the critical acclaim it generally received. Though, as we have seen, many critics disliked Conrad's sympathetic representation of "natives," they recognized the novel's originality and power (Sherry 1973; 55, 60). Here Conrad may have benefited from the same market forces that were to give rise to literary modernism in the twentieth century: Conrad's work was difficult at a time when difficulty was being increasingly appreciated, at least by cultural elitists.[38] Certainly, positive reviews gave Conrad much need encouragement. As his letters of the period indicate, it was at about this time that Conrad began to seriously consider committing himself fully to a career as a writer, in part because of the difficulty he was having in finding work on a ship.[39]

CHAPTER THREE

"But I Should Like to Sell Them": Conrad's First Stories and the Short-Fiction Market

According to Wincenty Lutoslawski, a zealous Polish nationalist who had arranged to meet Conrad in 1897 after reading *Almayer's Folly* and *An Outcast of the Islands,* "as a Pole," Conrad had a "very high conception" of a writer's political and moral duties:

> He knew that writers in Poland had been, in the nineteenth century, the chief leaders of national life, as no practical activity was open to Poles in politics, the army, public education or any kind of office. Writing, authorship, was considered as a kingly function of the highest kind, implying a supreme knowledge of aims and means in order to lead the reader to do the right things in the most difficult national circumstances of persecution, oppression, and treachery. (90)

Even though they met only briefly, Lutoslawski—who described Conrad as a "glowing Polish patriot"—was correct about Conrad's sense of moral duty as a writer. Like his father, Apollo Korzeniowski, a well-known Polish writer and insurgent who died when Conrad was eleven following exile for his political activities, Conrad regarded his writing as a social and political act.[1] Unlike his father, however, who had family money to rely on, writing was Conrad's only means of support once he ended his maritime career.[2] Although Conrad's "high conception" of his duties as a writer prevented him from writing simple entertainment, financial need forced him to adapt to the existing market for fiction. This was particularly important after he married in March 1896 and after the South African Mining Company he had invested his inheritance in failed (Najder 1983, 201). Desperate for income, Conrad began writing short stories while on his honeymoon in Brittany, completing "The Idiots," "An Outpost of Progress," and "The Lagoon" in May, July, and August of 1896, respectively. These early short stories reflect Conrad's efforts to fulfill what he felt were his political and moral duties as a writer even as he attempted to exploit popular demand for short fiction: rather than obfuscate his radical politics, Conrad continued to challenge imperialism and its supporting ideologies directly, just as he did in his first two novels, hoping that he could place the stories despite their content because of his literary reputation. Writing for the short-fiction market forced him to consider questions of audience more carefully, however, and as we shall see, had a marked effect on his work. In particular, the difficulties he had in placing "The Idiots" and "An Outpost of Progress" led him to experiment with the hybrid forms that were to become part of the early postcolonial aesthetic, something that becomes clear in "The Lagoon," a story in which alternative points of view are set against each other. Even though the tension in this story is ultimately resolved in favor of the more radical perspective, the techniques Conrad developed served him later when he began to create intentional hybrids such as "Karain" and "Youth."

Entering the Short-Fiction Market

Conrad's decision to begin writing short fiction was well timed, at least financially. As William Atkinson notes, as literacy increased in Great Britain and the United States in the late nineteenth century, the market for short fiction became increasingly lucrative (1997, xi).[3] Conrad, however, was new to this market and therefore insecure both about the quality of his work and its marketability, as a series of letters he wrote to his publisher, T. Fisher Unwin, and his editor, Edward Garnett, reveal. In a letter to Unwin that he sent on May 22, 1896, Conrad informed him that he had completed a story, "The Idiots," and offered to send it to him, hoping apparently that Unwin would assist him in placing it in *Cosmopolis*, an international review that Unwin's firm helped print and distribute. Of the story itself, Conrad wrote, "Fancy it, not at all bad" (*Letters* 1:279). That same day Conrad wrote to Garnett, telling him that he had sent the story to Unwin (*Letters* 1:281). Ten days later, Conrad again wrote to Garnett about "The Idiots," this time in more detail:

> The Patron [Unwin] got hold of my short story. It's a most damnable occurrence. . . . I wrote to him instructions to forward it to you. I *would not* have it published unless You see it and pass it as fit for the twilight of a popular magazine. I want to know what you think of it with an absurd intensity of longing that is ridiculous and painful. Often I think of the thing with shame—less often with pleasure—but I think of it every day. (*Letters* 1:284)

Conrad's hyperbole reveals both his disdain for popular periodicals and his insecurity about the story's quality. Although very much in need of the income that publishing short stories could bring, Conrad worried that he was compromising his art. Four days later, Conrad wrote to Garnett yet again: "I wrote to F[isher] U[nwin] urging him to forward 'Idiots' to you. Have you got them? What do you think? O! My friend speak the truth [even] if you do tear my entrails through my palpitating flank! From you even torture is sweet" (*Letters* 1:285).

Despite his repeated queries, Conrad did not learn his friend's opinion of the story until July, when Unwin mentioned in a letter that Garnett had been "pleased with it" (*Letters* 1:291); Conrad also learned in the same letter that the story had been rejected twice by *Cosmopolis*.[4] Conrad's disappointment at his story's repeated rejections was at least partially offset by Garnett's approval of it as a work of art.[5] Word from Garnett that *Savoy*, a new periodical edited by Arthur Symons, had asked to see his work further bolstered his confidence, as a letter he sent to Unwin on July 22, 1896, suggests (*Letters* 1:292): "The acceptance of my story [by *Cosmopolis*] would have given me pleasure. But its refusal is not without its compensations—for it is exactly what I did foresee. It shows me that I have judged the work rightly. I am not ashamed of it for all that. Bad or good I cannot be ashamed of what is produced in perfect single mindedness—I cannot be ashamed of those things that are like fragments of my innermost being produced for the public gaze" (*Letters* 1:293). Here, Conrad seems to be making a claim of artistic integrity that anticipates his preface to *The Nigger of the "Narcissus,"* where he writes, "The artist descends within himself, and in that lonely region of stress and strife, if he be deserving and fortunate, he finds the terms of his appeal" (145). In the letter, he goes on to emphasize his material needs, however: "But I must live. I don't care much where I appear since the acceptance of such stories is not based upon their artistic worth. It is probably right that it should be so. But in that case there is not particular gratification in being accepted *here* rather than *there*—If the 'Savoy' thing asks for my work—why not give it to them? I understand they pay tolerably well (2g[uinea]s per page?)" (*Letters* 1:293). Conrad's willingness to have his work published in *Savoy* is telling, particularly since he had indicated his dislike for Symons and his magazine to Unwin just two months earlier (Gordon 220). Clearly, Conrad realized that he would have to make certain compromises to earn money. He was unwilling to compromise his political and moral integrity, however, assuring the liberal Unwin in the passage that follows that "the stories will be worth[y] of your imprint—even if stones are cast at them" (*Letters* 1:293). He continues, sounding a little defensive about trying to profit from his work:

> But I should like to sell them. If you think I am greedy then consider I am greedy for very little after all. And if you knew the wear and tear of my writing you would understand my desire for some return. I writhe in doubt over every line.—I ask myself—is it right?—is it true?—do I feel it so?—do I express all my feeling? And I ask it at every sentence—I perspire in incertitude over every word!—Perhaps you will smile over all this fuss. But I am sure You will not smile unkindly. After all it is my work. The only lasting thing in the world. People die—affections die—all passes—but a man's work remains with him to the last.

Conrad's reference to one's "work" as "the only lasting thing in the world" affirms that to him, writing was not just a vocation or an artistic endeavor but a political and moral act. Although a lifelong religious skeptic,

Conrad had a strong ethical sense, as Najder observes (1983, 220):[6] "In Conrad's view, 'Each act of life is final' and therefore one had to take care to behave responsibly" (*Letters* 1:95; Najder 1983, 47–49).[7]

Fortunately for Conrad financially, Unwin managed to place "The Idiots" in *Savoy* soon after Conrad gave him permission to do so, and the story appeared in October 1896, earning Conrad fifty pounds, more than twice what he received for *Almayer's Folly.*[8] Although as Karl Beckson notes, he would have preferred to appear in *Cosmopolis* or some other more "respectable periodical," he did benefit from the *Savoy*'s relatively high pay scale, and because of the magazine's notoriety, his story probably reached a relatively wide audience, which must have offered Conrad some satisfaction (152).

Resistance and Responsibility in "The Idiots"

Thematically, "The Idiots" is not unlike Conrad's first two novels, even though it is set in rural France rather than the Malay Archipelago; in it, Conrad is as critical of Europeans and European culture as he is in *Almayer's Folly* and *An Outcast of the Islands.* More important, perhaps, the story also addresses the dynamics associated with domination and resistance through its representation of gender oppression. Conrad does not conflate colonial subjectivity with female subjectivity, of course, since the story makes no reference to colonies or colonization. By including the story in *Tales of Unrest,* however, a collection largely concerned with colonial subjectivity, he does suggest, as do a number of feminist postcolonial critics, that there are important similarities between the two types of subjugation and the possibilities for resistance.[9]

Essentially, the story is about a woman, Susan Levaille, who, having already borne four "idiots," stabs her drunken husband with a pair of scissors when he tries to force himself upon her sexually. Knowing that she will be charged with murder, she initially flees but ultimately decides to return and defend her actions to the authorities. Remarkably, given the dominating patriarchal attitudes of the times, the story gives voice to Levaille, presenting her thoughts verbatim: she will "tell them—tell the gentlemen in black clothes that there are things no woman can bear" (81). Before she can return to the village and take responsibility for her actions, however, she is startled by a would-be rescuer, whom she mistakes for her husband's ghost, and falls into the ocean and drowns.[10]

By presenting Levaille's reasons for killing her husband through her own consciousness at a number of points throughout the story, the narrative invites the reader to sympathize with her rather than her brutish husband, thereby legitimizing her use of violence in response to oppression.[11] That she decides to go back and explain her actions to the authorities is also significant, since as we shall see, it is consistent with the sense of moral responsibility Conrad attributes to the Malay protagonists of stories such as "The Lagoon" and "Karain." She takes responsibility for her actions even though doing so will certainly lead to her death: she has acted according to her beliefs and is willing to be judged accordingly.

"The Idiots" as a Critique of European Culture and Its Institutions

In addition to addressing issues of resistance and moral responsibility, "The Idiots" offers a critique of the corrupt, oppressive European social institutions that affirm both patriarchy and imperialist ideology. As Ted Billy suggests, "Conrad's primary concern is not the domestic turmoil involving the parents of four imbecile children but the idiotic sensibilities of three successive generations of a family set against a backdrop of wide-spread political, social, and religious corruption. . . . Like his chief models at the turn of the century—Maupassant, Flaubert, and Zola—Conrad derides the inhumanity of modern institutions, the corruption of their officials, and the foolishness and ignorance of their victims" (163).

The power of Conrad's critique is greatly augmented by the way it is presented. Rather than create a stable omniscient narrator, Conrad employs a first-person narrator who becomes omniscient by the end of the story so that he can exploit the sense of intimacy a first-person narrator creates and at the same time expose more fully the folly and corruption of the individuals and community he describes by representing his characters' thoughts as well as their words and actions.[12] Moreover, as Daniel Schwarz suggests, by moving to an omniscient narrator at the end of the story, Conrad is better able to pass "judgment" on the society he depicts in an authoritative manner (25):

> Rather than dramatise the process by which the narrator learns the information on which his telling is based, as he will in his later tales, Conrad has his narrator rather clumsily explain that he pieced together the story until it stood as a unified "tale formidable and simple." As in the more polished "Amy Foster," to which "The Idiots" looks forward, village life is indicted as petty and mean, and piety is seen to be shallow in a society where Christianity exists in name only. The people accept a simple pecking order where idiots are reduced to animals and where human relationships are conducted without feeling. The political and religious structures under the aegis of the marquis are revealed as corrupt. In both "The Idiots" and "Amy Foster," Conrad indicts a rural community for failing to respond humanely. (25)

If Schwarz's evaluation of "The Idiots" is correct, then it is easy to see how "corrupt" European social institutions relate to the corrupt institutions that are being created by Europeans in their colonies. Although the story is set in rural France, Conrad's critique of European society relates directly to his representations of imperialism in his first novels, since both are the products of the same social system. Colonial life—like "village life"—is "petty and mean, and piety is seen to be shallow in a society where Christianity exists in name only," as Schwarz puts it. Indeed, village life in "The Idiots" is comparable to colonial life in *Almayer's Folly,* where Nina faces similar pettiness and hypocrisy in both Singapore and Sambir. That Conrad should depict life in Brittany as being similar in some respects to life in Sambir should not be surprising. As he indicates in the author's note to *Almayer's Folly,* to him, people are essentially the same, whether they live "in houses or in huts, in the streets under a fog or in the forests behind the dark line of dismal mangroves that fringe the vast solitude of the sea": everyone, he asserts, is subject to heaven's gifts—"the curse of facts and the blessings of illusions; the bitterness of our wisdom and the deceptive consolation of our folly" (3–4). In *Tales of Unrest,* the volume in which "The Idiots" was first collected, Conrad makes a similar point by grouping together thematically related stories that are set in Europe, Africa, and the Malay Archipelago. Despite the varied settings, Conrad's primary focus is on Europeans and their corrupt institutions. As Schwarz observes, "Cumulatively, *Tales of Unrest* implies a vision of Western society impelled toward self-destruction" (33).

Idiots Abroad: Savagery and Civilization in "An Outpost of Progress"

Conrad's next story, "An Outpost of Progress," which was also collected in *Tales of Unrest,* attacks imperialist ideology directly, suggesting not only that imperialism is the product of a corrupt, immoral civilization but that its agents are more savage than the "natives" they have pretenses of civilizing. Most critics seem to regard "An Outpost of Progress" as a companion piece to *Heart of Darkness,* if not a dry run for it, arguing that both stories represent Africa as a corrupting influence. When read in the context of "The Idiots" and that story's critique of oppressive European social institutions, however, it becomes clear that in "An Outpost of Progress," the Europeans arrive in Africa already corrupted and that they are morally unfit to oversee others.[13]

Like "The Idiots," "An Outpost of Progress" is a simple story, at least in terms of plot. At a remote trading station on the Kassai River run by two novice Belgian traders, Kayerts and Carlier, an African clerk, Henry Price, trades the station's African laborers, along with some local tribesmen, to slave traders for ivory. Although the two Europeans initially object to the trade for moral reasons, they eventually agree not to report the incident to their superiors lest they lose their profits. Months later, the two Europeans fight over sugar for their coffee, and Kayerts shoots the unarmed Carlier. When the Company steamer arrives the next morning, Kayerts hangs himself. The story ends with Kayerts's superior finding his corpse with its tongue sticking out in scorn.

As the above synopsis suggests, "An Outpost of Progress" delivers an overt, unambiguous attack on imperialism and imperialists, prompting Garnett to comment that the story "directly challenged the fashionable imperialist propaganda and Kipling's gospel of 'the White Man's burden'" (1971, 9). In the story, the two white men and the colonial institutions they serve are represented as corrupt, immoral, and weak. Although in theme the story resembles *Almayer's Folly* and *An Outcast of the Islands,* it represents a departure from Conrad's earlier style because he relies largely on irony to challenge the legitimacy of European imperialism.[14] Even the title is ironic, for as the story's opening pages make clear, the trading station is anything but "an outpost of progress" and the two "imbeciles" who run it are hardly "pioneers of trade and progress" (87–88).[15]

Conrad's use of sustained, biting irony to indict both imperialist practices and imperialist ideology in "An Outpost of Progress" distinguishes it from typical British fiction of the mid-1890s. Certainly, Conrad realized that his story was distinct from the increasingly jingoistic fiction that was being published widely in various periodicals and that, therefore, the story might be impossible to place: accordingly, he told Unwin that if *Cosmopolis* rejected it, he would "put it by," adding that "A day may come for it" (*Letters* 1:294). As it turned out, his worries were unfounded: *Cosmopolis* accepted the story, where it appeared in June and July 1896, earning Conrad fifty pounds (*Letters* 1:301). Ultimately, the publication of the story benefited Conrad in another, unexpected way: on reading the second installment, R. B. Cunninghame Graham, a prominent radical and prolific writer, wrote to Conrad praising the story and challenging Conrad "to hold to [his] beliefs" (*Letters* 1:370). The two quickly became friends, forming, with Edward Garnett, the center of an anti-imperialist literary circle that lasted into the next century.[16]

Writing for Two Readerships: Convention and Unconventionality in "The Lagoon"

Unlike "An Outpost of Progress," which uses overt irony to offer a direct, sustained critique of imperialist ideology and practices, "The Lagoon" is a hybrid of sorts, a work that envelops one story within another, creating a narrative tension that subverts not only the conventions of the exotic fiction of the 1890s but their ideological implications. Written just after "An Outpost of Progress" was completed, Conrad sent the story, which, superficially at least, appeared to be an exotic tale of love and death, directly to the *Cornhill Magazine,* a well-established popular periodical, where it was accepted and published in October 1896. That Conrad sent it directly to *Cornhill* is significant, not only because the magazine was popular rather than literary, but also because it marks the beginning of Conrad's break with Unwin and the limited market he represented. Although the story is as critical of imperialism as his earlier works, a casual reader could easily miss its subversiveness since Conrad employs many of the conventions of the exotic adventure story even as he undercuts them. For the first time, Conrad seems to address two readerships: those who could appreciate his stories for what they were and the "arm-chair" imperialists who simply sought entertainment.[17]

At first "The Lagoon" seems to be a typical example of exotic colonialist fiction, complete with a jungle setting, passionate natives, and a white man of few words and great wisdom. Although the unnamed white man is neither the main character nor the narrator, the story begins with his arrival at the home of a Malay war comrade, Arsat, and ends with his departure. More important, the adventure story we read is the same story the white man hears from Arsat. Like many colonialist narratives, "The Lagoon" provides the reader with a subject position within the story—the reader witnesses the exotic tale through a peripheral white character. What makes "The Lagoon" unusual is the way it is framed. Rather than present Arsat's tale of love, death, and vengeance as a simple curio, the anonymous narrator uses Arsat's story to challenge not only European assumptions of superiority but also the legitimacy of European imperialism itself (Hampson 2000, 125).

As with "The Idiots" and "An Outpost of Progress," the plot of "The Lagoon" is not complex. Arsat, a warrior from the states of Wajo in the Malay Archipelago, has taken refuge on the mainland after he and his brother help Diamelen, a slave Arsat loved, escape from her royal masters in a small canoe. When the white man arrives at Arsat's lagoon at twilight, he learns that Diamelen is dying of fever. Over the course of the evening, Arsat tells the white man of the escape years ago and of his brother's death at the hands of their pursuers. Rather than fight alongside his brother, Arsat flees in order to be with Diamelen. After Arsat finishes telling the white man his tale, Diamelen dies, and the white man offers to take Arsat upriver with him. Arsat refuses, however, declaring that he will now return to his own country and avenge his brother's death. The story ends with Arsat standing alone, looking "beyond the great light of a cloudless day into the darkness of a world of illusions" (204).

Superficially, at least, the story seems to affirm European stereotypes about passionate "natives" and the brooding, silent "East," leading Daphna Erdinast-Vulcan to identify the story as "a rather crude specimen of Conrad's exoticism at its worst" (55).[18] A closer analysis suggests that Conrad ultimately subverts the conventional imperial romance, however, by employing a narrator who subtly criticizes the white colonist and the imperial system he represents. In particular, the unnamed narrator uses imagery, detail, and varying levels of omniscience to open up an alternative interpretive possibility, one that challenges the assumptions of Conrad's jingoistic readers rather than affirms them. In this sense, at least, "The Lagoon" is a linguistic hybrid, a story that operates on two levels at once, reproducing imperialist ideology only to undercut it.

Subversive Imagery in "The Lagoon"

One of the things that most clearly differentiates "The Lagoon" from colonialist fiction is its used of pointed imagery to undercut the imperialist claim that its mission is to civilize rather than exploit its subjects. For example, the narrator opens the story by describing the white man's approach to Arsat's house, which is built on piles above a remote lagoon. The white man leans his arms "over the roof of the little house in the stern of the boat," while the Malay steersman and the four oarsmen work the boat against the current. The white man gives an order, telling the oarsmen that they will stop at Arsat's clearing for the night, and then rests "his chin on his crossed arms and gaze[s] at the wake of the boat" (187). So far we have a generic colonial setting and scene: a white man leisurely gives orders to sulky natives who grudgingly do as they are told.[19] As the white man "gaze[s] at the wake of the boat," however, the narrator's loaded imagery suggests that in addition to being an adventure story or an exotic tale, the story offers commentary on imperialism itself:

> Nothing moved on the river but the eight paddles that rose flashing regularly, dipped together with a single splash; while the steersman swept right and left with a periodic and sudden flourish of his blade describing a glinting semicircle above his head. The churned-up water frothed alongside with a confused murmur. And the white man's canoe, advancing upstream in the short-lived disturbance of its own making, seemed to enter the portals of a land from which the very memory of motion had forever departed. (187–88)

According to Ruppel, the image of active Europeans penetrating a passive, primitive landscape is typical of nineteenth-century exotic fiction (179–80). Conrad subverts these exotic conventions, though, by suggesting that the imperialist "disturbance" will be "short-lived": the influence of imperialists will be as temporary as their motives are petty. In this story the white man is an adventurer rather than a nation builder. Like Lingard in Conrad's first novels and Stein, Brown, and Jim in *Lord Jim*, the white man regards colonial territories either as plunder or a private domain, a place that can be "squeezed" and then discarded.

Free Indirect Discourse and the Voice of the Subaltern

In addition to challenging imperialism through the careful use of imagery, the narrator offers an indigenous perspective on imperialism through the Malay boatmen in a manner reminiscent of *Almayer's Folly* and *An Outcast of the Islands*.[20] Not surprisingly perhaps, given the realities of the colonial existence, these subalterns are suspicious of outsiders. They do not like stopping at Arsat's clearing because he is an interloper, like the whites themselves:

> They would have preferred to spend the night somewhere else than on this lagoon of weird aspect and ghostly reputation. Moreover, they disliked Arsat, first as a stranger, and also because he who repairs a ruined house, and dwells in it, proclaims that he is not afraid to live amongst the spirits that haunt the places abandoned by mankind. Such a man can disturb the course of fate by glances or words; while his familiar ghosts are not easy to propitiate by casual wayfarers upon whom they long to wreak the malice of their human master. White men care not for such things, being unbelievers and in league with the Father of Evil, who leads them unharmed through the invisible dangers of this world. To the warnings of the righteous they oppose an offensive pretence of disbelief. What is there to be done? (189–90)

This passage is important not only because it reflects the subalterns' distrust of whites and their allies, whom they see as both invaders and infidels, but also because it conveys a sense of the cultural distance between subject peoples and colonists.[21] As subalterns, the boatmen have not been conditioned by colonial institutions and therefore have little understanding of colonists or sympathy for them. To the boatmen, the colonists are "in league with the Father of Evil" and therefore enemies. With this in mind, the question "What is there to be done?" becomes more than just a reflection of their sense of helplessness; it also suggests that the boatmen feel something should be done about the "unbelievers" who have invaded their world.

The fact that the story offers a dialogized, indigenous perspective makes it unusual, particularly since it initially represents itself as a typical imperial romance. What makes the passage remarkable, however, is the narrator's use of free indirect discourse, since it invites the reader to share an indigenous perspective: the narrator induces the reader to think and feel as the boatmen do. The free indirect discourse here is all the more remarkable because it is the only time the device is used in the story: the narrator never invites the reader to share the white man's perspective. Indeed, the narrator seems to be critical of the white man.[22] This becomes most clear when he describes the white man's attitude toward Arsat: "he liked the man who knew how to keep faith in council and how to fight without fear by the side of his white friend. He liked him—not so much perhaps as a man likes his favorite dog—but still he liked him well enough" (191). According to Gail Fraser, "The mildly sardonic tone of the comparison between the useful Malay and a man's faithful dog suggests that the narrator's conception of friendship is not limited by racial bias as the white man's" (1988, 30). The passage does more than simply offer commentary on the white man's racial prejudices, however. As Ruppel notes, "the disparaging comparison of Arsat to a dog opens an ironic space in the narrative" (186). Rather than promote imperialism, "The Lagoon" implicitly challenges the racist ideology that supports it. The white man's beliefs and values are called into question, not those of the subaltern boatmen.

A Tale of Two Tales

Although as we have seen, Conrad reproduces conventions of the exotic romance in order to subvert them, one could argue, as Erdinast-Vulcan does, that the story still belongs within the exotic tradition since it remains a tale of love and death in which subject peoples—unlike their imperial masters—are represented as savage creatures ruled by their passions (55).[23] Such tales tend to legitimate imperialism, since, in addition to contrasting the supposed rationality of Europeans to the supposed emotionality of indigenous peoples, they literally contain the alterity the "native" tale represents within a simple narrative framework that is dismissive of indigenous beliefs and values (Hampson 2000, 125). "The Lagoon" ultimately distinguishes itself from the exotic romance, however, by privileging Arsat's developing sense of morality over the white colonist's lack thereof through a complex process that involves both identification and differentiation.

As I suggested earlier, Arsat's attitudes are identified with those of the white colonist early in the story through the boatmen, who observe that, like whites, Arsat seems to have no fear of ghosts. That Arsat expects the white colonist's understanding and sympathy when telling the story of his betrayal of his brother also suggests a significant level of identification between them. As Arsat himself puts it, in telling his tale, he hopes "to lay down the heaviness" of his "trouble . . . in a friend's heart" (194). It is only when Arsat tells his tale, however, that he identifies his people with the white man's directly, asserting that he is of "a people who take what they want—like you whites" (196). Whites, too, Arsat implies, are people who betray anything or anyone while in pursuit of their desires.[24]

Despite similarities like those just outlined—similarities that suggest whites are not nearly as morally righteous as they would like to believe—an important difference between Arsat and the white colonist emerges toward the end of the story: unlike Arsat, who, as we shall see, comes to regret his past arrogance and selfishness, the white man seems incapable of remorse or moral growth. As Arsat finishes his tale, he hears a stirring within the house and, going in, finds that Diamelen has died of fever. Emerging from the house, Arsat says, "She burns no more," and then, "I can see nothing" (203). Signaling for his boat, the white man replies, "There is nothing" (203). The contrast between Arsat's words and those of the white colonist reveals a fundamental difference between them. In saying that he "can see nothing," Arsat acknowledges his own limitations: he may have been morally blind, but at least he recognizes that he has been so, and therefore, he has the potential, at least, to recover his morality. The white man, in contrast, remains amoral: to him, there is "nothing" because he is empty inside: he is a "hollow man," to borrow a phrase from *Heart of Darkness*.[25]

The story's closing scene seems to reinforce the moral difference between Arsat and the white colonist. When the white man offers to wait through the morning if Arsat wants to accompany him upriver, Arsat indicates that he will instead return to his homeland to avenge his brother's death: "There is no light and no peace in the world; but there is death—death for many. We are sons of the same mother—and I left him in the midst of enemies; but I am going back now" (203). He draws a breath and continues: "In a little while I shall see clear enough to strike—to strike. But she has died, and . . . now . . . darkness" (203–4). Finally, it seems, Arsat fully realizes that self-interest does not justify forsaking "loyalty and respect" (196): to do so is to be like whites, "who take what they want" (203). Arsat's realization is lost on the white colonist, of course: the latter simply resumes his advance upstream, an advance that, as we have seen, is futile, at least symbolically (187). Looking back, he sees that "Arsat had not moved": "He stood lonely in the searching sunshine; and he looked beyond the great light of a cloudless day into the darkness of a world of illusions" (204). Unlike the white man, who remains morally blind, Arsat can now see "into" the darkness. In the end it is the Malay who sees right from wrong, and who takes responsibility for his actions.

Clearly, "The Lagoon" is more than just a story about empire. As many of Conrad's critics have shown, it also addresses love, guilt, death, and even cultural difference.[26] Ruppel is correct, however, in relating it to the "popular exotic" stories of the late nineteenth century, since the story exploits the conventions of this genre even as it challenges them. Nonetheless, despite its exoticism, the story not only sympathizes with subject peoples but also suggests that imperialism will disappear as surely as the wake of a boat heading upstream. The story also attacks imperialists themselves by presenting Arsat as morally superior to the white colonist since he is willing to return home and take responsibility for his actions. Arsat ultimately realizes what the white colonist does not: that might does not make right, that one should not take what one wants just because one has the power to do so.

Conrad's efforts to write for two audiences in "The Lagoon"—both armchair imperialists and those who questioned imperialist ideology—resulted in a hybrid construct, a story that operates on two levels at once. Although it is not an "intentional hybrid" in the absolute sense of the term, since the story's ending resolves the tension between perspectives decidedly in favor of the anti-imperialist point of view, the story does represent Conrad's first experiment with the type of double-voicedness that characterizes much of his later work.[27] As we shall see in the chapters that follow, Conrad's efforts to expand his readership led him to develop narrative techniques that would allow him to obfuscate his radical, anti-imperialist politics. Unlike the stories of his "first phase"—which offer sustained critiques of imperialism through omniscient or nearly omniscient narrators—stories such as "Karain," "Youth," and *Heart of Darkness* provide multiple perspectives on imperialism, generating a narrative tension that is now associated with modernism.[28] Such changes in Conrad's style were not products of a modernist "will to style," as Fredric Jameson suggests in *The Political Unconscious* (225), but the result of Conrad's efforts to expand his readership and still be true to his political ideals. In effect, he develops a Trojan horse strategy similar to those adopted by other early postcolonial writers such as S. K Ghosh and Solomon Plaatje. Rather than "preach to the converted," to borrow a phrase Conrad used in a letter to Graham, Conrad begins to address a larger, more conservative audience in an effort to influence them and profit by them (*Letters* 2:69).

CHAPTER FOUR

Tricks of the Tale: Misdirection and Subterfuge in *The Nigger of the "Narcissus,"* "Karain," and "Youth"

> I confess to you I dream of peace, a little reputation, and the rest of my life devoted to the service of Art and free from material worries.
>
> JOSEPH CONRAD in a letter to Baroness Janina de Brunnow, October 2, 1897

Even though Conrad received nearly one hundred pounds for the magazine rights to "The Idiots," "The Lagoon," and "An Outpost of Progress"—more than he earned for his first two novels combined—and made another fifty pounds when the stories later appeared in a volume, he continued to have financial difficulties, not only because he was already in debt but because he lived beyond his means.[1] His problems were compounded when, early in 1897, he assumed financial responsibility for two nieces. Soon afterward, his wife, Jessie George Conrad, became pregnant. To meet his growing financial needs, Conrad was forced not only to write more but also to seek a larger audience, one that included conservatives as well as liberals, expansionists as well as Little Englanders. To acquire such an audience, Conrad altered both the style and content of his stories. Rather than openly challenge imperialism as he did in his first novels and short stories, Conrad began to obfuscate his radical, anti-imperialist politics through misdirection and subterfuge, a strategy that led first to the creation of "intentional hybrids," that is, texts in which alternative points of view are "set against each other dialogically," and then to what I term his Trojan horse fictions (Bakhtin 360). Conrad's next three works—*The Nigger of the "Narcissus,"* "Karain," and "Youth"—are thus important transitional texts: in creating them, he experiments with form in order to develop techniques that would allow him to succeed as a writer without compromising his political ideals.

Racial Prejudice as a Subject in The Nigger of the "Narcissus"

Conrad first employs misdirection in *The Nigger of the "Narcissus,"* a short novel that he completed in January 1897. Unlike *Almayer's Folly* and *An Outcast of the Islands,* both of which have colonial settings, this novel is set at sea and therefore does not present itself as a story about empire.[2] Moreover, although Conrad does explore colonial subjectivity in his depiction of James Wait, an English subject of African descent from St. Kitts, the story focuses primarily on the ship's European crew as it contends with not only Wait's terminal illness but also a dangerous storm and a near mutiny.[3] It also frequently shifts between an omniscient narrator and a character-narrator, making it difficult for the reader to deduce the author's perspective. Through such narrative misdirection, Conrad is able to study racial prejudice and colonial subjugation without appearing unpatriotic or subversive.[4]

Although *The Nigger of the "Narcissus"* has received considerably less critical attention than *Heart of Darkness,*" in many ways it is even more controversial. Some refuse to read it because they find the title racist and offensive.[5] Others, like Jeremy Hawthorn, are troubled by the story's content as well:

> When first I read *The Nigger of the "Narcissus"* as part of an undergraduate course in English literature, what I wanted most of all was a reaction to that word 'nigger' in the title and body of the work—either from within the work itself, or from critical responses to it. Why does Conrad make a black man the centre of the story, and draw attention to him and his blackness in the title? What is the narrative attitude to Wait and his blackness? What is the significance of Conrad's use of the word 'nigger' here? (Hawthorn 1990, 101)

Hawthorn goes on to report, "Nowhere could I find any answer to these questions. Critics and lecturers concentrated upon *The Nigger of the 'Narcissus'* as a sea story, a reflection of Conrad's years as a mariner and a distillation of the values and qualities this experience had led him to deem essential" (101). The criticism collected in the Norton Critical Edition of the novel seems to confirm Hawthorn's observation. Of the twelve articles Robert Kimbrough includes in the volume, only one, Eugene Redmond's "Racism or Realism? Literary Apartheid, or Poetic License? Conrad's Burden in *The Nigger of the 'Narcissus,'*" focuses on race and the novel's troubling title. The others concentrate primarily on elements such as symbol, myth, structure, and, in a few cases, social class.

In *Joseph Conrad: Narrative Technique and Ideological Commitment,* Hawthorn attempts to address the racial issues that he feels too many previous critics have ignored. After discussing critical debate over the story's supposed narrative weaknesses and ambiguities and identifying some additional inconsistencies, Hawthorn argues that Conrad's "narrative indecision" results from his own "ideological contradictions and uncertainties," that Conrad's own "prejudices . . . lie at the heart of the incoherence of *The Nigger of the 'Narcissus'*" (1990, 128). To Hawthorn, Wait is "the villain" of the story, or at least one of two villains, Donkin, the man who robs Wait on his deathbed, being the other (1990, 102). Hawthorn never explains what makes Wait villainous, however, and he does not discuss the ways in which Conrad presents Wait as a victim—not only of Donkin's villainy but also of racial prejudice and deadly illness. Although Wait certainly lacks some of the characteristics that British readers might have expected their heroes to have—including light skin and the ability to face his death bravely—he does not cause the storm that nearly sinks the ship, the near mutiny, or the doldrums that prevent him and his companions from reaching England as quickly as they would like to. The fact that Wait's shipmates believe him to be at least partially responsible for their troubles is important, though, since it brings their attitudes toward "niggers" into focus: they make Wait a scapegoat because of his race. By representing the crew's attitudes toward Wait in such a manner, Conrad makes racial prejudice a subject of the novel. Like his friend Cunninghame Graham, who in his satirical essay "Bloody Niggers" attacked the

British tendency to identify colonial subjects as "niggers" so as to justify their exploitation, Conrad challenges the racist underpinnings of imperialist ideology through his portrayal of Wait and his shipmates.[6]

"Nigger" as an Ideological Construct

Despite its troubling title, a title that leads many to conclude that the novel is racist, *The Nigger of the "Narcissus"* interrogates stereotypes about blacks, stereotypes that, as Homi Bhabha demonstrates in *The Location of Culture,* are part of a discursive strategy intended to "construe the colonized as a population of degenerate types on the basis of racial origin, in order to justify conquest and to establish systems of administration and instruction" (1994, 70). Although as a crewman aboard the *Narcissus,* Wait is removed from a colonial context, he remains a colonial subject and is understood by his companions through racist stereotypes. As Frantz Fanon puts it, "Wherever he goes . . . the Negro remains." Fanon continues: "The Negro is an animal, the Negro is bad, the Negro is mean, the Negro is ugly" (113). Wait, however, is represented as being quite the opposite of this racist stereotype—he is "calm, cool, towering, superb" (10). He is also extremely articulate, speaking English in a formal manner that contrasts sharply with the speech of his shipmates, particularly Donkin, who employs a lower-class dialect associated with "East-end trash" (25).[7] Indeed, if anyone is represented as being a "nigger" in the story, it is Donkin, who corresponds to what was known in late Victorian times as a "white nigger."[8]

To better understand Conrad's use of the term *nigger* as both a term and a conceptual category, it is important to consider the word in the context of late Victorian British culture. As Anne McClintock indicates in *Imperial Leather: Race, Gender and Sexuality in the Colonial Contest,* although terms like *nigger* were originally employed by Europeans to make racial distinctions between themselves and those with darker skins, in the late nineteenth century "the rhetoric of race was used to invent distinctions between what we would now call *classes.*" She continues:

"T. H. Huxley compared the East London poor with the Polynesian savage, William Booth chose the African pygmy, and William Barry thought that the slums resembled nothing so much as a slave ship" (54).[9] Since many of the so-called "white negroes"—"Jews, prostitutes, the working-class, domestic workers, and so on"—were as light-skinned as their supposed betters, English racialists looked for other ways to differentiate them from the middle and upper classes (McClintock 53–54).[10] In particular, they focused on what McClintock terms "domestic barbarism," considering things such as accent, clothing, hygiene, morality, and productivity (53).[11] Donkin's function as a "white nigger" becomes clear since he has virtually all the characteristics McClintock identifies:

> He looked as if he had been cuffed, kicked, rolled in the mud; he looked as if he had been scratched, spat upon, pelted with unmentionable filth . . . His ears were bending down under the weight of his battered felt hat. The torn tails of his black coat flapped in fringes about the calves of his legs. He unbuttoned the only two buttons that remained and every one saw that he had no shirt under it. It was his deserved misfortune that those rags which nobody could possibly be supposed to own looked on him as if they had been stolen. (5)

By presenting Donkin in such a manner, Conrad suggests that *nigger* is as much a social and economic category as it is a racial one: "niggers" are products of imperialism and the capitalistic system upon which it is based.[12] Conrad does not suggest that all working-class people are "niggers," of course: although characters like Singleton and Belfast are uneducated and speak in lower-class dialects, they are not petty, slothful, or unkempt. If such characters are represented as being "savages," to borrow Huxley's term, then they are "noble savages," a point Conrad underscores by having the narrator note that Singleton "resembled a learned and savage patriarch" (3). Like Donkin, Singleton and Belfast are part of an exploited class, but unlike him, they are not fully degraded by their low status. Rather, they resemble Wait, whom, ironically, they look down on because of his race.

That Singleton, Belfast, and the rest of the crew consider themselves superior to Wait is evident from their initial reaction to him: "The boy . . . raised the light to the man's [Wait's] face. It was black. A surprised hum—a faint hum that sounded like the suppressed mutter of the word 'Nigger'—ran along the deck and escaped into the night" (10). To the crew of the *Narcissus,* Wait is lower than they are on the social hierarchy and therefore, in theory at least, subject to their abuse and exploitation. Wait does not act according to their expectations, however, and he refuses to be subjugated by the rest of the crew. Indeed, he treats them as if they were his inferiors: "He was naturally scornful, unaffectedly condescending, as if from his height of six foot three he had surveyed all the vastness of human folly and had made up his mind not to be too hard on it" (10). Wait acts that way even toward his officers, speaking to the first mate in "disdainful tones" as he explains to him that the mate was the one who "misapprehended" when he mistook Wait shouting out his name for the command "Wait!" (11).

Although Wait refuses to accept his status as a "nigger," the crew persists in regarding him as such, though none dare use the word in front of him until he is debilitated by illness (49). Even then he resists, telling Belfast, "You wouldn't call me nigger if I wasn't half-dead, you Irish beggar!" (49). Stung by Wait's reference to his own colonial identity—the suggestion that as an Irishman, he is a "white nigger"—Belfast replies, "You wouldn't be white if you were ever so well." Belfast's words represent more than just a racist taunt: he attempts to subordinate Wait by reminding him that "white niggers" have a higher status than "black" ones.

The unusual relationship that develops between Wait and Belfast proves to be one of the most important in the novel since it highlights the social dynamics that occur on a larger scale between Wait and the rest of the crew. Belfast, like his white shipmates, is both drawn to Wait and repelled by him. To Belfast, Wait is black and therefore beneath him, and yet as a crewmate, he is entitled to "the unspoken loyalty that knits together a ship's company" (6). He is a part of "the brotherhood of the sea," and therefore, no matter how much they despise him because of his race, the crew feels compelled to support and protect him (18). The tension between these dual attitudes toward him becomes most apparent when the crew tries to rescue the debilitated Wait from the partially submerged sick bay after the ship nearly sinks. As Belfast desperately tries to locate Jimmy, he cries, "For the love of God, Jimmy, where are ye? . . . Knock! Jimmy darlint! . . . Knock! You bloody black beast! (42). As the juxtaposition of the words "darlin[g]" and "beast" suggests, Belfast, like the rest of the crew of the *Narcissus,* is both attracted to and repulsed by Wait. Because Wait is a fellow seaman, they identify with him and his situation as a dying man: he makes them more aware of their own mortality, as a number of critics, including Albert Guérard, have noted. Because they consider him a "nigger," however, they cannot help but suspect that he is "shamming sick," that he has been "malingering" (45). Their conflicted attitude is reflected in the narrator's repeated references to him as "our nigger" (21, 23): the word *our* suggests that on some level they accept him as one of their own even as the word *nigger* suggests that to them he is merely a thing.

The tension between the crew's conflicting attitudes toward Wait exposes the ideological function of *nigger* as a concept. Although the crew has been conditioned to think of racial others as inferiors, they cannot quite reconcile that belief with their experiences with Wait aboard the *Narcissus.* The novel thus implicitly challenges imperialist ideology to the extent that the latter relies on racism to justify the subjugation of others. *Nigger* may exist as a conceptual category, but that does not mean that the category is legitimate.

Colonial Subjectivity and the Reader

If the crew's attitude toward Wait tells us something about how people near the bottom of the social hierarchy use race to subordinate others to themselves, Wait's words and actions tell us something about what it is like to be a colonial subject. As I noted earlier, Wait does his best to resist being identified as a "nigger," not only by expressing a willingness to fight those who call him that, but by attempting to look and act white. In *Black Skin, White Masks,* Frantz Fanon terms such efforts "denegrification." He writes: "Every colonized people—in other words, every people in whose soul an inferiority complex has been created by the death and burial of its local cultural originality—finds itself face to face with the language of the civilizing nation; that is, with the culture of the mother country. The colonized is elevated above his jungle status in proportion to his adoption of the mother country's cultural standards. He becomes whiter as he renounces his blackness, his jungle" (18). Wait's attitude, clothing, demeanor, and language all suggest that he is attempting to "denegrify," that he has renounced his black identity in an effort to become white. His physical features, however, prevent him from succeeding: no matter how he speaks and acts, his shipmates identify him by his dark skin, "misshapen" head, and "flattened face" (11). Having refused a black identity and been refused a white one, symbolically at least, Wait resembles the "smudge" that marks his name on the ship's roster (10): he is an unreadable signifier, a smear of black ink on white paper. When he dies, it is as if he never existed, a point the narrator underscores by reporting an exchange between the captain and the clerk after the ship has returned to England and the crew has been paid off: "James Wait—deceased—found no papers of any kind—no relations—no trace" (105). The irony, of course, is that even as the text seems to deny the very existence of its title character, it impresses that existence on the reader through its sensitive representation of him. Wait, with all of his fear, pride, and anger, is represented as being very human—so human that the shipmates who dismiss him as a "nigger" identify strongly with him as a man. Conrad may well have hoped that the book would have a similar effect on some of his readers.

Misdirection, Subterfuge, and the Marketing of The Nigger of the "Narcissus"

Although *The Nigger of the "Narcissus"* can be read as a subversive text to the extent that it examines and implicitly decries the dehumanization of the title character, few of Conrad's contemporaries recognized it as anything but sea story.[13] The *Spectator,* for example, describes it as "an extraordinarily vivid picture of life on board of a sailing-vessel in the merchant marine," and the *Academy* writes that the book "compels us to look at life as it appears to an ordinary mariner" (Sherry 1973, 93, 95). Such reviews suggest that Conrad's nineteenth-century readers had difficulty accepting a black man from St. Kitts as the primary subject of a story.[14] Even the *Daily Chronicle,* which finds in the story "a freshness, reality, and peculiar interest which raise the book far above the ordinary level of tales of the sea," recognizes nothing extraordinary in the portrayal of Wait: "The story is simply an account of an ordinary voyage made by an ordinary sailing ship from Bombay round the Cape to the Thames. Nothing particular happens. There is a big storm, some dissatisfaction among the crew, which never ripens into anything like mutiny, and the least admirable of the men dies and is shot into the water. That is all" (Sherry 1973, 89–90). That the reviewer finds Wait rather than Donkin "the least admirable" character is telling, since it suggests how deeply ingrained racial prejudices were at the time: Donkin may be vicious and dishonest, but at least he is not black, the implication seems to be. The fact that the very same reviewer finds the story to be of "peculiar interest" is significant as well, since it raises the possibility at least that the writer was affected by the piece in a way he or she could not quite account for.[15]

The response that Conrad evoked in this reviewer might well be the one he desired from his readers in general, for he succeeded in inducing him or her to recognize the humanity of someone whose humanity imperialist ideology denies. For Conrad, the challenge is to do this without appearing to be radical and subversive. In part, he succeeds through misdirection, as I suggested earlier: the story opens on the deck of the *Narcissus* as it prepares for its voyage from Bombay to London and ends as a tribute to English seamen: "Good-bye, brothers! You were a good crowd. As good a crowd as ever fisted with wild cries the beating canvas of a heavy foresail; or tossing aloft, invisible in the night, gave back yell for yell to a westerly gale" (107).[16] By framing the novel in such a manner, Conrad leads the reader to believe that the *Narcissus* and its crew are the primary focus, thus cloaking the novel's radical social message.

Misdirection is only one of the strategies Conrad experiments with in *The Nigger of the "Narcissus."* He also utilizes subterfuge to disguise his ideological agenda, employing an unstable narrator who is sometimes omniscient and sometimes a character within the story. As Jakob Lothe notes, because of the way Conrad deploys these dual narrators, "it is often unclear which voice is speaking" (1989, 96). By intertwining the two narrative voices in such a manner, Conrad is able to distance himself from the radical elements of the text.[17] Toward the beginning of chapter 2, for example, the *Narcissus* is described as follows as it begins its voyage:

> The passage had begun, and the ship, a fragment detached from the earth, went on lonely and swift like a small planet . . . She had her own future; she was alive with the lives of those beings who trod her decks; like that earth which had given her up to the sea, she had an intolerable load of regrets and hopes. On her lived timid truth and audacious lies; and, like the earth, she was unconscious, fair to see—and condemned by men to an ignoble fate. The august loneliness of her path lent dignity to the sordid inspiration of her pilgrimage. (18)

The narrator's assertion at the end of this passage that the colonial trade the *Narcissus* is involved with is "sordid" subtly calls into question the morality of the colonialism itself.[18] Whether the assertion should be attributed to the omniscient narrator, who, by convention, at least, might be associated with Conrad, or the character-narrator is unapparent, however.

Many of the passages pertaining to Wait and his situation are presented in a similar manner. One example of this occurs in the passage cited earlier in which Wait's face is described as a "mask" that is at once "pathetic," "brutal," and "tragic" (11). As disturbingly racist as this passage is, when considered in the context of late nineteenth-century discourse on race and empire, its subversiveness becomes evident as well, since the passage acknowledges that "niggers" have souls and that their situation is "tragic."[19] Moreover, as Hawthorn notes, it is impossible to determine who describes Wait in such a manner: it could be the omniscient narrator or the character-narrator (1990, 107). Again, by making it indeterminable, Conrad effectively distances the omniscient narrator, whom readers would presumably associate with the author, from the story's subversive content and thereby avoids appearing to have an overt ideological agenda.[20]

Because he had so effectively cloaked the subversive content of *The Nigger of the "Narcissus"* through misdirection and subterfuge, Conrad was able to market this novel more effectively than he could his first two. In the fall of 1896, he sent a partial draft to W. E. Henley, the notorious conservative and imperialist who had reported to Unwin just a year and a half earlier that he could not "read more than sixty pages" of *Almayer's Folly* (*Letters* 1:211).[21] Henley was impressed by *The Nigger of the "Narcissus"* and expressed interest in serializing it in the *New Review*, where it appeared from August to December 1897.[22] Because Henley serialized the novel, Conrad was, in effect, able to sell it twice: to the *New Review* and to Heinemann, who published it as a volume in December 1897. The narrative strategies Conrad experiments with in the novel thus proved successful: Conrad learned that he could sell his work to conservatives as long as he concealed his radical politics.

A Return to the Colonies: "Karain: A Memory"

In "Karain: A Memory," Conrad returns to subject matter and setting similar to the ones he used in his earlier colonial fiction, this time employing a character-narrator to obfuscate his radical anti-imperialist politics. As many critics have observed, Conrad's extensive use of a character-narrator represents a significant change in his narrative technique, one that he was to employ in later, more celebrated works such as *Heart of Darkness* and *Lord Jim*.[23] Typically, such critics treat Conrad's use of such narrators as a modernist technique for presenting multiple points of view or as a means of figuring himself as English (Watt 1979, 213; Najder 1983, 230–31). When considered in the context of Conrad's efforts to expand his readership while remaining true to his anti-imperialist politics, it becomes evident that the technique was at least in part pragmatic: the creation of character-narrators provided Conrad with a means of inflecting a story's meaning without taking an implied authorial position within the text, a position that might put off imperialistic readers. As we shall see, in stories like "Karain," Conrad begins to develop a Trojan horse strategy, one in which he sets multiple points of view in a dialogic relationship with one another so as to obfuscate the story's more radical implications.

Karain's Narrative as an Alternative Perspective on Imperialism

Before examining the implications of how the character-narrator frames the story, it is important to have a clear understanding of the story he frames, particularly since it is through this story, which the narrator repeats verbatim, that Conrad gives voice to an alternative perspective on imperialism. Superficially at least, "Karain" resembles "The Lagoon," which is also set in the Malay Archipelago. Both stories focus on Malay men who feel tremendous guilt for having betrayed a male companion because of their desire for a woman, in Karain's case a friend's sister who has betrayed her family and her people by eloping with a Dutch trader. Karain, a subject of one of the independent states of Wajo, accompanies his friend Pata Matara as he searches the archipelago for the couple, whom they agree to kill "to cleanse the dishonour" (32). Upon finding them, however, Karain shoots Matara instead of the Dutch trader, saving the sister, with whom he has become obsessed, from her brother's *kriss.* Unlike Arsat, who represses his guilt for his role in the death of his brother until Diamelen dies, Karain's guilt manifests itself immediately in the form of Matara's ghost, who urges him to "Kill! kill! kill!"—an admonition that drives Karain to fight European imperialism, first in Aceh, then in Sula (43). Ultimately, Karain is able to find peace with the help of a Moslem pilgrim who wards off the ghost, and Karain settles in an "isolated corner" of Mindanao, where he becomes "war-chief" of three villages (43, 4). When the pilgrim suddenly dies, however, Karain is again haunted by Matara's ghost until Hollis, an English gunrunner, fashions him a charm out of a gilt Jubilee sixpence featuring an engraving of Queen Victoria. Karain returns to his people with the coin around his neck and resumes his war against the Spanish and their allies, presumably making it "hot for the caballeros," as another one of the gunrunners observes (54).

Karain's narrative about his betrayal of Matara is important not only because it explains how Karain came to be an insurgent leader but because it supplements European histories of the conquest of the Malay Archipelago, effectively "provincializing them," to borrow Dipesh Chakrabarty's phrase. In particular, when recounting his travels in search of the sister, Karain describes how imperialism has transformed the archipelago, focusing primarily on Java, which lives "under the edge of a foreign sword" (31). There he finds "Stone campongs, full of white faces . . . surrounded by fertile fields" while every Malay he meets is "a slave" (31). He sees that the Dutch have not only gained control of the island's resources but changed the social order to the point that even chiefs are "no better than slaves" and "low born wretches" challenge their betters on behalf of their white masters (32, 33). He also senses that local values have been transformed, as evidenced by the fact that most of the Javanese they meet cannot understand Matara's desire to revenge the elopement of his sister with a Dutch colonist, one old man even beseeching him to "Desist!" (32). As his travels continue "East" and "West," Karain sees that not only Java has been transformed but the whole archipelago (33). He also learns something about what it is to be a subaltern as Europeans heap "curses" upon his head and "rough white faces" issue orders to him as if he himself were a slave (32–33).

By having his English narrator present Karain's narrative verbatim, Conrad gives voice to an insurgent perspective on imperialism, a point of view generally unavailable to British readers in the late nineteenth century. Through Karain, the reader is able to see that colonization involves both military and cultural subjugation, and that indigenous peoples are at least as willing to fight and die for their beliefs as Europeans are. Karain's narrative also provides an indigenous perspective on the physical and societal transformations that occur as a once-independent region is transformed into a European colony. Finally, Karain puts the colonizers themselves under his gaze, so to speak, when, in asking for one of their "charms," he suggests that their world is as full of ghosts—and guilt—as his own.

Despite such radical implications, many critics dismiss "Karain" as little more than a traveler's anecdote about a "slightly ridiculous, superstitious native" who uses a sixpence as a fetish to ward off a ghost (Graver 33).[24] To do so is to miss the story's subversive elements, though, not only because the title character shows how imperialism has made the Malays "slaves" (31)—a point that the Indonesian writer Pramoedya Ananta Toer feels is extremely significant (GoGwilt 1998, 98)—but because, as we shall see, the frame narrative fails to contain the alterity that Karain's story represents.

The Framing of "Karain"

Initially, the narrator presents his story as a reminiscence—a memory, as it were: "We knew him [Karain] in those unprotected days when we were content to hold in our hands our lives and our property" (3). The narrator immediately returns to the present, however, suggesting a strong connection between the story he is about to recount and the world he is living in now: "None of us, I believe, has any property now, and I hear that many, negligently, have lost their lives; but I am sure that the few who survive are not yet so dim-eyed as to miss in the befogged respectability of their newspapers the intelligence of various native risings in the Eastern Archipelago." Although the narrator acknowledges no direct relationship between his past activities and current troubles, the juxtaposition suggests it: the people represented as "we" in the story are at least partially responsible for the unrest the papers report. The sentence that follows—"A strange name wakes up memories"—seems to affirm this, connecting the narrator and his gunrunning comrades to the Malay insurgents whose names are now appearing in English newspapers.

The narrator goes on to describe Karain, a Malay leader to whom he had sold arms years earlier. Rather than represent Karain as ignorant savage, however, the narrator presents him as an "actor" and the three villages he controls as a "stage":

> It was the stage where, dressed splendidly for his part, he strutted, incomparably dignified, made important by the power he had to awaken an absurd expectation of something heroic going to take place—a burst of action or song—upon the vibrating tone of a wonderful sunshine ... His smallest acts were prepared and unexpected, his speeches grave, his sentences ominous like hints and complicated like arabesques. He was treated with a solemn respect accorded in the irreverent West only to the monarchs of the stage, and he accepted the profound homage with a sustained dignity, seen nowhere else but behind the footlights and in the condensed falseness of some grossly tragic situation. (7)

The narrator's persistent use of theater imagery has a number of functions. On one level it reveals his patronizing attitude toward Malays, since he uses it to ridicule a man he calls a "very good friend" (8). To the narrator, even though Karain "filled the stage with a barbarous dignity," he is still nothing more than a "petty chief" with delusions of grandeur. This becomes most clear when the narrator contrasts his assessment of Karain's position with Karain's: after asserting that Karain's domain is "an insignificant foothold on the earth," the narrator highlights Karain's "theatrical" sweep of the arm as he gestures towards his land, declaring it "All mine!" (4–5). On another level the theater imagery invites the reader to reconsider his or her own beliefs and values and therefore has a subversive function. Like "The Mousetrap" in *Hamlet,* Karain's story is framed so as "to catch the conscience of the king." In the case of this story, however, the king corresponds to Conrad's imperialist readers: the story is designed so that they will unconsciously recognize their own guilt in the action of the players and respond accordingly.

The second and third sections provide more detail about Karain and the Europeans who sell him weapons, highlighting the ethical issues involved. The narrator and his comrades have been running guns to Karain for "two years at short intervals" (18). The Europeans know he is preparing for a war against Spanish imperialists—a war the Europeans believe he cannot win—but they continue to supply him with weapons as long as he can pay for them: "We tried to enlighten him, but our attempts to make clear the irresistible nature of the forces which he desired to arrest failed to discourage his eagerness to strike a blow for his own primitive ideas . . . He was absurd and unanswerable . . . All we could do for him was to see to it that the powder was good for the money and rifles serviceable, if old" (18). That the narrator describes imperialism as being "irresistible" is significant, since it reveals his own ideological assumptions: like many Europeans in the late nineteenth century, he believed that European domination was inevitable because of Europeans' inherent superiority over subject peoples. That he and his companions are willing to provide weapons to Malay insurgents is also important; the gunrunners are "moral cannibals," to use a term for profiteers that Conrad employs in "The Tale" (234). Violating the "law against the traffic in firearms and ammunition with the natives" is more than a matter of illegal commerce (7); since white imperialists depended in part on the perception that they could not be effectively resisted because of their military superiority, selling weapons to "natives" represented a form of racial treason. The narrator and his companions are all the more culpable because they know that Karain "has a sombre, glowing sense of fury within him—a brooding and vague sense of wrong, and a concentrated lust of violence which is dangerous in a native" (18): he is an anticolonial insurgent, one who "will make it hot" not only for the Spanish but for all imperialist interests in the archipelago, if only because he would serve as a demonstration that resistance to imperialist domination was possible (54). The gunrunners and their backers—the "very respectable people sitting safely in counting houses" (19)—have no qualms about selling firearms for profit, however; they live in a "land of unbelief, where the dead do not speak," to borrow Karain's words (44). Like the white colonist in "The Lagoon," they are troubled neither by ghosts nor their own consciences, especially when money is involved.

In the next section, the narrator repeats Karain's narrative about his travels and his betrayal of Pata Matara verbatim, breaking at the beginning of section 5 to emphasize that Karain's illusions have led to his treachery and the guilt that haunts him: "I looked at that man, loyal to a vision, betrayed by his dream, spurned by his illusion, and coming to us unbelievers for help—against a thought" (40). In the passage that follows, however, the narrator concedes that he and his gunrunning comrades have ghosts of their own: "The silence was profound; but it seemed full of noiseless phantoms, of things sorrowful, shadowy, and mute, in whose invisible presence the firm, pulsating beat of the two ships' chronometers ticking off steadily the seconds of Greenwich Time seemed to me a protection and a relief" (40). As Hampson suggests, the reference to Greenwich time reminds readers that Europeans have their illusions as well, in this case the illusion that they have "mastery over time and space" (Hampson 2000, 126). According to Robert J. C. Young, the prime meridian also represents imperialist ideology, since arbitrarily dividing the world into hemispheres involves asserting mastery over people as well (1–2): people are defined as being either "Western" or "Eastern" and are conceptualized accordingly. With this in mind, the narrator's reference to Greenwich time takes on a new significance: it is imperialist ideology that keeps ghosts—and the guilt they represent—at bay. Why should Europeans feel guilt about the consequences of imperialism when they believe that, as men of the "West," they have been given dominion over peoples of the "East"?

Karain resumes his narrative with an account of his haunting and his efforts to assuage his guilt by fighting imperialism throughout the Malay Archipelago. Finally, he reports that with the death of the Moslem pilgrim, his comrade-in-arms and spiritual protector, he has once again been hearing Pata Matara's voice whisper, "Kill! kill! kill!" (43). Recognizing that they themselves might be attacked by the guilt-stricken insurgent, the European crew becomes alarmed: "For the first time that night a sudden convulsion of madness and rage passed over his [Karain's] face . . . he looked so dangerous that we all three leaped to our feet, and Hollis, with the back of his hand, sent the *kriss* flying off the table. I believe we shouted together" (43). Karain soon recovers his equanimity, leaving the "three white men standing over him in rather foolish attitudes." They, of course, are "a little ashamed" of themselves: as white men, they are never supposed to show their fear before subject people. Jackson picks up the kriss and returns it to Karain, who "stuck it in the twist of his sarong, with punctilious care to give his weapon a pacific position. Then he looked up at us with an austere smile. We were abashed and reproved" (43). When Karain finally speaks, he again surprises the Europeans: "With you I will go. To your land—to your people. To your people who live in unbelief; to whom day is day, and night is night—nothing more, because you understand all things seen, and despise all else! To your land of unbelief, where the dead do not speak, where every man is wise, and alone—and at peace!" (44). Karain's desire to live among the infidels—"where the dead do not speak"—where there are no ghosts reveals not only how desperate his past actions have made him but his perspective on Europeans: to him they are people without morals, people never haunted by ghosts of conscience. When the Europeans attempt to dismiss Karain's proposal, he presses them: "'I can toil, and fight—and be faithful,' he whispered, in a weary tone, 'but I cannot go back to him who waits for me on the shore. No! take me with you . . . Or else give me some of your strength—of your unbelief . . . A charm! . . .'" (44, ellipses in original). Noting that they cannot possibly take Karain to Europe, Hollis expresses his fears that if Karain remains in Mindanao, he "will run amuck amongst his faithful subjects" (45).[25] The narrator agrees, knowing that something must be done for their Malay friend. As the three white men ponder the problem in silence, the narrator again notes "the steady tick of the chronometers" (45). Suddenly, Hollis has an idea: as if prompted by the clocks, which, as I noted earlier, symbolize imperialist ideology, Hollis decides to employ another imperial symbol as a charm for Karain—a gilt Jubilee sixpence with Queen Victoria's image on it.

Although the narrator describes Hollis opening the small leather box of personal possessions that holds the coin in section 5, he tells of the coin itself only in section 6, drawing out what amounts to a presentation ceremony. Looking "grave" for the benefit of Karain, Hollis searches for the coin. As he rummages through his mementos—which the narrator calls "Amulets of white men! Charms and talismans!" (48)—the white men's ghosts seem to appear, at least to the narrator: "And it seemed to me, during that moment of waiting, that the cabin of the schooner was becoming filled with a stir invisible and living as of subtle breaths. All the ghosts driven out of the unbelieving West by men who pretend to be wise and alone and at peace—all the homeless ghosts of an unbelieving world—appeared suddenly round the figure of Hollis bending over the box" (48). It is at this point that the relationship between ghosts and guilt becomes most clear. The passage continues: "all the exiled and charming shades of loved women; all the beautiful and tender ghosts of ideals, remembered, forgotten, cherished, execrated; all the cast-out and reproachful ghosts of friends admired, trusted, traduced, betrayed, left dead by the way—they all seemed to come from the inhospitable regions of the earth to crowd into the gloomy cabin, as though it had been a refuge and, in all the unbelieving world the only place of avenging belief" (48–49). That the narrator describes friends who have been "betrayed" and "left dead" as "reproachful ghosts" is, of course, important: in addition to indicating that ghosts are products of guilt, he suggests that Karain's betrayal of Pata Matara is no worse than the betrayals of which he and the other European gunrunners are guilty. Even more significant, perhaps, is the fact that the narrator includes "ideals" among the list of things that Europeans have "betrayed": like the white colonist in "The Lagoon," the gunrunners have forsaken whatever ideals they had for the sake of profits. If the Europeans feel guilt for their past misdeeds, it is only briefly, because Hollis's charm drives the ghosts away: "'It lasted a second—all disappeared. Hollis was facing us alone with something small that glittered between his fingers. It looked like a coin . . . 'A charm for our friend,' he said to us. 'The thing itself is of great power—money, you know'" (49).

The Power of a Fetish: The Gilded Sixpence and Imperialist Ideology

Hollis's use of a gilt Jubilee sixpence as the charm suggests that money functions as a fetish for Europeans, one that protects them from both spirits and their consciences.[26] The fact that the coin is inscribed with "the image of the Great Queen" wearing the imperial crown suggests that the empire itself has become a fetish, an object that has become invested with ideology. Hollis's next utterance makes the latter point more clear, for as he presents the coin to Karain, he says more about Victoria and the nation she rules in an aside: "She commands a spirit, too—the spirit of her nation; a masterful, conscientious, unscrupulous, unconquerable devil . . . that does a lot of good—incidentally . . . a lot of good . . . at times—and wouldn't stand any fuss from the best ghost out for such a little thing as our friend's shot" (50, ellipses in original). The fact that Hollis describes the "spirit" of the English nation as "unscrupulous" is, of course, significant, as is the way he qualifies his assertion that the nation does "a lot of good" by adding the phrase "at times." He, at least, is not fully blinded by ideology and is willing to concede that the Empire exists for profit as well as morality.

The power of such a charm is not lost on Karain, who stands "rigid, with head thrown back; his eyes rolled wildly, flashing; the dilated nostrils quivered" (50): he believes that the charm will free him from his conscience—give him the strength that comes from being morally unaccountable (44). Accordingly, when Hollis places the coin—which he has put in an amulet—around Karain's neck, the latter seems "to wake from a dream," shaking "himself as if throwing off a burden" (51). He then looks around with the "assurance," transformed, as it were, into a European. Soon afterward, he declares that the ghost is gone: "He has departed again—forever!" (51). Then he returns to his "conquered foothold of earth," "the glorious splendour of his stage," to renew his war against the Spanish (52).

That the narrator reinvokes stage imagery at this point is particularly important; it reminds the reader that there is a story within the story. As in *Hamlet,* the interpolated story is designed to "catch the conscience" of its audience. This becomes clear in the very next paragraph when, after describing Karain's return to his people, the narrator refers directly to the reader: "I wondered what they thought; what he thought; . . . what the reader thinks?" (52, ellipsis in original). In this story what the reader thinks is very important. The story is designed so that imperialist readers will unconsciously identify with the players and recognize their own culpability. Those who support imperialism and the capitalist system of exploitation are no better than gunrunners who sell weapons to rebellious natives. They are all people without consciences, people who use money and empire as fetishes to ward of the ghosts of their victims.

Contesting Interpretations: "Karain" as an Intentional Hybrid

If the story were to end here, "Karain," like "The Lagoon," would read as a straightforward attack on European imperialism. In the final paragraphs of "Karain," however, Conrad distances himself from this critique by having his Anglocentric character-narrator reject the story's subversive implications, making it an "intentional hybrid" to the extent that the story's critique of imperialist ideology is dialogized. Years after his final encounter with Karain, the narrator happens to meet Jackson in London. The two walk together, exchanging stories, until Jackson stops in front of a gun shop to look through the window at the weapons. Jackson suddenly asks the narrator if he remembers Karain:

> "The sight of all this made me think of him," he went on, with his face near the glass . . . and I could see another man, powerful and bearded, peering at him intently from amongst the dark and polished tubes that can cure so many illusions. "Yes; it made me think of him," he continued, slowly. "I saw a paper this morning; they are fighting over there again. He's sure to be in it. He will make it hot for the caballeros." (53–54, ellipsis in original)

Like the narrator, Jackson acknowledges the connection between his earlier activities as a gunrunner and the present unrest in the Philippines. More important, perhaps, Karain's people are being killed for a cause that appears to be hopeless, since the "forces" they are contesting are of an "irresistible nature" (18).[27] Apparently, the guilt Jackson feels for his earlier gunrunning activities makes him think of Karain and the ghost that haunted him: "I wonder whether the charm worked—you remember Hollis's charm, of course. If it did . . . never was a sixpence wasted to better advantage! Poor devil! I wonder whether he got rid of that friend of his. Hope so . . . Do you know, I sometimes think that—" (54, ellipses in original). Karain's "friend," of course, is the spirit of Pata Matara, the spirit of his betrayed countryman. Jackson seems to be wondering whether ghosts—as manifestations of conscience—are real and whether they can indeed be kept at bay with a fetish.

The narrator, representing the "English" point of view, dismisses Jackson's question, implying that he has gone native: "My dear chap," I cried, "you have been too long away from home. What a question to ask! Only look at all this" (54). He then gestures towards the London cityscape with its "sombre and ceaseless stir": "Our ears were filled by a headlong shuffle and beat of rapid footsteps and an underlying rumour—a rumour vast, faint, pulsating, as of panting breaths, of beating hearts, of gasping voices. Innumerable eyes stared straight in front, feet moved hurriedly, bland faces flowed, arms swung" (54). The rhythm the narrator describes, with its "rapid beat of footsteps" and "beating of hearts," subtly recalls that of the chronometers aboard the ship: the mechanized imperial metropole will truck neither ghosts nor conscience.[28] "Ye-e-e-s," Jackson replies, acknowledging the narrator's point but not conceding it. The narrator goes on to describe hansom cabs moving slowly through the streets, a "pale-faced youth," horses stepping "gingerly," vivacious girls with "shining eyes," a "fine old fellow" who struts, "stroking a white moustache," and a series of sandwich boards: to him London is alive and always moving, a place of activity, energy, and commerce. Jackson again says, "Ye-e-es," still unwilling to concede the narrator's point. He sees London differently: "His clear blue eyes looked about, contemptuous, amused and hard, like the eyes of a boy. A clumsy string of red, yellow, and green omnibuses rolled swaying, monstrous and gaudy; two shabby children ran across the road; a knot of dirty men with red neckerchiefs round their bare throats lurched along, discussing filthily; a ragged old man with a face of despair yelled horribly in the mud the name of a paper" (55). Where the narrator saw luxury and the wealth of empire, Jackson sees unconscionable squalor and misery.[29] "Yes; I see it," Jackson finally says: "It is there; it pants, it runs, it rolls; it is strong and alive; it would smash you if you didn't look out; but I'll be hanged if it is yet as real to me as . . . as the other thing . . . say, Karain's story" (55). Jackson's insistence that Karain's worldview is as valid as the narrator's generates an ideological tension in the story, one not resolved by the narrator's final words: "I think that, decidedly, he had been too long away from home"

(55).[30] Although the narrator rejects Jackson's views, he does not do so convincingly, instead resorting to an ad hominem attack.[31] As Hampson argues, the narrator's suggestion that Jackson has been away from London for "too long" and possibly has gone native hardly contains the "alterity" that Karain's story—and Jackson's response to it—represent (2000, 128).[32] His off-hand dismissal of Jackson's views does allow Conrad to insulate himself from the story's anti-imperialist content, however. Although the story suggests that as "moral cannibals," Europeans are morally inferior to those they rule, it does not do so unequivocally since the narrator rejects the implication, albeit unpersuasively.

Conrad's effort to distance himself from the critique of empire in this story distinguishes "Karain" from his earlier short fiction. Although he employed a character-narrator in "The Idiots," the unnamed narrator's interpretation in that story is neither ironized nor challenged by an authorial voice, the story's content, or another character. In "Karain," however, he calls the character-narrator's authority into question by having another character contest it, opening up alternative interpretive possibilities. Although ironizing techniques like this are now associated with modernism, Conrad subverts his narrator's authority for practical reasons rather than aesthetic ones, just as other early postcolonial writers do: by constructing an intentional hybrid—that is, a narrative in which alternative perspectives are "set against each other dialogically" (Bakhtin 360)—Conrad is able to subtly question imperialist ideology without necessarily alienating imperialist readers. In this, Conrad seems to have succeeded: acting on Edward Garnett's advice, he managed to place the story in *Blackwood's*, a respectable periodical that, as Ian Watt notes, was "very conservative" (1979, 131).[33] Indeed, the editor, William Blackwood, was so pleased with the story that he paid Conrad more than he normally would, on the condition that Conrad would give him "first refusal on any future short story" Conrad might write (131).[34]

As his letters of the period indicate, Conrad was glad to have his work appear in *Blackwood's* since it gave him the opportunity to build a larger readership, albeit a more conservative, pro-imperialist one.[35] To avoid alienating this audience, Conrad went to even greater lengths to distance himself from the anti-imperialist elements in the stories that followed. Accordingly, in "Youth: A Narrative," the first story written specifically for *Blackwood's,* Conrad uses misdirection just as he did in *The Nigger of the "Narcissus,"* setting the story primarily at sea and focusing, ostensibly at least, on English mariners. In this story, the main character, Marlow, tells of his first voyage to "the East," a disastrous journey in which his ship, the *Judea*—which he describes as being "all rust, dust, [and] grime"—encounters a variety of problems before finally sinking near Sumatra after its cargo catches fire (4, 70). The ship's crew, which is made up entirely of men from Liverpool, salvage everything they can from the wreck and make their way ashore, with Marlow, the second mate, commanding one of the boats. Their perseverance throughout—which is underscored by the ship's motto, "Do or Die"—is presented as a key component of what it is to be English (5): as the story's frame narrator asserts at the very beginning of the story, "This could have occurred nowhere but in England, where men and sea interpenetrate, so to speak" (3).

As Gail Fraser notes, the version of the story that was published in *Blackwood's* "has a clear ideological intention"—one that is absent from the book version that was published four years later: this intention, according to Fraser, was "to endorse the traditionalist values celebrated by *Blackwood's* since the early 1800s" (1996, 33). Fraser goes on to demonstrate how the magazine version's "most dramatic episode" functions as "Marlow's strongest appeal to patriotic feeling":

> When the *Judea*'s cargo of coal catches fire and explodes, her crew of "Liverpool hard cases" responds with impressive discipline and will: "But they worked," Marlow says, "That crew of Liverpool hard cases had in them the right stuff. *It's my experience they*

> *always have.* It is the sea that gives it—." The italicized sentence, which asserts that "the right stuff" will never diminish, is one of the many similar additions made after the manuscript stage and before serial publication. (33–34, emphasis in original)

Clearly, Conrad tailored his story to suit the conservative readers of *Blackwood's.* Indeed, a casual reading might lead one to conclude that the story celebrates not only the English but their empire. To read it in such a manner is to miss the subversive elements concealed within the story's final pages, however, elements that generate an ideological tension similar to the one found in "Karain." Once Marlow lands in the Dutch East Indies, he sees British imperialism for what it really is. Rowing from the wharf where he landed out to an inbound English steamer, he is taken for a Malay boatsman:

> And then, before I could open my lips, the East spoke to me, but it was in a Western voice. A torrent of words was poured into the enigmatical, fateful silence; outlandish, angry words, mixed with words and even whole sentences of good English, less strange but even more surprising. The voice swore and cursed violently; it riddled the solemn peace of the bay by a volley of abuse. It began by calling me Pig, and from that went crescendo into unmentionable adjectives—in English. The man up there raged aloud in two languages, and with a sincerity in his fury that almost convinced me I had, in some way, sinned against the harmony of the universe. I could hardly see him, but began to think he would work himself into a fit. (39)

If the young Marlow had any illusions about English imperialists being any less abusive than their Dutch and Spanish counterparts in the Malay Archipelago, the captain's invective quickly dispels them. Indeed, Marlow reports being "almost convinced" by the words intended for a Malay that he himself is of a lower order, that his very existence was some sort of unpardonable sin.[36] When Marlow indicates that he is English, however, it is the captain who becomes discomfited: "Oh, my goodness! I say . . . did you hear me just now?" Marlow then reveals that he has heard him, causing the captain to become defensive:

> I thought you were a shore-boat. Now, look here—this infernal lazy scoundrel of a caretaker has gone to sleep again—curse him. The light is out, and I nearly ran afoul of the end of this damned jetty. This is the third time he plays me this trick. Now, I ask you, can anybody stand this kind of thing? It's enough to drive a man out of his mind. I'll report him . . . I'll get the Assistant Resident to give him the sack, by . . . ! (39–40)

Marlow's reply—"There was a light"—infuriates the English captain even further, and Marlow again hears the "voice" of the imperialist "West": "But it's out, man! What's the use of talking like this? You can see for yourself it's out—don't you? If you had to take a valuable steamer along this God-forsaken coast you would want a light too. I'll kick him from end to end of this miserable wharf. You'll see if I don't. I will—" (40). The dialogue between Marlow and the captain is significant not only because it suggests the brutality of imperialism but also because Marlow challenges the captain, albeit mildly, by insisting that he is in the wrong because the light was on. Marlow's refusal to see things the captain's way invites the reader to do the same, to judge the captain and the imperialist system he represents as vicious and cruel. Although Marlow does not speak for Conrad any more than the frame narrator does, he does represent an alternative perspective on imperialism, one capable of recognizing imperialism for what it is.

The young Marlow is also able to see imperialists for what they are, at least briefly. The next morning, when he is awakened by the sunlight after finishing the night in an open boat, he encounters "men of the East" for the first time: "They were looking at me. The whole length of the jetty was full of people. I saw brown, bronze, yellow faces, the black eyes, the glitter, the colour of an Eastern crowd. And all these beings stared without a murmur, without a sigh, without a movement. They stared down at the boats, at the sleeping men who at night had come to them from the sea" (40–41). The unusual circumstances of his first encounter with the local populace allow him to see himself and his comrades as the "men of the East" do.[37] The experience of being "othered" shocks him: "I sat up suddenly. A wave of movement passed through the crowd from end to end, passed along the heads, swayed the bodies, ran along the jetty like a ripple on the water, like a breath of wind on a field—and all was still again" (41). Marlow's use of sea imagery to describe the crowd of locals is telling, since throughout the rest of the story the sea is represented as an antagonist of sorts, one that nearly capsizes the ship before its cargo of coal is loaded, pours through leaks in the hull once the *Judea* is underway, and finally claims the ship when the coal explodes.[38] The suggestion seems to be that colonial peoples, like the sea, will eventually overwhelm those who try to dominate them. The passage that follows seems to reinforce this idea since it not only again connects subject peoples to the sea but also emphasizes the vulnerability of the English crew:

> I see it now—the wide sweep of the bay, the glittering sands, the wealth of green infinite and varied, the sea blue like the sea of a dream, the crowd of attentive faces, the blaze of vivid colour—the water reflecting it all, the curve of shore, the jetty, the high-sterned outlandish craft floating still, and the three boats with the tired men of the West sleeping, unconscious of the land and of the people and the violence of sunshine. They slept thrown across the thwarts, curled on the bottom-boards, in the careless attitudes of death. (41)

To an extent, the crew of the *Judea* resembles Tennyson's Lotus-Eaters. It is not self-indulgence that overcomes this crew, however, but their limited strength. Even this stoic, persevering group of Englishmen will not be able to withstand the "stealthy Nemesis" that "lies in wait, pursues, overtakes so many of the conquering race, who are proud of their wisdom, of their knowledge, of their strength" (41–42).[39]

As the passages I have just quoted suggest, Marlow's narrative, which began as a dissertation on youth, has also become a story about empire. Although Marlow stops short of criticizing European imperialism directly, the shift in emphasis makes such a critique implicit, as does the reversal of the colonist's gaze. All this seems to be lost on the naïve frame narrator, however, who, like Half-a-Crown in Solomon Plaatje's *Mhudi,* misses the story's radical implications. As the story's last paragraph suggests, he still regards the story as a paean to lost youth: "And we all nodded at him . . . our faces marked by toil, by deceptions, by success, by love; our weary eyes looking still, looking always, looking anxiously for something out of life, that while it is expected is already gone—has passed unseen, in a sigh, in a flash—together with the youth, with the strength, with the romance of illusions" (42).

Intentional Hybridity and Conrad's Trojan Horse Strategy

Ultimately, the difference between Marlow's understanding of his own experiences and that of the frame narrator generates a tension similar to the one in "Karain": both stories are intentional hybrids to the extent that they set alternative perspectives against one another dialogically. By structuring the texts in such a manner, Conrad is able to express his anti-imperialist attitudes even as he distances himself from them through his frame narrators, effectively cloaking his radical politics. The narrators of both stories, however, are unconvincing in their dismissal of their stories' radical implications, and as a result, these implications are not entirely contained. As I have argued in chapter 1, such subterfuge is characteristic of the early postcolonial aesthetic, as evidenced by novels such as *Ratanbai, The Prince of Destiny,* and *Mhudi.* Like Lal Behari Day, S. K. Ghosh, and Solomon Plaatje, Conrad had to be duplicitous were he to have any hope of reaching a broad, imperial audience. In "Karain" and "Youth," however, the radical never fully emerges as a pointed critique. As we shall see, this did not happen until his next works, *Heart of Darkness* and *Lord Jim,* texts in which Conrad's Trojan horse strategy reaches its full development.

CHAPTER FIVE

"You—Even You!—May Miss It": *Heart of Darkness* and Conrad's Trojan Horse Strategy

. . . the Danaan captains
By the divine handicraft of Pallas built
A horse of timber, tall as a hill,
And sheathed its ribs with planking of cut pine.
This they gave out to be an offering
For a safe return by sea and the word went round.
But on the sly they shut inside a company
Chosen from their picked soldiery by lot,
Crowding the vaulted caverns in the dark—
The horse's belly—with men fully armed.

VIRGIL'S *Aeneid*, translated by Robert Fitzgerald

There was censorship in the colonial world: no Marx or Lenin. But there was Conrad sneaking through . . .

PETER NAZARETH, "Out of the Darkness: Conrad and Other Third World Writers"

As we saw in the previous chapter, Conrad's use of both a frame narrator and a character-narrator in "Youth" allowed him to distance himself from the critique of imperialism implicit in the story. Although Marlow's narrative suggests that European imperialism is cruel and inefficient, the suggestion is never quite voiced because neither Marlow nor the frame narrator formally draws such a conclusion. In *Heart of Darkness*—another *Blackwood's* story that features Marlow as narrator—Conrad again uses multiple narrative perspectives to disassociate himself from the story's anti-imperialist content. In this story, however, the attack on imperialism is voiced, albeit subtly, through a frame narrator who, in addition to ironizing British imperialist history even as he invokes it, subverts Marlow's imperialist rhetoric of light and darkness, exposing him as an ideologue. As a result, even though *Heart of Darkness* is double-voiced to the extent that alternative perspectives are set against one another, the anti-imperialist perspective emerges and becomes dominant. In effect, the story functions like the Trojan horse Virgil describes in *The Aeneid:* like the Greeks, who concealed armed men in what appeared to be an offering rather than a war engine, Conrad hides his radical critique of imperialism within a story that appears to celebrate the British Empire.[1] By adopting such a strategy, Conrad is able to "sneak" his radical critique "through," to borrow Peter Nazareth's phrasing, reaching a broader audience without compromising his radical ideals (Nazareth 1982, 178).

Imperialism, Imperialist Rhetoric, and the Critics of Imperialism

To understand the subversive elements of *Heart of Darkness,* we must consider the story in the context of European imperialism in Africa and the rhetoric of light and darkness. Although Britain and France dominated Africa economically and politically in the late nineteenth century, a number of other nations—including Germany, Italy, Holland, and Portugal—hoped to establish themselves as colonial powers in the "Dark Continent." Leopold II, King of the Belgians, in particular had African ambitions, writing in 1877 that he, too, wanted "a share of this magnificent African cake" (Emerson 79). Remarkably, in less than a decade, Leopold managed to become "King-sovereign" of tens of millions of Africans and nearly a million square miles of Central African territory. Leopold was successful for a number of reasons: he was skilled as a statesman, he had a huge personal fortune, and he was adept at exploiting his relationship with his cousin, Queen Victoria. Furthermore, since Belgium was a neutral, minor power, Leopold's personal empire did not threaten the interests of England, France, or Germany. Finally, and perhaps most important, as Barbara Emerson suggests, Leopold was a brilliant propagandist who was able to use a variety of media to build support for his endeavors in the United States and Great Britain.

Leopold's strategy for obtaining control of the Congo involved creating "an innocuous-seeming international structure for the opening up of Central Africa behind which he could pursue his own ends" (Emerson 79). Recognizing the value of philanthropic propaganda, in 1877 Leopold organized the International African Association, an agency dedicated to ending the slave trade, establishing free trade, and eventually "civilizing" Africa. Although in Leopold's words, the association's goal was "to open to civilization the only part of the globe where Christianity had not penetrated and to pierce the darkness which envelops the entire population," in reality, Leopold was planning to turn the Congo into a profitable business (Hennessy 13).

As the passage just quoted suggests, the rhetoric of light and darkness played an important role in Leopold's propaganda campaign. Like the American slave lobby, which earlier in the century had used light/dark imagery to support their contention that slavery actually benefited Africans since it brought them the "light" of Christianity, Leopold appealed to Europeans as fellow Christians, suggesting that he was actually doing God's work.[2] Soon after the leading European powers gave Leopold, as chair of the International African Society, permission to police the Congo in 1877, he hired Henry Morton Stanley, the celebrated explorer and journalist who is credited with finding Dr. Livingstone, to establish three stations along the Congo River. With Stanley, Leopold got more than a capable explorer; although he can hardly be called altruistic, Stanley was committed to the "cause of civilization" and to the rhetoric of light and darkness, as the titles of his major works, *Through the Dark Continent* and *In Darkest Africa,* suggest. Working for the association, Stanley not only established stations and acquired land from local rulers but, on returning to Europe, used his rhetorical skills on behalf of the association and, later, the Congo Free State. In a speech in London in 1884, for example, he invokes the light/dark opposition, accusing English politicians of misunderstanding the spirit of Leopold's mission in Africa: "They [the politicians] cannot appreciate [it] rightly, because there are no dividends attached to it, this restless, ardent, vivifying and expansive sentiment, which seeks to extend civilizing influences among the dark races, and to brighten up with the glow of civilization the dark places of sad-browed Africa" (Morel 15). Speaking in Manchester one month later, Stanley discusses the "bright and happy" future of the Congolese in similar terms. According to him, the gold star in the center of the International African Association's flag represents "the morning star, forerunner of the light that was to shine over the Dark Continent" (Morel 13).

Proponents of European imperialism in Africa were not the only ones to use light/dark rhetoric: by the end of the nineteenth century, even those who opposed the Congo Free State tended to use light/dark imagery in their attacks on it. Rather than question European assumptions of white superiority, Congo reform leaders such as Edmund Morel criticized Leopold and his agents for the way they conducted the "campaign of light against darkness" (Morel 179). Ironically, even though he himself used phrases such as "angels of light," "sea of darkness," and "torchlight of truth" when talking about the white man's duty in Africa, Morel charges Leopold and his agents with prejudice, racism, and immorality. In effect, Morel accuses Leopold of dropping the "White Man's Burden" rather than challenging the legitimacy of the "duty" identified by Kipling in his celebrated poem of 1899.[3]

Despite having attitudes that, by today's standards at least, are racist, Morel proved to be a very effective advocate for reform, collecting information regarding European atrocities in the Congo and disseminating it through the *West African Mail,* a publication he founded in 1903. The very next year, he began the Congo Reform Association, a popular political organization that pressured the Belgian, American, and British governments to force Leopold to relinquish control of the Congo Free State. Within four years, the Congo Reform Association had succeeded. By documenting the abuses of Leopold and his agents and accusing Leopold of misconducting the "campaign of light against darkness," Morel and his allies forced Belgium to annex the Congo and take responsibility for "civilizing" the Congolese.

Morel was not the only European to question the legitimacy of the "scramble for Africa" or decry the exploitation and abuse of Africans, of course, and the Belgians were not the only ones to be criticized. Olive Schreiner, for example, attacks British imperialism directly in *Trooper Peter Halket of Mashonaland* (1897), and Mary Kingsley argues for "the government of Africa by Africans" in *West African Studies* (1899) (358).[4] In Conrad's own circle, Cunninghame Graham and Edward Garnett were both vociferous opponents of British imperialism, the two of them working together to develop "The Over-Seas Library," a series of books dedicated to countering the "Imperial drum-beating" that had become so prevalent in England in the late 1890s.[5] Conrad's good friend Ford Madox Ford was also a committed anti-imperialist, collaborating with Conrad on *The Inheritors,* a biting satirical attack on imperialism and imperialist ideology.[6]

Conrad's Trojan Horse Strategy

Conrad's circumstances were very different from Graham's, Garnett's, and Ford's, of course, since he was the only one of the four supporting himself entirely with his writing: as a result, Conrad felt compelled to cloak his radical content once he began working with conservative publishers. Accordingly, when, in December 1898, William Blackwood invited Conrad to contribute a story for the special thousandth issue of *Blackwood's,* Conrad sent him *The Heart of Darkness,* a story, like "Youth," that uses multiple narrators to obfuscate its radical anti-imperialist implications.[7] Despite his use of what Brian Richardson terms "ideological camouflage," Conrad still worried that the as yet uncompleted story might be judged unsuitable for such a highly visible issue of the conservative monthly, and so he describes it to Blackwood in terms that downplay its radical content:[8]

> It is a narrative after the manner of *youth* told by the same man dealing with his experiences on a river in Central Africa. The *idea*

> in it is not as obvious as in *youth*—or at least not so obviously presented. I tell you all this, for tho' I have no doubts as to the *workmanship* I do not know whether the *subject* will commend itself to you for that particular number . . . . The title I am thinking of is "*The Heart of Darkness*" but the narrative is not gloomy. The criminality of inefficiency and pure selfishness when tackling the civilizing work in Africa is a justifiable idea. (*Letters* 2:139–40)

Conrad's letter is significant not only because it indicates how careful he felt he had to be with the conservative Blackwood but also because it suggests that Conrad was willing to misrepresent the radical nature of his work in order to get it published.[9] The latter becomes more clear when Conrad's letter to Blackwood is compared with a letter he wrote to Graham after the first installment of the story appeared in *Blackwood's* two months later, a letter that suggests *Heart of Darkness* contains a covert, radical content: "I am simply in seventh heaven to find you like *H of D* so far. You bless me indeed. Mind you don't curse me by and bye for the very same thing. There are two more instalments in which the idea is so wrapped up in secondary notions that You—even You!—may miss it" (*Letters* 2:157). In describing *Heart of Darkness* as a story in which the main "idea" is "wrapped up in secondary notions," Conrad seems to suggest that he adopted a Trojan horse strategy to expose the jingoistic readers of *Blackwood's* to an anti-imperialist story.[10] Although he concedes that the story's radical content may be difficult to discern—that even those with similar ideas "may miss it"—the very next passage makes it clear that he expected Graham to approve of the story's implicit politics: "So far the note struck chimes in with your convictions—mais après? There is an après. But I think that if you look a little into the episodes you will find in them the right intention though I fear nothing that is practically effective" (*Letters* 2:157–58). Conrad's confidence in his radical friends' ability to find "the right intention" in his work appears to have been well-founded, for after reading the final installment of the story in *Blackwood's*, Graham wrote Conrad to tell him that he liked the story very much, and Conrad credits Garnett with being able to "detect the shape of a mangled idea and the shadow of an intention in the worst of one's work" (*Letters* 2:222).[11]

Although he had the understanding and support of his most radical friends, Conrad's letters suggest that writing for an imperialist readership—however "right" his "intention"—made him feel uncomfortable and even a little guilty. Just after completing *Heart of Darkness,* for example, he writes to Garnett of *Lord Jim,* another Trojan horse novel, in terms that reveal his discomfort with writing stories designed to appeal to imperialists, at least on the surface: "I am writing—it is true—but this is only piling crime upon crime: every line is odious like a bad action. I mean odious to me—because I still have some pretences to the possession of a conscience though my morality is gone to the dogs" (*Letters* 2:198). Although it might be tempting to interpret the passage as referring to the odiousness of the writing process itself, a process Conrad always found difficult, the references to "conscience" and "morality" suggest that he worried about the real-world effects of his work. Here Conrad seems to recognize a potential problem in his method that many later critics would come to identify: to challenge imperialist ideology, he had to reproduce it and thereby risk inadvertently promoting it, something he found unconscionable.[12]

Conrad's worries about reproducing imperialist ideology seem to have been compounded by the fact that his method was entirely new and that, therefore, he could only hope it would ultimately have the "right" effect upon readers. His letter to Garnett continues: "My efforts seem unrelated to anything in heaven[,] and everything under heaven is impalpable to the touch like shapes of mist . . . All is illusion—the words written, the mind at which they are aimed, the truth they are intended to express, the hands that will hold the paper, the eyes that will glance over the lines. Every image floats vaguely in a sea of doubt—and the doubt itself is lost in an unexpected universe of incertitudes" (*Letters* 2:198). In a letter written to Ted Sanderson just ten days later, Conrad reiterates his doubts about his methods and himself in even more direct terms:

> It is great to hear you talk like this of my work . . . If You knew how ambitious I am, how my ambition checks my pen at every turn. Doubts assail me from every side. The doubt of form—the doubt of tendency—a mistrust of my own conceptions—and scruples of the moral order. As if my soul mattered to the universe! But even

> as the ant bringing its grain of sand to the common edifice may justly think itself important, so I would like to think that I am doing my appointed work." (*Letters* 2:212)

As his reference to "scruples of the moral order" indicates, Conrad continued to have doubts about his new methods, possibly because it involved pandering to the tastes of imperialists, at least on one level. His reference to his "appointed work" suggests that he found a way to rationalize his efforts, however, since his words recall those of an earlier letter to Unwin in which he insists upon the moral value of writing (*Letters* 1:93). Although his worries about whether his work would have the desired effect remained, apparently Conrad took solace in the fact that he had the "right intention."

Conrad's anxieties about whether his meaning would ever be perceived by any but the most perspicacious readers seem to have been justified: most of Conrad's contemporaries, like generations of critics to follow, appear to have identified Conrad's viewpoint with Marlow's and concluded that Conrad approved of British imperialism.[13] Identifying Conrad too closely with Marlow is a mistake, though, for as Najder notes in his introduction to Conrad's *The Congo Diary*, "Marlow is not the author's mouthpiece but one of two main characters of the story, a co-hero, whose point of view is markedly different from the authorial perspective and whose attitudes are even subjected to irony" (1988, 156).[14] Marlow might be one of the story's main characters, but that does not mean that his views reflect Conrad's any more than Kurtz's do. To identify an author too closely with a character is to ignore Conrad's dialogism: Marlow's words exist in relation to those of other characters, including the anonymous frame narrator, and must be considered in a broader discursive context.[15]

Irony, the Anonymous Narrator, and Intentional Hybridity

Until recently, critics missed the importance of the frame narrator of *Heart of Darkness*. Some ignore him entirely, and others dismiss him as a meaningless convention typical of late nineteenth-century adventure fiction. Others still consider him a proponent of imperialism since, among other things, he seems to refer approvingly to Sir Francis Drake and Sir John Franklin as representatives of the British imperial tradition (8). Anthony Fothergill, for example, discusses the anonymous narrator's words as a "eulogy to the Thames and the glorious history it has witnessed and serviced" (66), and Jakob Lothe describes them as "imperialistic rhetoric" (1996, 168). As Robert Hampson demonstrates, however, although the frame narrator offers "the kind of nationalist history and imperialist rhetoric with which his first readers would have been familiar," his very words "lull them into a false sense of security at the outset" (1995, xxix). Hampson continues:

> for the careful or experienced reader, hints of a different version are suggested towards the end: "Hunters for gold or pursuers of fame, they had all gone out on that stream, bearing the sword, and *often* the torch, messengers of the *might* within the land" . . . Just as the words used subtly subvert the narrator's confident rhetoric, the reference to Sir Francis Drake might also have reminded some of Conrad's readers of a less than flattering article on Drake that appeared in *Blackwood's* six months earlier, while references to Sir John Franklin's expedition arguably implants an allusion to European cannibalism at the start of the novel. (emphasis added by Hampson)[16]

Hampson's point about the frame narrator's choice of heroes is particularly important, for the frame narrator could hardly have chosen more controversial figures than Drake and Franklin to represent those "men of whom the nation is proud" (47). For all his accomplishments Drake was a privateer who obtained a large part of his "treasure" through piracy and murderous raids on Spanish settlements (47). As James Anthony Froude comments in *English Seamen in the Sixteenth Century,* in which are published lectures he delivered at Oxford in 1893–94, historically Drake was allowed only "qualified praise" by the British since "he was a robber and a corsair, and the only excuse for him is that he was no worse than most of his contemporaries" (103). To the late nineteenth-century British imperialists, many of whom were increasingly coming to value the rule of law since they were often the ones making the laws, Drake was even more suspect because of his lawlessness, and therefore his status as a hero was in the process of being reevaluated, as evidenced by the *Blackwood's* article on Drake's summary execution of a member of one of his expeditions, to which Hampson refers.[17]

Franklin was controversial for different reasons. Though recognized "as one of the most conspicuous of the naval heroes of Britain, and as one of her most successful explorers" in the 1890 edition of the *Encyclopedia Britannica,* during his first Arctic expedition he lost eleven men to various causes, including murder and cannibalism, and after publishing a popular book on the subject, he became known as "the man who ate his shoes" (Berton 63). His final Arctic expedition was even more disastrous, leading to the deaths of almost a hundred and fifty men, including himself.[18] Although rescue expeditions found no survivors, they did find evidence of cannibalism, evidence that was published not only in official reports but also in popular magazines such as *Household Words* and the *London Illustrated News* (Hampson 1995, xxxviii–xxxix). With Franklin and his men's horrific end so widely publicized, mention of it must have reminded at least some of Conrad's readers that those who claimed to represent civilization were not always so far removed from acts like cannibalism as they would like to believe.

Because Franklin and Drake were controversial figures, one might conclude that in alluding to them as "men of whom the nation is proud," the frame narrator is simply being obtuse.[19] Certainly, Hampson seems to believe so, as does Andrea White.[20] A careful analysis of other details in the passage suggests that the frame narrator is, in fact, being ironic. For example, in noting that Queen Elizabeth went to the docks to meet "the *Golden Hind* returning with her flanks full of treasure" (47), the frame narrator unmistakably connects Drake to Kurtz, whose ambition, we later learn, is "to have kings meet him at railway-stations" (148).[21] By relating Drake to the murderous Kurtz in this manner, the narrator implicitly disparages Drake and the imperial tradition he represents. The passage's closing words—"What greatness had not floated on the ebb of that river into the mystery of an unknown earth! . . . The dreams of men, the seed of commonwealths, the germs of empires" (47, ellipsis in original)—also seem to be ironic since they follow a list of "knights-errant of the sea" that includes pedestrian elements, including settlers and stock traders. Although settlers and stock traders certainly were necessary to British imperial expansion, they were hardly knights-errant, and the reference to them as such tends to undercut the frame narrator's inflated rhetoric. Indeed, the term *knights-errant* operates on two levels, since it suggests that knights like Drake and Franklin not only wandered but erred. Because of such ironies, what appears to be a celebration of British imperialist history simultaneously functions as a critique of it, a critique that is particularly important since it immediately precedes Marlow's own celebration of the British Empire and thereby invites the reader to regard Marlow's narrative more critically. To put it in Bakhtinian terms, the frame narrator's speech marks *Heart of Darkness* as an intentional hybrid to the extent that one voice unmasks another. The story functions as a Trojan horse as well, however, since, as we shall see, the radical critique represented by the frame narrator not only fully emerges by the end of the novel but becomes dominant. Like S. K. Ghosh and Solomon Plaatje, Conrad uses irony to create a text that operates on two levels at once so that he could attack imperialism without offending imperialists.

The Horse's Exterior: Marlow and the Liberal Critique of Ideology

Since Marlow himself is an imperialist, it should not be surprising that he misses the frame narrator's irony, taking his opening words at face value and reacting to them accordingly.[22] Looking toward London, which the narrator describes as a "monstrous town" marked by a "lurid glare," Marlow begins by asserting that it, too, "has been one of the dark places of the earth" (48). As the change in tense suggests, Marlow sees London very differently than the disparaging frame narrator: to Marlow, London is no longer a place of darkness but a source of light. He continues, "I was thinking of very old times, when the Romans first came here, nineteen hundred years ago—the other day. . . . Light came out of the river since" (49, ellipsis in original). By reducing almost two thousand years to a "day," Marlow implies that there is a direct relationship between ancient Rome and present-day England, an implication he reinforces a few sentences later by asserting, "But darkness was here yesterday": for all its horrors, Marlow seems to suggest, the Roman conquest, which he later describes as "robbery with violence, aggravated murder" (50), led to the development of the British Empire, which he identifies with the "light" that "came out of the river since."[23]

Marlow, of course, is quick to differentiate imperialisms that are "merely a squeeze" from British imperialism, with its "devotion to efficiency" (50). British imperialism, he believes, confers immediate benefits on subject peoples through modernization and is therefore preferable to cruder, more brutal imperialisms like that of the Romans. And it is not just Roman imperialism that Marlow is critical of, for later, when he sees a map marking colonial territories, he remarks, "There was a vast amount of red [denoting British territory]—good to see at any time because one knows that some real work is done in there" (55). Of all the many types of imperialism, Marlow seems to suggest, the British kind is the best since the British do more than simply grab "what they could get for the sake of what is to be got" (50).[24]

As his narrative proceeds, Marlow continues to criticize the imperialist practices of other nations, disparaging the "lager-beer" drinking German "pioneers of progress," remarking on the futility of the French man-of-war shelling the bush, and implicitly condemning Belgian atrocities in the "grove of death" scene where he describes a living graveyard of discarded African workers (55): "They were dying slowly—it was very clear. They were not enemies, they were not criminals, they were nothing earthly now, nothing but black shadows of disease and starvation lying confusedly in the greenish gloom. Brought from all the recesses of the coast in all the legality of time contracts, lost in uncongenial surroundings, fed on unfamiliar food, they sickened, became inefficient, and were allowed to crawl away and rest" (66). Conquest, Marlow admits, is not pretty "when you look at it too much," and as a liberal British critic, he forces us to look.[25] Moreover, as a character in his own narrative, he even acts at times to prevent such ugliness, blowing the steamer's whistle, for instance, in an attempt to scatter Kurtz's native followers before the "pilgrims" can shoot them on "a jolly lark" (146). He fails, however, to speak or act against imperialism in principle or to question its legitimacy. In fact, it would seem that as the captain of a river steamer, he participates in it, serving not only his own interests but also those of the Company and European imperialism at large.

Seeing in Black and White: Marlow and Imperialist Ideology

Marlow's participation in the exploitation of Africa goes beyond his duties as a ship's captain, of course, for as Benita Parry notes, he uses imagery that privileges light over darkness, white over black, in an attempt to legitimate the colonization of Africa by whites. According to Parry, such imagery is traditional in European culture:

> It is a commonplace that in western thought the contrast between black and white has for centuries stood for the good, true, pure, and beautiful as opposed to the evil, ignorant, corrupt, and atrocious. When the actions of modern imperialism brought the white world into organised confrontations with the other continents, the existing accretions of dark and black were thickened and extended to establish an equivalence between "primitive," "barbaric," or "savage" societies and moral perversity, and by inference between black people living amidst jungle, forest and wilderness and a condition of aboriginal depravity. (1983, 5)

Marlow's imagery does not merely reflect European imperialism's extension of "darkness" along racist lines. Light, too, as a category is extended to include not only whiteness but also the "white" race and European civilization in general. Accordingly, Marlow calls Europeans "whites" in his narrative and refers to Africans as "black shapes," "black figures," "black shadows," and "black fellows." He even emphasizes differences in clothing, contrasting Africans, who are "mostly black and naked" (63), to Europeans like the chief accountant, who wears "white cuffs," a "light alpaca jacket," and "snowy trousers" (67).

Marlow also uses "light" as a metaphor for things such as civilization, reason, and discourse. As we have seen, he suggests, for instance, that since the Roman conquest, "light" has "come out of" the Thames (49), meaning that the once "dark" Britain is now a source of civilization. Light also represents reason when he says things such as "It seemed somehow to throw a kind of light on everything about me" (51), and "Light dawned upon me" (79). Finally, he associates light with language, describing Kurtz's writings as "illuminating" and his speech as a "pulsating stream of light" (113–14). He relates darkness, in contrast, to savagery: Africans, according to Marlow, are not men and women but howling "black shadows" that inhabit the "dark-faced" forest (133–34). Rather than speak, the Africans shout "strings of amazing words that resembled not sounds of human language" (146). Moreover, the continent itself is an area "impenetrable to human thought" (127), a "lightless region of subtle horrors" (132). In his view, European imperialists are like the torch-bearing woman in Kurtz's oil-sketch who walks, blindfolded, through a dark background: they bring light to a "lightless" region, if only inadvertently (79). Like the figure in Kurtz's painting, they are both "sinister" and "stately": although conquest itself is ugly, it ultimately results in progress, just as the Roman conquest of England did.

The Belly of the Horse: The Frame Narrator and the Deconstruction of Marlow's Tale

The novel's frame narrator offers a very different perspective on European imperialism, one that challenges it by contesting Marlow's interpretation of his own experiences in Africa. Like a spin doctor in a political campaign, this narrator puts a spin on Marlow's narrative that discredits Marlow and the ideology he serves: he frames Marlow's narrative with his own, interrupting it at critical points, contradicting it, and ultimately deconstructing it, or at least suggesting to the reader that it deconstructs itself.[26] The frame narrator, who indicates at the beginning of the story that the "convictions" of those aboard the *Nellie* differ (46), begins his assault immediately, interrupting Marlow's "yarn" after only one sentence to suggest that the "meaning" of Marlow's tale is "not inside . . . but outside, enveloping the tale which brought it out only as a glow brings out a haze" (48). It does not have the "direct simplicity" of a typical seaman's yarn and, therefore, cannot be taken literally. To comprehend such a tale, the narrator suggests, we have to consider the form as well as the content, something Conrad seems to confirm in his author's note, writing that his rhetorical strategy in the story "was like another art altogether" (xi); he continues, "the somber theme" of the story "had to be given a sinister resonance, a tonality of its own, a continued vibration that, I hoped, would hang in the air and dwell on the ear after the last note had been struck." It is to such a "sinister resonance" that the frame narrator seems to refer when he suggests that we explore the rhetorical "haze" that envelops Marlow's narrative: rather than simply see Africa "through" Marlow's eyes, the frame narrator hopes that we will "see through" Marlow's effort to justify the colonization effort.[27]

A few paragraphs after suggesting that the reader consider form as well as content, the narrator again interrupts Marlow's narrative, this time questioning whether the story Marlow is about to relate is the "culminating point" of his existence, as Marlow claims, or just another one of his "inconclusive" experiences (51). Marlow, the narrator suggests, is not to be trusted, particularly when it comes to interpreting his own experiences in Africa.[28] As the product of imperialist ideology as well as its servant, Marlow tends to see things in black and white, privileging the latter. Even when he recognizes color, he tends to polarize it, emphasizing shade rather than hue. Blue, for example, becomes "dark blue," and "green" becomes "dark green" and even "so green as to be almost black" (60). Such polarization is not only perceptual but also conceptual for Marlow; everything he associates with Africa is "dark": the natives, the jungles, the rivers, the villages, and even the sun, while things he associates with Europe are bright. The narrator, in contrast, insists that there is a full range of colors. To make this point, the narrator juxtaposes Marlow's reaction to the sunset to his own: while dusk prompts Marlow to speak at length about "light" and "darkness," the narrator comments on how light "colors" the river: "Flames glided on the river, small green flames, red flames, white flames, pursuing, overtaking, joining, crossing each other—then separating slowly or hastily" (51). Marlow, the frame narrator seems to suggest, is, in a sense, color-blind; he does not "see" things as they are but as imperialist ideology would have them—in black and white.

Because he sees things only in terms of light and darkness, Marlow is, at best, a liberal critic of imperialism, one who supports the system as a whole even as he criticizes its excesses. As the frame narrator suggests, however, Marlow's own rhetoric undercuts the very ideology he promotes, for as Marlow consciously attempts to distinguish light from darkness, his own words suggest that they are essentially the same, or at least closely related. Sunlight, for instance, is described repeatedly as "blinding" (19, 20), as is the "white fog" on the river (101, 105). A dying African worker's eyes, too, are described as both "blind" and "white," again suggesting that light and darkness are inseparable. Marlow also describes light as a source of darkness and darkness as a source of light: Kurtz's eyes "shine darkly," for example, and a "black creek" has "shiny patches." Taken as a whole, Marlow's rhetoric suggests that light and dark are not opposites but complements, thereby subverting the imperialist ideology that employs the light/dark opposition to justify the subjugation of "nonwhite" people.

Marlow's rhetoric undermines not only the basic opposition between light and dark but also those oppositions subordinate to it. For instance, although he uses the terms *white* and *black* when referring to the race of Europeans and Africans, respectively, he uses both colors when describing the physical appearance of members of either race. He calls the first Africans he sees "black fellows," for example, only to note then that "from afar" he could see "the whites of their eyes glistening" (61). When describing a dying African worker a little later, he combines black and white imagery in a more complex way: "The black bones reclined at full length with one shoulder against the tree, and slowly the eyelids rose and the sunken eyes looked up at me, enormous and vacant, a kind of blind, white flicker in the depths of the orbs which died out slowly . . . He had tied a bit of white worsted round his neck . . . It looked startling round his black neck this bit of white thread from beyond the seas" (66–67). Since normally bones are white, Marlow's use of "black bones" as a metaphor for the dying African is striking since it suggests not only that the man is starving but that, on some level, white can appear as black, a suggestion that the references to the "blind, white flicker" of his eyes and the "white thread" around his neck seem to support. Like all the "blacks" Marlow describes, the dying worker is, in reality, both black and white.

Marlow also unites black and white imagery when describing Europeans, whose skin is "white" and mustaches are "black" (72). Kurtz, too, although white-skinned, not only shines "darkly," as noted earlier, but is repeatedly called a "shadow" and a "shade" (134, 143, 147). Marlow also describes the Intended in terms of both light and darkness: "She came forward all in black with a pale head, floating before me in the dusk . . . This fair hair, this pale visage, this pure brow, seemed surrounded by an ashy halo from which dark eyes looked out at me" (156–57). The Intended, it seems, like the other Europeans, is in reality no "lighter" than the Africans are "dark," and therefore, the ideology that privileges whites over blacks is again questioned.

Another opposition Marlow asserts only to undercut rhetorically is that between Europe and Africa. For example, when describing the neighborhood of the Company headquarters in the city, he uses images that, elsewhere in the novel, are associated with Africa: namely, shadows, blindness, and death: "A narrow and deserted street in *deep shadow,* high houses, innumerable windows with venetian *blinds,* a *dead* silence, *grass* sprouting between the stones, imposing carriage archways right and left, immense double doors standing ponderously ajar" (55, emphasis added). As the pun on "blinds" suggests, Marlow's use of such imagery is at least partly unconscious: although in this passage, *blinds* functions as a noun, it is the same word he uses in describing sunlight and fog in Africa. *Grass,* too, is strongly associated with Africa elsewhere in the novel; on the very same page, for example, he says that in Africa, the "grass growing through [Fresleven's] ribs was tall enough to hide his bones." This near juxtaposition highlights the connection between Africa and Europe.

Nature cannot be repressed, despite European efforts to do so. Grass sprouts between the stones of European roads just as it reclaims the abandoned machinery and outposts of the Europeans in Africa.

Marlow's rhetoric also suggests that language, which he frequently associates with light, can also be a source of darkness. According to Marlow, when he was a boy, Central Africa was represented by "blank space" on maps because it was unexplored by Europeans. With the arrival of the Europeans, however, the blank spaces become dark: "It had got filled in since my boyhood with rivers and lakes and names. It had ceased to be a blank space of delightful mystery—a white patch for a boy to dream gloriously over. It had become a place of darkness" (52). Central Africa is partly darkened, at least on the globe, by language that, elsewhere, is associated with light rather than darkness. Just as the written word can literally darken a page, the spoken word can darken a room. In describing his encounter with the Intended, for example, he says that "with every word spoken the room was getting darker" (158), suggesting that their words were, in some sense, the cause of darkness. This, of course, parallels what is happening on the *Nellie,* where Marlow's tale is strongly related to the growing darkness.

Marlow's opposition of European technology to African primitivism also deconstructs itself. Although on the one hand, Marlow matches every sophisticated European tool with a primitive African counterpart (steamships to canoes, guns to spears, and so forth), on the other, he uses animal imagery when describing European machines. For example, to him, a broken boiler appears to be "wallowing in the grass," and an overturned railway car looks "as dead as the carcass of some animal" (63), as does his broken steamer (81). Furthermore, rather than rust, the abandoned machinery "decays" as if it were once alive.

Finally, Marlow's rhetoric calls into question the distinction between European science and African magic. For the Europeans, science is a product of reason that, in turn, is associated metaphorically with light; accordingly, in Marlow's narrative it comes to represent European superiority. Marlow's Africans, in contrast, believe in magic rather than science; in fact, according to Marlow, they can understand technology only in terms of magic, as his description of his fireman makes clear:

> He was an improved specimen; he could fire up a vertical boiler . . . He ought to have been clapping his hands and stamping his feet on the bank, instead of which he was hard at work, a thrall to strange witchcraft, full of improving knowledge. He was useful because he had been instructed; and what he knew was this—that should the water in that transparent thing disappear the evil spirit inside would get angry through the greatness of his thirst and take a terrible vengeance. (97)

Although Marlow finds his fireman's superstitious understanding of technology amusing, later in the passage he admits, "the boiler seemed indeed to have a sulky devil in it." If, in this instance, Marlow is being ironic, his frequent references to "devils," "demons," "phantoms," "apparitions," and "shades" elsewhere in the text suggest that he himself depends on the language of superstition and the supernatural. In fact, by the end of the narrative, darkness itself seems supernatural to him, an evil from which he must protect the Intended; it is no longer merely the absence of light but its enemy. Accordingly, when darkness threatens to become "triumphant" during his encounter with the Intended, Marlow lies to protect her from it, despite his self-avowed hatred of lies. Feeling that women must be kept "out of it," Marlow shields the Intended from the knowledge that darkness pervades even Europe; to tell her "would have been too dark—too dark altogether."[29]

The Tension Between Two Endings

Marlow's treatment of darkness as an antagonist at the end of his narrative confirms that he is indeed a liberal critic of European imperialism rather than a radical one, for while he is critical of the Company and its employees, he shares their belief that darkness is an evil that must be dispelled. Although he refuses to see himself as an "emissary of light" personally, he believes that it is the duty of Europeans to bring light to Africa, just as earlier the Romans had brought light to England, however inadvertently (59). If "sunlight can be made to lie," as he concedes in the last scene of his narrative, it is because darkness has corrupted the bearers of light. Sunlight itself does not lie; rather, men like Kurtz and the Station Manager "make" it lie. The problem with European imperialism is the involvement of hypocrites like the so-called pilgrims, according to Marlow: imperialism itself promises to bring light to "the dark places of the earth," just as the Roman conquest, though brutal, brought light to England.[30]

The frame narrator sees imperialism and its consequences very differently. As Marlow finishes his narrative, the frame narrator reports that the tide has reached its ebb and is flowing back out to sea, "leading to the uttermost ends of the earth." The fact that the narrator repeats the very words he used at the beginning of the story when offering his ironic account of imperialist history is, of course, important since it reminds the reader that his attitudes are very different from Marlow's, that to him Drake and the British imperial tradition he represents are as culpable as Kurtz and Continental imperialisms. That the anonymous narrator notes that the tide has ebbed is also significant since it recalls his earlier words regarding the "greatness" that has "floated on the ebb" of the Thames, "the [h]unters for gold," the "pursuers of fame" (47). His implication seems to be that, far from being a source of light as Marlow would have it, England's "tranquil waterway" leads to horrors like those in Africa, that the Thames is a source of darkness rather than light (94).

The tension between the story's two endings—Marlow's, with its liberal implications, and the frame narrator's, with its radical ones—is consistent with the tension that runs throughout the entire text. *Heart of Darkness* is an intentional hybrid to the extent that the points of view it represents are "set against each other dialogically" (Bakhtin 360). Were Conrad to privilege the radical critique in a more obvious way as he does in earlier works such as *Almayer's Folly* and "The Lagoon," the story would have been unacceptable to Blackwood and his readers. The story's radical content emerges more fully than it does in "Karain" and "Youth," however, making it a Trojan horse of sorts. By adopting such a strategy, Conrad was able to reach a broader, more profitable conservative audience and have a chance, at least, of influencing them.

Determining a work's ideological effect with any exactitude is, of course, impossible, as Catherine Gallagher and Stephen Greenblatt note.[31] Certainly, Conrad was very much concerned with the possibility that even his most sympathetic readers might "miss" the radical implications of *Heart of Darkness* and that, therefore, the story would not be "practically effective" (*Letters* 2:157). Contemporary reviews suggest that his concerns were justified. Reviewers recognized the story as an attack on "the Belgian ivory-hunt" even though the story makes no explicit reference to either Belgium or the Congo (Sherry 1973, 139), and Morel himself considered it "the most powerful thing ever written on the subject" (Louis and Stengers 205).[32] They seem to have missed the radical critique of imperialism, however, and in an unsigned review that appeared in *Academy and Literature,* Garnett seems to deny that the story offers any critique of imperialism at all: "There is no 'intention' in the story, no *parti pris,* no prejudice one way or the other; it is simply a piece of art, fascinating and remorseless, and the artist is but intent on presenting his sensations in that sequence and arrangement whereby the meaning or the meaninglessness of the white man in uncivilized Africa can be felt in its really significant aspects" (Sherry 1973, 133). On the surface, Garnett's insistence that the story has no political "intention" or "prejudice" seems odd, particularly since he was not only Conrad's good friend and confidante but also a fellow anti-imperialist. The fact that the review was unsigned suggests an explanation, however: Garnett hoped to help market his friend's story not only by writing a positive review but by downplaying the story's radical anti-imperial content.[33] In a sense, he wrote a Trojan horse review.

Although it is difficult to ascertain whether Garnett's laudatory, if misleading, review had a significant effect upon the sales of *Youth—A Narrative and Two Other Stories* (1902), the collection of short stories in which *Heart of Darkness* appeared, Garnett's focus on the story's aesthetic qualities rather than its political context "considerably influenced later criticism," as Najder notes (1983, 286).[34] Whether they praised or condemned Conrad's extravagant artistry, critics in the 1940s and 1950s all but ignored the story's political content.[35] It was only in the 1960s that critics again began to consider the story in the context of nineteenth-century European imperialism in Africa, beginning with Eloise Knapp Hay's *The Political Novels of Joseph Conrad: A Critical Study* (1963) and Avrom Fleishman's *Conrad's Politics: Community and Anarchy in the Fiction of Joseph Conrad* (1967). Even then, political approaches like Hay's and Fleishman's were unusual: for the most part, *Heart of Darkness* was considered an apolitical modernist text that was either nihilistic, psychological, or both. As Adam Hochschild, the author of *King Leopold's Ghost: A Story of Greed, Terror, and Heroism in Colonial Africa,* recalls, when he was in college the story was taught in terms of "Freudian overtones, mythic echoes, and inward vision" rather than as a political text (3).

As political criticism became more popular in the 1970s, critical responses to *Heart of Darkness* began to change, particularly after Chinua Achebe's celebrated 1975 lecture on racism in *Heart of Darkness* was published in essay form in 1977.[36] In this essay, an amended version of which is now included in the widely used Norton Critical Edition of *Heart of Darkness,* Achebe argues that Conrad was both a racist and an imperialist and that *Heart of Darkness* calls into question the very humanity of black Africans. Ironically, although Achebe's response to the story is more political than aesthetic, like most critics before him, he seems to regard the story as a modernist text, charging Conrad with using Africa "merely [as] a setting for the disintegration of the mind of Mr. Kurtz," a "metaphysical battlefield" (256).

Heart of Darkness *as an Intervention*

Despite its limitations, Achebe's essay provoked a much-needed reassessment of *Heart of Darkness* and Conrad's work in general as Conradians, postcolonial critics, and specialists in modern British literature debated Conrad's attitudes toward race and empire.[37] Few, however, consider the text in its original context or analyze its ideological function. Even Peter Firchow, who details the story's discursive context, focuses more on its "aesthetic power" than its ideological effect, analyzing it as "a modern work of art" rather than as a social text (x, 29). That *Heart of Darkness* is a work of art is, of course, undeniable: it has been canonized as a great literary work. As Alan Sinfield observes, however, literature—like every cultural production—has an ideological function, one that is at least potentially subversive since literary works do not "necessarily promote the dominant viewpoint" (35). In *Heart of Darkness,* Conrad develops this "radical potential" through the construction of a text in which one voice ironizes another (Sinfield 35). By creating a Trojan horse of sorts, a text in which a radical critique of imperialist ideology is hidden within a liberal critique of certain imperialist practices, Conrad is able to reach readers who would otherwise ignore or reject his work. As Peter Nazareth notes, Conrad does this in part through innovation: he "invent[s] devices for getting his anti-colonial texts published by the very forces profiting from imperialism." Such devices, according to Nazareth, were his only means of "slipping the story past the mental defenses of those benefiting from imperialism" (Nazareth 1990, 107). The irony, of course, is that for most critics, the devices themselves have become the object of study rather than the content, and as a result, this most political of texts is now widely regarded as "a tour de force of condensed modernist highjinks" (Wallenstein 205). It is as if critics are themselves Trojans, admiring the magnificent horse that has appeared outside their walls. Although they can hear the spears rattling inside, they choose not to interpret the sounds in the context of war. To them, the horse is a statue rather than a war engine, an exquisite work of art to be enjoyed for its own sake.

CHAPTER SIX

"The Onlookers See Most of the Game": Marlow, Jim, and Postcolonial Patusan

In *Culture and Imperialism,* Edward Said argues that Joseph Conrad could not "imagine a fully realized alternative to imperialism" because he did not recognize that those living in India, Africa, and South America had existences independent of those proscribed for them by imperialism (xviii, 25). Although he concedes that Conrad is critical of certain aspects of imperialism, he suggests that in representing subject peoples as unable to see beyond imperialist domination, Conrad reveals his ideological blindness. Ironically, in identifying Conrad's supposed blindness, Said reveals a blind spot of his own, for in assessing Conrad's works, he overlooks those set in the Malay Archipelago even though they make up the overwhelming majority of Conrad's colonial fiction. Like most other postcolonial critics who identify Conrad as an apologist for imperialism if not a proponent of it, Said ignores novels such as *Almayer's Folly* and *An Outcast of the Islands,* both of which offer alternative perspectives on imperialism. Such an oversight is even more surprising in the case of *Lord Jim:* one would expect postcolonial critics to at least acknowledge the significance of a major canonical text that depicts a successful anticolonial insurgency and the formation of a postcolonial state. That they do not can, perhaps, be explained by Conrad's subterfuge. Apparently, critics like Said are deceived by the same textual features that fooled many of Conrad's contemporaries and have come to regard the novel as an imperial romance—that is, as a narrative that celebrates imperialism.[1] What these critics seem to miss is that although the novel features many of the conventions of the imperial romance, ultimately, it challenges imperialism rather than promulgates it:

as Linda Dryden observes, in *Lord Jim,* as in his other Malay novels, "Conrad consciously manipulated the genre of imperial romance to force a reassessment of the imperial cause and its heroes" (195).

Deploying the conventions of the imperial romance in order to deconstruct them is only one element of Conrad's Trojan horse strategy in *Lord Jim:* he also employs misdirection by having his character-narrator, Marlow, insist that Jim is simply a "romantic" and that the events that occur in Patusan have little social or political significance. As in "Karain," however, the character-narrator's rejection of the radical implications of his own narrative is unconvincing, in this case because Marlow's narrative is framed by a primary narrator who suggests an alternative interpretive possibility: that Jim is more fool than hero, a man whose death marks the beginning of a postcolonial period in Patusan. The primary narrator does more than just offer an alternative interpretation of Jim's life and death: he also undercuts Marlow's interpretive authority by representing him as a comic figure and sometimes even a foolish one. Marlow may be a "skeptic," as Dryden, Stephen Ross, and others indicate, but he is nonetheless taken in by Jim and his deluded idealism, at least in part, and therefore, his judgments regarding Jim are open to challenge (Dryden 192; Ross 113). It is the tension between Marlow's interpretation of events and that of the primary narrator that makes *Lord Jim* a double-voiced text. As in *Heart of Darkness,* however, the tension is ultimately resolved in favor of the radical anti-imperialist perspective as the Patusanis free themselves from European domination and establish themselves as an independent people.

Jim, the White Man's Code, and the Colonization of Patusan

Before addressing the ways in which Conrad cloaks the novel's radical content, I will first consider that content itself, the radical implications of which, as Linda Dryden demonstrates, become most clear when *Lord Jim* is compared to the imperial romances of R. M. Ballantyne, G. A. Henty, and Rider Haggard. In novels such as *Coral Island, The Tiger of Mysore,* and *King Solomon's Mine*, white men go out to the periphery of empire to prove themselves honest, brave, true, and just—and to make their fortunes. The title character of *Lord Jim* has a different reason for going into the imperial frontier: he hopes to reestablish what Dryden terms his "white imperial manhood" (146). By abandoning the *Patna* when it appears to be sinking, Jim betrays not only the eight hundred Moslem pilgrims but the mariner's "standard of conduct" and the white man's code, according to which whites are never to show fear before their colonial subjects (34).[2] This last betrayal is most important to understanding the novel's ideological function since it represents a sort of racial treason: by proving himself a coward, Jim has betrayed his "own kind," to borrow Marlow's phrase, particularly those who depend on their "racial prestige" to govern in places where they are tremendously outnumbered (214).

Given Jim's desire to prove himself white, it is easy to see why he regards coming to Patusan as a "magnificent chance" (145): settling in a place where "utter insecurity of life and property was the normal condition" affords him the opportunity to reestablish himself in the white community, or so he believes (138). Jim's task is to "civilize" Patusan—that is, to transform it into a place where European lives and properties are safe. "You—shall—hear—of—me," he boasts to Marlow as he leaves for Patusan (147): apparently, he believes that he can redeem his "good name" by single-handedly transforming a distant, "native-ruled state" into a profitable colony (198, 133).

Upon arriving in Patusan, Jim behaves like the typical protagonist of an imperial romance. Armed only with a pistol, he organizes a local faction, the Bugis, into a military force in order to drive his Arab competitors from the region (214).[3] He then uses his Bugis allies, and what he calls his "own people" (202)—those he frees from Sherif Ali—to intimidate the local Rajah and establish himself as a power in Patusan. After his initial successes, Jim maintains his position by playing one faction off another. Even though he is formally allied with the Bugis, he keeps them from becoming too powerful by preventing them from "pay[ing] off old scores" and by recognizing the legal authority of the now innocuous Rajah (164, 152). Soon afterward, he makes himself the district's dominant military power by building a fort that commands the town square and then convincing Doramin to provide him with artillery while keeping control of all the gunpowder himself (215). Once he secures himself politically and militarily, he begins to develop Patusan commercially. As Marlow notes, Jim has cleared ground for a coffee plantation and has in mind "ever so many experiments" (191).[4] Clearly, Jim has no intention of remaining a "trading clerk" in a "place with no trade" (142); he wants to be lord of a flourishing colony, a man who is respected by the "world outside" (181).

Jim's success in Patusan is based on more than just his "energy" and "enterprise," of course (191). He succeeds as a colonist because he acts like one, treating indigenous peoples as servants and inferiors. Upon arriving in the district, Jim demands "inflexibly" that the Malays take him upriver (147); afterward, when he lands in Patusan and the Rajah's spearmen surround him, he "strike[s] them dumb" with his audacity and then marches into the Rajah's stockade as if of his own volition (148). As he tells Marlow, he has determined to never again reveal when he is "afraid" (148). Indeed, he seems resolved to demonstrate the "open" courage expected of white men, using it to promote the "Jim-myth," as McClure suggests (157, 121). He even shows courage when fleeing the Rajah's stockade: rather than use stealth or bribery to escape, Jim leaps over a palisade with "two spearman in attendance" and then lives openly in the village with "an utter disregard for his personal safety" (152, 170). Such demonstrations continue after he establishes himself as a colonist in Patusan, as evidenced by the fact that he drinks the Rajah's coffee, knowing it might be poisoned, to prove that he is "not afraid" (151).

Jim also adopts the lifestyle and trappings of a successful white colonist, as Dryden suggests (177). Unlike the failed colonist, Cornelius, who lives in a "wretched" house with half a roof and "wisps of dry grass sticking out and the corners of broken mats flapping on every wall" (171), Jim builds an impressive house complete with a palisade and cannons that command the village square (202). Recognizing that it takes more than guns to rule Patusan, Jim enhances his prestige by acquiring a light-skinned consort, Jewel, and a dark-skinned body guard, Tamb' Itam (133).[5] He also takes care to dress like a white man, complete with a "white helmet," "canvas leggings," and "pipe-clayed shoes" (225). Jim's "white apparel" maximizes the contrast between himself and his "dark-faced" subjects (138): as Marlow notes, Jim appears "like a creature not only of another kind but of another essence" (140). Jim's "white," machine-made clothing does more than simply distinguish him from Malays, Bugis, and Dyaks, of course; it also serves as a reminder to his subjects that he is backed by the "overwhelming force" (225). If he can get pipe clay for his shoes, he can get more gunpowder, and the transports that bring him new shirts could easily be gunboats. Jim does more than just dress the part of a colonist, however: he also acts like a "white lord," not only administering justice but taking tea with the Rajah, exploring the interior, and even hunting game (157).

Jim's attitude, attire, and lifestyle make it clear that, rather than "go native," Jim becomes a model colonist. As Boo Eung Koh notes, "Jim's colonization of Patusan is not an act of immersion in the native community but one of domination of the natives in the interests of the European world. . . . Not only does he restore the 'free trade' which was endangered by Rajah Allang who was a sort of protectionist in international trade, he also plans a colonial economic policy (e.g. a coffee plantation) which would exploit the land and labor of the natives" (171). If, as Koh suggests, Jim exploits his subjects, he also demonstrates a genuine if patronizing concern for their welfare; he considers the establishment of peace and prosperity to be "his work" (229). Jim believes that he rules the indigenous peoples for their own good, just as Lingard does in *Almayer's Folly* and *An Outcast of the Islands.* Accordingly, when at the end of his visit to Patusan, Marlow offers Jim the opportunity to leave, Jim refuses, saying, "Only try to think what it would be if I went away. Jove! can't you see it? Hell loose. No!" (198). Jim has convinced himself that he cannot leave Patusan because to do so would be to betray a trust again. He considers governing Patusan an "awful responsibility" but a necessary one (161). Like the hero of a conventional imperial romance, he believes that it is his sacred duty to bring light to the dark places of the earth.

Lord Jim as Unconventional Romance

Although the Patusan section of *Lord Jim* initially presents itself as a "paradigm of romance," to borrow Jameson's phrase, the romance becomes highly unconventional once Gentleman Brown appears, initiating a series of events that expose Jim's selfish interests and the limits of his power as a "white lord" (Jameson 207). Here, an important parallel between *Lord Jim* and *Heart of Darkness* surfaces, for the relationship between Jim and Brown parallels that between the philanthropic Kurtz who went into the bush and the misanthropic Kurtz who leaves it. In *Lord Jim,* as in *Heart of Darkness,* Conrad implies that there is a connection between those who want to "exterminate" the "brutes" and those who want to "civilize" them: both are in it for "greater profit," as Marlow suggests (132). Brown, who, as many critics suggest, represents Jim's darker self, forces this realization on Jim when the two negotiate. Quick to recognize Jim for what he is—a white adventurer living among "natives" for personal gain—Brown hopes to form a temporary partnership with him in order to better "squeeze" Patusan dry (218). His hopes "vanished at once," however, when he sees Jim's imperial bearing and manner of dress—not because he sees Jim as the protector of Patusan but because he sees that Jim has already secured power (218). As he later tells Marlow, "He did not look like a man who would be willing to give anything for assistance. He had all the advantages on his side—possession, security, power; he was on the side of an overwhelming force!" (225). Realizing that he will never talk Jim into sharing his "plunder," Brown instead tries to save his own life by shaming Jim into guaranteeing safe passage when the two meet (219). He begins by suggesting that Jim has gone native and then challenges him to prove otherwise by offering either a fair fight or freedom: "Either bring your infernal crowd along or let us go out and starve in the open sea, by God! You have been white once for all your talk of this being your own people and you being one of them. Are you?" (226). Seeing that his words are having an effect, Brown next accuses Jim of hypocrisy, of pretending to act in his subjects' interest while really exploiting them. When Jim suggests to Brown that he and his men deserve ignominious deaths in the bush, Brown shouts, "And what do you deserve . . . you that I find skulking here with your mouth full of your responsibility, of innocent lies, of your infernal duty? What do you know more of me than I know of you? I came here for food. D'ye hear?—food to fill our bellies. And what did you come for? What did *you* come here for?" (227). In effect, Brown presents himself to Jim as a mirror image, emphasizing their "common blood," "common experience," and "common guilt" (229). To Brown, there is no moral difference between Jim's "slow, cautious, risky cheating" and his own, quicker method (219): both are trying to steal "the whole country" (217).

Brown's tactics prove to be very effective, though not for the reasons he imagines. Owing in large part to the guilt he feels for his failures aboard the *Patna,* Jim accepts Brown's assertion that there is little moral difference between himself and Brown and then decides that Brown should be given another chance just as he himself received one; he agrees to provide safe passage so long as Brown and his men relinquish their arms. Sensing the advantage, Brown pushes for a further concession: he challenges Jim to assert his authority as white lord and allow him and his men to leave fully armed. When Jim expresses doubt as to whether he has "the power," Brown mocks him: "'You don't know! And you wanted me just now to give up my arms! That's good, too . . . Suppose they say one thing to you, and do the other thing to me.' He calmed down markedly. 'I dare say you have the power, or what's the meaning of all this talk?' he continued. 'What did you come down here for? To pass the time of day?'" (230). Brown's words amount to a dare: he challenges Jim to prove he has not "gone native" by acting against the interests of Patusan. As Avrom Fleishman argues, Jim's eventual decision to let Brown and his men leave with their arms represents a betrayal of the Patusani community (110). Even though Jim believes that he can balance his subjects' interests with his obligations to the white community, his actions prove that he cannot. *Lord Jim* thus challenges the very idea the imperial romance celebrates: that colonizers act in the best interests of the colonized.

The "difficulty" Jim has in persuading Doramin and his followers to let Brown escape also differentiates *Lord Jim* from the conventional imperial romance. In novels such as *King Solomon's Mines,* so-called good natives blindly follow the orders of their white rulers. Jim, in contrast, has "to affirm his will in the face of out-spoken opposition" (232). Jim may be able to settle disputes in Patusan "by crooking his little finger," as he boasts to Marlow, but he does not command Patusan in the absolute sense (164): his power has limits despite his "racial prestige." Certainly, Doramin is neither awed nor intimidated by Jim. Indeed, he accepts Jim's decision only after Jim announces that he "shall not lead" an assault on fellow Europeans and that, therefore, Doramin's son, Dain Waris, will have to do it (233). Although Ross and others argue that Doramin acquiesces only to protect his son, they do not take into account Doramin's evident qualities as a leader, qualities that even Marlow acknowledges (92). When reporting a conversation he had with Doramin about Jim, for example, Marlow describes the Bugis chief as a forward-looking leader who is preoccupied with the welfare of his people: "Doramin was anxious about the future of the country, and I was struck by the turn he gave the argument. The land remains where God had put it; but white men—he said—they come to us and in a little while they go. They go away. Those they leave behind do not know when to look for their return. They go to their own land, to their people, and so this white man, too, would" (164). Doramin's words demonstrate that he sees beyond Jim's rule in Patusan even at the height of Jim's power: he realizes that colonists—even "good" ones like Jim—put outside interests before those of their subjects and that, therefore, they cannot be trusted to protect Patusani interests.[6] With all this in mind, it should not be surprising that he is reluctant to accept Jim's decision to let Brown go. As an "elected" leader, however, Doramin is obliged to listen at least to the counsel of the assembled chiefs, many of whom were selected by Jim and Dain Waris (233). Furthermore, since Jim negotiated with Brown alone and in English, Doramin only has Jim's words as to Brown's disposition. Finally, and most importantly perhaps, as the leader of the Bugis, Doramin cannot afford to alienate the man who not only controls all the gunpowder in the district but has at least the tacit support of the Dutch: Doramin must remain on good terms with Jim as long as Jim remains the dominant power in Patusan. Even though Doramin seems to have no choice but to accept Jim's will, he still expresses reservations: "Doramin raised his heavy head and said that there was no more reading of hearts than touching the sky with the hand, but—he consented" (233).

Doramin's words suggest that he doubts not only Jim's decision but also his motives; he acquiesces only because he must.

Doramin is not the only Patusani who questions Jim's decision: Jim's announcement that he "shall not lead" creates "an immense sensation" among the chiefs, and when Jim again insists that Brown be granted safe passage, there is "silence," and then "subdued whispering" and "the shuffling of many people" (233). Jim's decision not only surprises the Patusanis but troubles them. Even Tamb' Itam, Jim's most loyal follower, seems to recognize that Jim's decision goes against the interests of the community. This becomes evident when Jim orders him to inform Dain Waris, who is stationed downriver with an armed contingent, "that the whites were to be allowed to pass out unmolested" (235). Rather than leave immediately, Tamb' Itam asks for a token so that Jim's seemingly outrageous order will be believed (235). Jim is forced to use Stein's silver ring—which represents not only friendship and good faith but the commercial pact between Stein and Doramin—to vouch "for the truth of the messenger's words" (238). Tamb' Itam's concerns seem to be justified, for Dain Waris does seem to have difficulty believing Jim's orders, questioning Tamb' Itam closely (238). It is only after Tamb' Itam "reported the proceedings of the last council" that he takes the ring, which he has been "toying with," and slips it "on the forefinger of his right hand." Like his father, in the end Dain Waris has little choice but to accept the decision of the powerful white colonist, however foolish it might seem.

Revolutionary Consciousness in Patusan

Jim's dominance in Patusan ends with the death of Dain Waris and the others at the hands of Brown and his men. Jim is held responsible for the massacre, not because he has "taken it on his own head," as Marlow believes, but because the Patusanis' suspicions of Jim and his motives have proven true. Even though Jim's military position remains strong—after all, he still commands the fort and all the gunpowder in Patusan—he can no longer be an effective colonist since he no longer controls the labor and resources of Patusan. Indeed, Jim seems to have lost even the support of those he considers "his own people," the ones he and the Bugis freed from Sherif Ali (202). As it turns out, they are not his people at all but Doramin's. Like the Bugis, these Malays feel anger, not understanding the "exact relation" between Brown and "their own white man" (245). Rather than support Jim, they join the "armed Bugis and their followers" in Doramin's courtyard awaiting his commands (245). It is at this point that Patusan attains revolutionary consciousness, something that would be unimaginable in a conventional imperial romance: the people of Patusan—Malays and Bugis alike—are finally ready to risk their personal safety for the greater good, and to assault Jim in his own fort.[7] Although this reading is necessarily speculative, since the attack is preempted by Jim's surrender to Doramin at the end of the novel, Jewel and Tamb' Itam do make preparations for a siege, and Tamb' Itam tells Jim, "We shall have to fight" (245). If, as it appears, the Patusanis are ready to revolt, the question becomes, How have they attained such consciousness? Part of the answer is that there is already resentment on their part toward whites. Although up until Brown's appearance, many Patusanis seem to accept Jim's authority as a white colonist, and even recognize that it affords them certain benefits, they certainly have no love for whites, who they feel are as bad as the Arabs. The Rajah and his followers are more extreme; they hate the "new order" that Jim establishes, since it directly interferes with the day-to-day administration of Patusan (217). To them, Jim is more than a single white adventurer: he represents European imperialism itself and thus threatens the Rajah's authority. The Dyaks—or the "bush-folk," as Jim calls them—are the most extreme of all. They actively resist European incursions, considering all whites "infidels" (176). Once Jim betrays Patusan's interests, general resentment turns to resolve: the various peoples of Patusan come together to free themselves from European domination.

A resolve to change the social order is only one of the components necessary to broad revolutionary consciousness; most people are unwilling to risk their lives or well-being for a cause unless they believe that the cause has a chance of succeeding. Even Marlow seems to recognize this, remarking in another context that to sacrifice oneself for others, "you must believe there is a chance, one in a thousand, at least, some ghost of a chance" (58). In Patusan such a belief is impossible as long as the myth of white superiority is intact. Although whites enjoy a certain "racial prestige" because they are backed by overwhelming military force, in *Lord Jim* at least, the myth of white superiority has a supernatural element as well, one that Jim actively promotes. The myth begins to be dispelled, however, with Dain Waris's initial defeat of Brown. Although the Patusanis later suffer great losses, this is owing to white treachery rather than white strength, and the community itself survives. The fact that Brown's threat was contained while Jim was away is also important: the Patusanis do not need whites to protect them from other whites. That one of Brown's white followers is killed is significant as well, especially since he dies after a night of shrieking and complaining; like Cornelius, who screeches "like a frightened hen" before Tamb' Itam executes him, the white invader proves to be neither invulnerable nor fearless (240).

Jim's actions following the massacre, however, do the most to diminish whites' racial prestige: to the Patusanis, he seems to be treacherous, vulnerable, and even frightened. To appreciate this fully, we must imagine how the events that followed Brown's appearance might seem to the Patusanis:

1. Brown and his men appear in Patusan while Jim is away, and they are defeated by Doramin's forces. They retreat to a small knoll where the Patusanis can destroy them "without the risk of battle" (215). After "crying—in English—for permission to come up," Cornelius—the only white man in Patusan besides Jim—meets with Brown and remains in his camp overnight.
2. Jim returns to Patusan and negotiates with Brown, alone and in English. When Brown returns to his camp, Cornelius leaves it, spending the next afternoon in Jim's fort. Cornelius then returns to Brown's camp bearing a written message from Jim.
3. Jim informs Doramin and the assembled chiefs that he has decided that Brown and his men should be allowed to leave fully armed. When Doramin refuses his consent, Jim indicates that he will not lead an attack on fellow Europeans. Doramin

and the other leaders finally agree to support Jim, although they express reservations.

4. The next morning, Brown and his men leave their camp fully armed. Just before they disembark, Jim is overheard talking again to Brown. Since Brown and Jim speak in English, "not one of the many attentive listeners understood what the words meant" (236). Cornelius accompanies Brown and his men downriver.
5. Assisted by Cornelius, Brown and his men kill Dain Waris and many others in a surprise attack. Jim's most trusted follower, Tamb' Itam, witnesses the massacre and then returns to Jim's fort; immediately afterward, the gates are locked. (241)

Appearances, at least, suggest that Jim acts in collusion with Brown. As Marlow notes, the Patusanis fear that Brown and his men will return, "bringing many others with them, in a great ship, and there would be no refuge in the land for any one" (243). The fact that Jim is locked within his fort only confirms their suspicions: he appears to be awaiting Brown's return with more men and guns. Even the most charitable interpretation of Jim's actions is damning: if Jim's decision to allow Brown and his men to leave fully armed results from a misplaced trust rather than collusion, Jim has still betrayed the community, since his trust in Brown is apparently based on "their common blood." Once the massacre occurs, Jim appears to betray the community again, this time out of fear; rather than immediately answer "with his own life," as he promised, Jim remains within his impregnable fort, refusing to communicate with Doramin or the other chiefs. Either way Jim has betrayed the Patusanis' trust.

The Decolonization of Patusan

Jim, of course, is as oblivious to the true state of affairs in Patusan as the British were in India before the Sepoy rebellion of 1857: he believes not only that he rules the "natives" for their own good but that he governs with their consent. Accordingly, when Tamb' Itam returns with news of Dain Waris's death, Jim quickly laces his boots, ordering his servant to "assemble a fleet of boats for immediate pursuit" (241). It is only when Tamb' Itam says, "It is not safe for thy servant to go out amongst the people," that Jim realizes that he can no longer be the "white lord" of Patusan (242). At this point, Jim seems to have two obvious choices: he can either "fight" or "fly," as Jewel puts it (244). A third choice—to honor his word and "take it on his own head" is unthinkable to Jim, at least at this point.

Not surprisingly, perhaps, given his tendency to romanticize Jim's conduct, Marlow believes that Jim embraces this third option immediately in some sort of epiphany. Marlow's belief, though, is not consistent with the facts that he himself reports. Rather than decide at "that very moment" to face Doramin, as Marlow suggests, Jim sits "before the long table, at the head of which he was accustomed to regulate the affairs of his world, proclaiming daily the truth that surely lived in his heart" (242). The fact that he sits "before" the table instead of at its "head" suggests that he has made no decision yet; rather than act, he equivocates, just as he did aboard the *Patna,* remaining alone throughout the morning and afternoon, not making a sound. When he finally emerges, it becomes apparent that he still has hopes that the crisis will pass. "Well?" he asks Tamb' Itam, trying to ascertain popular sentiment: "'There is much weeping. Much anger, too,' said Tamb' Itam. Jim looked up at him. 'You know,' he murmured. 'Yes, Tuan,' said Tamb' Itam. 'Thy servant does know, and the gates are closed. We shall have to fight'" (242). Suddenly, Jim seems despondent and asks, "Fight! What for?" "For our lives," Tamb' Itam replies. "I have no life," Jim declares, realizing that his colonization effort has failed. Tamb' Itam interprets Jim's self-pitying statement as a tactical assessment and replies accordingly: "'Who knows?' said Tamb' Itam. 'By audacity and cunning we may even escape. There is much fear in men's hearts, too.'" Tamb' Itam's words finally prompt Jim to make a decision: his suggestion that Jim, "too," is afraid convinces Jim that he must differentiate himself from the "natives." Jim feels he must prove his courage, just as earlier in the novel he feels compelled to prove to Marlow that he was not a "wretched cur" by threatening him with violence (46).

That Jim has only now made his decision seems to be confirmed by his actions once Tamb' Itam leaves: it is only then that he informs Jewel of his resolve. Having lost everything in his attempt to prove his "power" by forcing his will on the Patusanis as Brown dared him to do, Jim indicates to the uncomprehending Jewel that he will "prove his power in another way and conquer the fatal destiny itself" (242). In a sense, Jim is again trying to prove himself "white," as he did before. The irony is that this time, he must relinquish his authority as a white colonist in order to do so.

As Hunt Hawkins notes, most critics interpret Jim's surrender to Doramin "as a positive gesture, one in which he regains his honor and affirms his allegiance to the native community" (79). Fleishman, for example, argues that Jim's decision represents "an individual act of identification with the higher claims of the community," that "Jim gives himself back to the group by accepting its justice" (110). Such readings are not consistent with the facts as reported by Marlow, however. Jim cannot give "himself back" to the community because he was never a member of that community—he has not gone native. Rather, as I argued earlier, Jim holds himself above the community to maintain his authority as a white colonist. Even when he finally relinquishes that authority at the end of the novel, he does so as a proud white man. Rather than fight, Jim hopes to prove his superiority by martyring himself.[8]

Despite Marlow's insistence that Jim's death is "romantic," by presenting his death in the context of what amounts to the decolonization of Patusan, Conrad departs sharply from the conventions of the imperial romance and the ideology it represents. Indeed, that ideology is contested directly to the extent that Jim's failure as a colonist anticipates the failure of colonization in general. Jim may have been a good colonist, but he was not "good enough," to borrow Marlow's phrase. No one could be. The colonial system—which is primarily concerned with "greater profit," as Marlow concedes—is as flawed as its agents, the novel suggests, and therefore, its end is inevitable (132).

Marlow, His Limitations, and the Function of the Frame Narrator

So far I have discussed the radical implications of Marlow's narrative as if *Lord Jim* were overtly anti-imperialist like *Almayer's Folly* and *An Outcast of the Islands.* It should be remembered, however, that Marlow is a character-narrator who, like the character-narrator in "Karain," rejects the story's anti-imperialist implications, thereby obfuscating the text's radical elements.[9] As he is in *Heart of Darkness,* in *Lord Jim,* Marlow is a man who, though critical of certain imperial practices, believes that the British variety of imperialism—with its "devotion to efficiency"—will ultimately benefit subject peoples (50). Bearing his Anglocentrism in mind, it should be no surprise that Marlow interprets Jim's surrender to Doramin as the act of a brave Englishman sacrificing his life for the sake of principle; like General Gordon at Khartoum, a man whose story Conrad's original readers would have been familiar with, the steadfast Jim faces death bravely, a true English hero, at least as Marlow tells it.[10] Marlow's views, however, do not represent Conrad's any more than they did in the earlier Marlow stories. Rather, in *Lord Jim,* as in *Heart of Darkness,* Marlow's views are undercut by a frame narrator who exposes Marlow's ideological blindness, thereby opening up alternative interpretative possibilities.[11] Like Homer's Odysseus, the frame narrator springs the "trapdoor" of the Trojan horse, allowing that which is concealed to emerge.

One of the ways in which the narrator exposes Marlow's limitations is by presenting him in a comic manner. Although Marlow seems to be convinced that his narratives are interesting if not edifying, the frame narrator suggests that Marlow's auditors regard him as a bore. Upon the first break in Marlow's narrative, for example, the narrator reports that Marlow's storytelling has nearly put his audience to sleep: "[Marlow] leaned his back against the balustrade and faced a disordered array of long cane-chairs. The bodies prone in them seemed startled out of their torpor by his movement. One or two sat up as if alarmed; here and there a cigar glowed yet" (190). The auditors' indifference—and Marlow's obliviousness to it—becomes even more apparent a few pages later when Marlow breaks off his narrative with a question only to be met by silence by his dozing audience: "Marlow paused, as if expecting an answer. Nobody spoke" (193). The very next line indicates just how deluded Marlow is: "'Quite right,' he began again," somehow interpreting his auditors' silence as an answer. Marlow, it seems, hears what he wants to hear in his auditors' silence—just as in Jim he sees what he wants to see.

Interactions such as these between Marlow and his auditors perform an important function, for they indicate just how deluded Marlow is: about his narrative, about the auditors' response to it, and about Jim himself. At the very least, they call into question the reliability of a man who proclaims indignantly that he "declined to meddle" in Jim's affairs and then meddles in just about every way possible, a man who announces that his "last words about Jim shall be few" and then continues speaking for twelve more chapters (45, 136). In effect, the frame narrator reminds us that Marlow is "profoundly, dynamically, and grotesquely unreliable," to borrow Alan Warren Friedman's characterization (73). Like Half-a-Crown in Solomon Plaatje's *Mhudi,* Marlow is an obtuse man who does not understand the implications of the story he himself tells.

From the Belly of the Horse: The Other Reading of Lord Jim

If, as I suggest, the frame narrator intervenes in Marlow's narrative for ideological reasons, it is only in a limited way. As J. Hillis Miller observes, although the frame narrator's intrusions "suggest that the reader might be wise to put in question Marlow's interpretation of Jim . . . the narrator cannot or will not provide the reader with any solid alternative ground on which to stand" (Miller 1982, 32). Were he to provide such ground, of course, *Lord Jim* would not be a Trojan horse fiction, since the critique of imperialism would be overt rather than covert. What the frame narrator does do is invite the reader to interpret Jim's actions independently of Marlow, marking the novel's double-voicedness. On one level, the ending follows the conventions of the imperial romance: Jim's ideals are more important than his life and so he faces his death with courage and dignity as an Englishman should. On another level, however—the one I will explore here—Jim is a histrionic fool whose vanity leads to a needless death.

As Jameson and Dryden observe, Jim's efforts to "conquer" his "fatal destiny" are nothing if not melodramatic (242).[12] He tells Jewel he "should not be worth having" if he did not face Doramin, causing her to fling "herself upon his breast" and clasp "him round the neck," crying, "Ah! But I shall hold thee thus. . . . Thou art mine!" (244, ellipsis in original). In response, Jim "catch[es] her arms, trying to unclasp her hands," but Jewel holds on "with her hair fallen back," "her hair touch[ing] the ground" (244). Tamb' Itam helps "ease her down," and Jim looks her "earnestly upon her face" before running to his canoe without looking back at Jewel, who is "on her knees . . . in a supplicating attitude" (244–45).

Jim's death is equally melodramatic. Entering Doramin's campong, Jim marches proudly, with "measured steps," as if he were a general defeated honorably in battle or a deposed monarch bravely facing his execution (245). Hearing a voice say, "He hath taken it upon his own head," only adds to Jim's sense of self-martyrdom: he turns to the crowd and says, "Yes. Upon my head." He then becomes ceremonious: "I am come in sorrow . . . I am come ready and unarmed." As his formal, almost poetic diction suggests, Jim is living out the bookish fantasy he identified earlier when he first learned about Patusan and exclaimed, "It's like something you read of in books" (141). Like Don Quixote—or Catherine Morland in *Northanger Abbey*—Jim has read too many romances, as the frame narrator suggests in the novel's opening pages. In Jim's case, though, the results of his delusions are deadly: his weakness leads to his death.

If Jim's delusions make the novel's final scene seem comic as well as tragic, Marlow's account of Jim's end soon reminds us of its political significance, even though Marlow himself seems to miss it. As ridiculous as he is, Jim still represents the model colonist, while Doramin represents his indigenous adversary. As Doramin rises "like an ox under yoke," leveling a flintlock at Jim's breast, the ring that had earlier represented not only Jim's good faith but the trade compact between Doramin and Stein, between Patusan and the outside world, drops from his lap and rolls "against the foot of the white man" (246). According to Marlow, Jim seems to recognize the symbolic importance of this, "glanc[ing] down at the talisman that had opened for him the door of fame, love, and success within the wall of forests fringed with white foam, within the coast that under the western sun looks like the very stronghold of the night" (246). Jim realizes that he has had an opportunity to prove his worth to the "outside world" by transforming Patusan into a profitable colony and that he has failed; now, he must do the right thing—what he considers to be the "white" thing—and face his death bravely. In this, at least, Jim succeeds. He stands "stiffened . . . with bared head" when he is shot and then sends "right and left at all those [Patusani] faces a proud and unflinching glance," falling "forward, dead" (246). Like General Gordon, who was reputed to have died with "unresisting disdain," Jim's final act is an assertion of superiority (Strachey 338).

The significance of Jim's melodramatic death is not entirely lost on Marlow. Even though he considers Jim to be "excessively romantic" and wonders whether it was worth it for Jim to sacrifice his life for the sake of honor, he acknowledges that Jim's end was in one sense at least an "extraordinary success" since it was consistent with the "ideal of conduct" Jim had established for himself (246). To Marlow, it seems, Jim has finally redeemed himself by facing his death bravely. "He is one of us," Marlow declares again, this time with authority: in dying for his ideals, he suggests, Jim has proven himself white.[13]

Marlow, of course, is not Conrad. Although Marlow regards Jim's death as proof of his "eternal constancy" (246)—and by extension, the constancy of white men in general—Conrad suggests that Marlow is ultimately as deluded as the imperialists who celebrated George Gordon's death fifteen years earlier. He accomplishes this by having Jim's vainglorious end both parallel and parody that of Dravot in "The Man Who Would be King," another story that seems to be based in part on Gordon's death. Both stories concern themselves with white men trying to prove their worth on the imperial frontier. Whereas Kipling's story suggests that Dravot indeed accomplishes something noble in the end—he is able to prove his mettle as a white man by accepting responsibility for his actions and facing his death bravely—in *Lord Jim,* the title character remains as deluded as he was in the beginning of the novel when he had adolescent fantasies about confronting "savages on tropical shores" (9):[14] Jim still imagines himself as "unflinching as a hero in a book" (9). The fact that we are told about Jim's bookish fantasies by the frame narrator rather than Marlow is significant, since it calls into question Marlow's interpretation of Jim's story: whereas Marlow considers Jim a "romantic," the frame narrator implies that he is a fool.[15] Like the frame narrator of *Heart of Darkness,* the frame narrator of *Lord Jim* puts a spin on Jim's story, again making Marlow's limitations apparent. If, as Marlow himself asserts, "the onlookers see most of the game" (136), it is the frame narrator who tells the onlookers what to look for: that in the end Jim, like all those claiming to bring light to the dark places of the earth, is deluded if not selfish and hypocritical.

Postcolonial Patusan

Lord Jim is more than just the story of a white man who is destroyed by the imperialist system he serves, however, for the situation of Patusan at the end of the novel is as significant as Jim's death. Although Said claims that Conrad could not imagine "a fully realized alternative to imperialism" and that "the natives he wrote about in Africa, Asia, or America were incapable of independence," at the end of *Lord Jim,* we witness both (Said 1990, 25). Consider what has happened in Patusan: Sherif Ali and his forces have been destroyed; the Rajah, whom the Dutch officially support, has proven himself ineffectual by refusing to act when Brown first came; Brown, the white adventurer, has been driven away; Cornelius, Brown's treacherous collaborator, is dead; and finally, Jim, the "good" colonist, is executed by Doramin. In short, for the time being, at least, Patusan has freed itself of invaders and imperialists alike; it is a postcolonial society with a new form of government. Doramin, who entered the district as an invader himself, emerges as the leader of a new postcolonial people:[16] he has repudiated the trade compact with Stein, as the fallen ring suggests; assumed command of the people previously aligned with Jim; and seized control of the river. The last scene of the novel, in which Doramin's "courtyard is full of armed Bugis with their followers and of Patusan people," anticipates the emergence of a national consciousness in which the many peoples of the Malay Archipelago form a combined identity so as to resist external domination (245). Jim's execution before the assembled peoples of Patusan is a rite of purification, the first act of a new state:[17] by holding Jim accountable despite his abilities and his "racial prestige," to borrow again Marlow's phrase, Patusan asserts its newly acquired sovereignty (214). To be free, Conrad seems to suggest, every last European has to be driven away or killed, even the "good" ones like Jim.

Marlow, of course, cannot apprehend the significance of the gathering in Doramin's courtyard; he can imagine "savages" as warriors, even rebels, but not as nationalist revolutionaries. "I do not know what this gathering really meant," he declares: "Were these preparations for war, or for vengeance, or to repulse a threatened invasion?" (245). Whether or not Marlow recognizes it, however, the colonial period ends in Patusan with Jim's death. Despite Said's claims to the contrary, Conrad helps us imagine an indigenous society "not totally controlled by the gringo imperialists and reformers of the world" (Said 1993, 25). If he has not created a fully realized alternative to imperialism, he has depicted its end and the formation of a new national consciousness, writing what is, in effect, a postcolonial novel long before the genre was established.[18]

Postcoloniality, Difficulty, and the Marketing of Lord Jim

Despite generally positive reviews, *Lord Jim* sold poorly, in part because rather than celebrate imperialism unequivocally, it depicted a successful revolution in which an English colonist is executed and a postcolonial state is established.[19] The novel's postcoloniality is not the only reason it failed to attain a popular audience, however: it is also a long, difficult book whose complex narrative structure tended to confuse readers.[20] It is not a modernist novel, however, if by "modernist" one means a novel in which experimentation is an end in itself.[21] As in *Heart of Darkness,* in *Lord Jim,* Conrad's experiments were motivated more by a desire to cloak his radical intent from Blackwood and his readers than any "will to style," to borrow Jameson's phrase. Such a position contradicts Leavis's famous remark about Conrad "making a virtue out of not knowing what he means," of course (207). When considered in the context of Conrad's other colonial fiction, it becomes clear that Conrad knew exactly what he meant, for he exhibits in *Lord Jim* the same attitude toward imperialism and imperialist ideology that he does in his early works. The difference between *Lord Jim* and the works written before *The Nigger of the "Narcissus"* is that in *Lord Jim,* Conrad is less direct so as not to offend jingoistic readers. Rather than challenge imperialism overtly, he again adopts a Trojan horse strategy by presenting the story as an imperial romance only to deconstruct it and by having the character-narrator reject the story's radical implications. Although Conrad's technique was to have a tremendous influence on modernists, as Gene Moore demonstrates, Conrad's concerns, both writerly and political, were very different from those of Ford Madox Ford, Virginia Woolf, Malcolm Lowry, and other avant-garde writers (Moore 226–30). As a writer who had yet to establish an audience for himself, Conrad could not afford to be any more difficult than he had to be: at the same time, however, like other early postcolonial writers working with imperialist publishers, Conrad had to obfuscate his radical politics if he were to be published at all.

CHAPTER SEVEN

Irony upon Irony: The Changing World and Changing Techniques in *Nostromo*

If, as I argue in chapter 3, "The Lagoon" marks the end of Conrad's first phase as an author since it was the last of his early stories to attack imperialism directly, *Lord Jim* marks the end of his second phase since it is the last of his great Trojan horse fictions. *Nostromo,* his next novel, represents the beginning of a third phase, since once again Conrad develops a new narrative strategy in response to changes he perceived in the fiction market and his own standing as a writer.[1] Rather than conceal a radical critique of imperialism within a seemingly innocuous story, as he did in *Heart of Darkness* and *Lord Jim,* in *Nostromo,* Conrad attacks imperialism directly, targeting the global system of exploitation upon which it is based. In terms of narrative technique, *Nostromo* resembles *Almayer's Folly* in that it employs an omniscient narrator who uses irony to establish a perspective that is critical of imperialism. Conrad's narrative technique in *Nostromo* differs from that in his first novel in one important respect, however: whereas in *Almayer's Folly,* the narrative point of view gradually shifts from a colonizing one to a colonized one, privileging the latter, as Allan Simmons (1997) demonstrates, in *Nostromo,* the narrator is consistently ironic, challenging every political and social position so as to expose the contradictions inherent in capitalism and the system of imperialist exploitation it engenders.

Conrad and the Critique of Global Capitalism

As Zdzislaw Najder notes in *Joseph Conrad: A Chronicle,* Conrad's critics have traditionally identified him as a political and social conservative, arguing, as Jocelyn Baines does, that his "outlook was essentially aristocratic" (198). Even critics like Patrick Brantlinger and Andrea White, who find in Conrad's work unequivocal attacks on imperialism, conclude that Conrad was a conservative, albeit of a "particular" kind (5).[2] A careful examination of Conrad's published and unpublished writings in the late nineteenth and early twentieth centuries suggests that he was anything but a conservative, however, at least as the term is understood today, since he opposed not only imperialism and the global capitalist system upon which it was based but also the social and cultural institutions, including religion, that legitimated various forms of oppression. Although some of his views were consistent with the conservatives of his day—including his distrust of socialism, which he feared would "inevitably end in Caesarism"—he neither supported the existing socioeconomic order nor worked for a return to one that preceded it (*Letters* 1:16).[3] On the contrary, Conrad anticipates Lenin in recognizing that the international competition for resources and new markets would inevitably lead to the destruction of capitalism itself, a view that is reflected in his essay "Autocracy and War":[4]

> Industrialism and commercialism . . . stand ready, almost eager, to appeal to the sword as soon as the globe of the earth has shrunk beneath our growing numbers by another ell or so. And democracy, which has elected to pin its faith to the supremacy of material interests, will have to fight their battles to the bitter end, on a mere pittance—unless, indeed, some statesman of exceptional ability and overwhelming prestige succeeds in carrying through an international understanding for the delimitation of spheres of trade all over the earth, on the model of the territorial spheres of influence marked in Africa to keep the competitors for the privilege of improving the nigger (as a buying machine) from flying prematurely at each other's throats. (107)

That Conrad should have what were then considered such extreme beliefs should not be surprising, since many of his friends and associates at the time were liberals, socialists, or radicals. His first publisher, T. Fisher

Unwin, for example, was a well-known liberal, and Edward Garnett, Unwin's reader who went on to become Conrad's lifelong friend and literary advisor, was a committed leftist with anarchist sympathies. In the 1890s, Conrad also established relationships with socialists such as H. G. Wells and George Bernard Shaw. It is Conrad's correspondence with Graham, a notorious radical who, as a member of Parliament, was a "champion of laws protecting factory and farm workers, an advocate of nationalized industry and of free universal education, and a fierce critic of colonialism," that reveals the most about Conrad's views, however, since Graham prompted Conrad to articulate the political positions that were implicit in his work (Najder 1983, 209). As I noted in chapter 3, Graham initiated the correspondence in 1897 after reading "An Outpost of Progress" and recognizing in it views that were consonant with his own. He asked Conrad in a letter whether he meant to hold to his political beliefs, and Conrad assured him that he did, though he added that he did not think his beliefs mattered "in the least" (*Letters* 1:370). Graham went on to become not only Conrad's close friend and confidante but also someone who, as Watts and Christopher GoGwilt demonstrate, had a tremendous influence on him.[5]

In his earliest letters to Graham, Conrad indicates that although he generally agrees with Graham's radical principles, he believed political activism to be futile. In a letter of December 20, 1897, for example, Conrad labels Graham a "hopeless idealist," since Graham believed that society could be reformed (*Letters* 1:424). Conrad strongly disagreed, using an industrial metaphor to describe the socioeconomic system he so despised:

> There is a—let us say—a machine. It evolved itself (I am severely scientific) out of a chaos of scraps and behold!—it knits. I am horrified at the horrible work and stand appalled. I feel it ought to embroider—but it goes on knitting. You come and say: "this is all right; it's only a question of the right kind of oil. Let us use this—for instance—celestial oil and the machine shall embroider a most beautiful design in purple and gold." Will it? Alas no. You cannot by any special lubrication make embroidery with a knitting machine. (*Letters* 1:425)[6]

Conrad's use of the knitting-machine metaphor is significant, not only because it expresses Conrad's belief at the time that direct political action is pointless, but also because Conrad takes a position that is in some ways at least even more radical than Graham's. Unlike Graham, whom Friedrich Engels described as a "Marxian" (quoted in Watts 1993, 152), Conrad thought that international capitalism and the cultural institutions that supported it were simply beyond reform, a view that becomes clear in his letter to Graham of February 8, 1899: "L'homme est un animal méchant. Sa méchanceté doit être organisée. Le crime est une condition nécéssaire de l'existence organisée. La société est essentielment criminelle—ou elle n'existerait pas. C'est l'égoisme qui sauve tout—absolument tout—tout ce que nous abhorrons tout ce que nous aimons" (*Letters* 2:159).[7] For Conrad, the problem with modern society was that it reflected human nature itself.

Conrad's pessimism about the possibility of reforming either human nature or society did not prevent him from criticizing both in his writing. Indeed, as I argued at the beginning of chapter 3, Conrad seemed to regard it his duty as a writer to act as a moral guide for others. Conrad simply believed that no matter how much criticism he offered, in the end, there was nothing in his work that was "practically effective" (*Letters* 2:158). Whether he was correct in this assessment is, of course, difficult to determine, since it is virtually impossible to quantify the ideological effects of literary works. It is clear, however, that Conrad, along with Garnett, Graham, W. H. Hudson, and Olive Schreiner, among others, was part of a now largely unrecognized minor literary movement that regarded imperialism as a product of international capitalism and challenged the legitimacy of both.[8] Conrad's early attitudes toward capitalism and imperialism are reflected in his writing of the period, most obviously in "Karain," where a gilt sovereign featuring the image of Queen Victoria symbolizes capitalist greed and lack of conscience; in *Heart of Darkness,* where the "horror" that occurs in Africa results from the capitalist accumulation of commodities; and in *Lord Jim,* where Jim attempts to transform Patusan into a model colony by creating a plantation and organizing the local people into a labor force.

It is in *Nostromo,* however, that Conrad offers his most comprehensive study of imperialism as a product of global capitalism. As Watts demonstrates, the writing of *Nostromo* was almost certainly influenced by the secession of Panama from Columbia, which was supported by the United States so that it could acquire control of the territory necessary to build a canal linking the Pacific and Atlantic oceans (Watts 1969, 37–41; Watts 1993, 147–48). What happens in Costaguana over the course of the novel parallels what happened in Panama. Indeed, in her introduction to the Broadview edition of *Nostromo,* Nadelhaft goes so far as to suggest that the novel, which began as a short story about Italian immigrants in South America, developed into a critique of what she calls "the annexation of Panama" by the United States (Nadelhaft 1997, 16). While there is little direct evidence to support this claim—since the correspondence of Conrad's that survived the period refers only once to events in Panama—Conrad's earlier letters to Graham regarding the Spanish-American War make his attitudes toward U.S. imperialism clear (Watts 1969, 39). It is therefore not unreasonable to interpret *Nostromo* in part as a response to the U.S.-sponsored division of Columbia into two nations, one of which was controlled by the United States. Set in the imaginary postcolonial South American nation of Costaguana, the novel suggests that a nation's political independence does not ensure economic independence or even self-determination. On the contrary, even though Costaguana has been free of Spanish rule for fifty years, the nation's resources and markets are still controlled by foreign interests, as are its government and even its territorial boundaries.

Material Interests and a Novel without a Hero

Most of the novel's action takes place in Sulaco, a western province that is separated from the rest of Costaguana by nearly impassable mountains. Despite its inaccessibility, Sulaco is of great strategic importance because it contains the San Tomé silver mine, "the biggest thing in Sulaco, and even in the whole republic" (38). The mine does not belong to Costaguana or its people, however. Rather, it is controlled by an American-based company led by a man named Holroyd that has invested in the mine, and Charles Gould, a Costaguanero of English descent whose family has been granted rights to it in perpetuity. To the capitalist Holroyd, the San Tomé mine is just a "hobby" (81). To the people of Costaguana, however, the mine is a determining factor in their lives. Casual decisions Holroyd makes from within his "eleven-story-high factory of great affairs" in San Francisco, California, affect everyone in Costaguana whether or not they have any interest in the mine (124). Holroyd's decision to extend financial credit to Don Vincente Ribiera and his supporters, for example, enables Ribiera to establish himself as "president-dictator" of the nation, one who will protect the interests of foreign investors rather than those of Costaguaneros, and five years later, when Ribiera's government falls, Holroyd's tacit support for a "provincial revolution" leads to Sulaco's secession from Costaguana and its emergence as a new nation that will again protect foreign interests (124).

Ironically, even though Holroyd's "unlimited means" give him a "long reach" that touches everyone in the novel, he himself is only a minor character (317). By limiting his role, Conrad keeps the narrative's focus on Holroyd's economic function rather than his personality: who he is matters less than what he is: a capitalist who works to amass more capital for himself and other investors. As a character Holroyd is one-dimensional, a man entirely defined by the capital he controls. According to the narrator, Holroyd "had entered into Costaguana affairs with a sort of passion" and found it had "become necessary to his existence" (378). He has, in effect, become an acquisition machine, something totally inhuman.[9]

Holroyd is not the only character who becomes possessed by possessions: virtually every character who seeks to control the mine's treasure is instead controlled by it, including General Sotillo, Pedrito Montero, Martin Decoud, and, of course, the title character, Nostromo. Charles Gould is most obviously obsessed by the mine, though, if only because the narrator repeatedly emphasizes the fact. We are told, for example, that Gould had "fallen under the spell of the San Tomé mine" by age twenty and that ten years later, its "grip" on him is even more "deadly" than the one it had on his father (59, 400). Since the narrator emphasizes Gould's

English identity, the suggestion seems to be that the English are no less susceptible to avarice than anyone else, despite their claims of altruism. Although he tells himself and others that he operates the mine in order to secure "order and justice" in Costaguana (521), in reality he does so for selfish reasons, as Martin Decoud recognizes, writing to his sister, "Those Englishmen live on illusions which somehow or other help them to get a firm hold of the substance" (239).

The manner in which the narrator establishes Gould's English identity is also significant since it prevents him from emerging as a heroic figure. Rather than simply assert that Gould is a third-generation Costaguanero who looks and acts English, the narrator repeatedly emphasizes Gould's English identity so as to make him seem almost absurd. After introducing him as someone who looks "like a new arrival from over the sea," he adds that he "looked more English than a casual tourist . . . He looked more English than the last arrived batch of young railway engineers, than anybody out of the hunting-field pictures in the numbers of *Punch*" (46–47). Later in the same long paragraph, the narrator adds that Gould looked "thoroughly English even on horseback" and that "in his English clothes and with his imported saddlery [he looked] as though he had come this moment to Costaguana . . . straight out of some green meadow at the other side of the world" (48). The narrator's repeated references to Gould's ultra-English identity mark him as absurd rather than heroic. Like Barath in S. K. Ghosh's *The Prince of Destiny,* an Indian prince who wears a cricketing shirt beneath his toga (515), Gould is a mimic man in V. S. Naipaul's sense of the term and therefore, he cannot possibly be the hero of a serious novel.

The fact that Gould does not qualify as a hero does not necessarily mean that the novel does not have one, of course: some assume that the title character is the hero, and others regard Emilia Gould as such. As I will show, however, the ideological positions represented by every character in the novel, no matter how extensively or sympathetically portrayed, are undercut by the narrator, thereby making those characters ironic heroes at best. Even Emilia Gould, the novel's "most inviting and sympathetic character," as John Cooper notes, is dehumanized by material interests (154).[10]

Materialist History and Nostromo

In addition to illustrating the dehumanizing effects of global capitalism on individuals, *Nostromo* identifies it as part of a larger historical process, suggesting that because of its inherent contradictions, it will eventually end. Although Conrad's letters to Graham make it clear that Conrad was no Marxist, his understanding of history was influenced by the British Left, as evidenced by "Autocracy and War."[11] Because of his unwarranted reputation for being politically conservative, however, many critics refuse to recognize Conrad's materialist view of history. As John Reilly suggests, in *Nostromo,* Conrad "reaches a Marxist conclusion through non-Marxist premises" (135). Summarizing Reilly's argument, Andrew Michael Roberts explains, "The Marxist conclusion is that history consists of relentless struggle, and that 'individual psychology is itself correspondingly riven with contradiction'; the non-Marxist premise is the priority which Conrad accords to human nature, since for Conrad it is the duality of that nature which produces historical conflict, not vice versa" (18). Conrad's premises are not as humanistic as Reilly suggests, however. Although Conrad certainly believed that people had to take moral responsibility for their actions, he recognized that individual lives were shaped by history, a sentiment reflected in *Nostromo* when, in providing an account of Decoud's suicide, the narrator observes that "independent existence" is only an "illusion" and that individuals are just a "helpless part" in the "whole scheme of things" (497).[12] As this narrative assertion suggests, Conrad's concept of history was as materialist as that of Graham. Both men believed that history was driven by economic forces, but whereas Graham believed that a more just society could be established through radical economic reform, Conrad suspected that such efforts were futile since human nature itself was corrupt.[13]

This sense of futility is what gives *Nostromo* an air of tragedy. In an 1898 letter to Graham, Conrad wrote, "What makes mankind tragic is not that they are the victims of nature, it is that they are conscious of it. To be part of the animal kingdom under the conditions of this earth is very well—but as soon as you know of your slavery the pain, the anger, the strife—the tragedy begins" (*Letters* 2:30). In *Nostromo,* Conrad incorporates this belief into fiction. Like Oedipus, the characters of this novel struggle against their destinies, even though they suspect that such struggles are pointless. The title character, for example, is fully aware that Mitchell, Gould, and others exploit him, but he serves them nonetheless, not only because he values the prestige that having a position of trust brings him, but because he enjoys exerting power over other workers as Capataz de Cargadores. Ironically, it is in part his desire to maintain his reputation for fidelity that leads him to steal the silver that he and Decoud are supposed to safeguard: as he explains to Emilia Gould as he is dying, he could not return the silver because four ingots were missing, and he knew people would assume he "purloined them" (559). Nostromo is thus caught in a bind—he cannot do the honest thing without appearing to be dishonest. This, combined with his desire for material wealth and his bitterness toward Gould, Mitchell, and the others, who he feels do not fully appreciate him, leads him to steal the treasure and thus become its "slave" (523). What distinguishes Nostromo from the protagonists of Conrad's earlier novels is his "full self-knowledge" of his slavery (523). Unlike Jim in *Lord Jim,* who seems to believe that he has "mastered his fate" (193), Nostromo dies knowing that he has failed to master his.[14]

Insurgency and Revolution in Nostromo

Another important point of distinction between *Nostromo* and Conrad's earlier works is his representation of insurgency and insurgents. As I noted in previous chapters, *Almayer's Folly* concludes with Nina Almayer joining the anticolonial insurgency in the Dutch East Indies, and *Lord Jim* ends with the emergence of Patusan as a postcolonial state. Even in works such as *Heart of Darkness,* where indigenous characters and their points of view are presented in only a limited way, Conrad posits a potential at least for insurgency and liberation through the woman frequently identified by critics as "the African mistress." As Sid Ray has recently demonstrated, this "barbarous and superb woman" is a Dido-like warrior and chief rather than a kept woman (146).[15] "Stately and ominous," she does "not so much as flinch" when Marlow pulls the whistle that causes the other Africans to flee, and the Harlequin is so frightened by her that he would rather shoot her than face her (136). In *Nostromo,* a novel conceived of and written after he met Graham, Conrad represents insurgency in a very different manner. Rather than focusing on anti-imperialist insurgencies, Conrad addresses decolonization and the social unrest associated with it, anticipating many of the themes that were to be addressed by postcolonial writers of the 1960s. On the surface at least, Conrad's pessimism about the ability of recently liberated peoples to establish just societies resembles that of writers like Chinua Achebe, Wole Soyinka, and even Ngugi wa Thiong'o.[16] As Baines notes, *Nostromo* seems to close off any real possibility of social justice for the inhabitants of Costaguana, since "by the end of the book we are virtually back where we started" (301).[17]

Virtually back to where we started, but not quite. Although Baines's conclusions about *Nostromo* are consistent with Conrad's professed views of the late 1890s, by the time the novel was published in 1904, Conrad's attitudes toward social revolution had changed, in part because of Graham's influence (Watts 1993, 152). In a 1905 essay entitled "Books," Conrad stresses that the artist should "cherish . . . an undying hope," adding that to "be hopeful in an artistic sense it is not necessary to think that the world is good. It is enough to believe that there is no impossibility of its being made so" (8–9). Conrad could not have made such a statement in the 1890s: as his letters of the time to Graham reveal, Conrad had little hope for humanity, writing in 1898, for example, that its "fate" is "not worth troubling about" (*Letters* 2:17). By 1904, however, Conrad recognized that there was at least some hope for improving the human condition by ending economic oppression, perhaps because of Graham's influence. Ironically, his newfound hope seems to be based on a belief that capitalism would produce the conditions that would lead to its own destruction, a belief he expresses very clearly in "Autocracy and War" (107). Although Conrad certainly did not expect that a socialist utopia would follow the demise of capitalism, he apparently allowed for at least the possibility that something better would follow.

Locating such hope in *Nostromo* is difficult since the novel ends not only with the title character's death but also with the foreign capitalists establishing control over the newly independent nation of Sulaco and its resources. As Benita Parry suggests, however, the novel's resolution "acknowledges that radical politics may be a means of deliverance from an intolerable present" (1983, 121). She continues: "This viewpoint connects with the Epigraph, 'So foul a sky clears not without a storm,' to register a prospect on the initiation of change as not only inevitable but desirable, and in this version Costaguana's history is not witnessed as an endless spiral of failure rooted in human fallibility, but as a story of successive forms of exploitation bringing into existence altered material conditions and class relationships which generate new forms of consciousness, new ambitions, and new goals" (121). Conceding that such an interpretation is "unsupported by narrative sanction and obscured by a rhetoric scornful of revolutionary aims and practices," Parry nonetheless argues that the novel ends with the "promise" of a better future, since Nostromo, despite his corruption, "live[s] on in the minds and hearts of Costaguana's poor as exemplar of their [radical] aspirations" (127).[18]

Certainly, Parry is justified in rejecting the narrator's implied judgments, since, like all of Conrad's narrators, he has biases of his own. Her argument that potential for real social change exists at the end of the novel would be more compelling, however, if she were to focus more on the emerging working class, a group that the narrator himself recognizes as a new and potentially subversive phenomenon in Sulaco. It is in organized labor that Conrad finds the potential for social change, not because he believes that laborers will eventually create a worker's paradise, but because unions are a product of one of capitalism's inherent contradictions, the inevitable conflict between labor and capital. Early on in the narrative, the narrator indicates that once Sulaco secedes from Costaguana, it has "quite serious, organized labour troubles" (95). According to Captain Mitchell, these troubles result in part from the influence "socialistic Italians" have had on "the natives" (478–79): apparently, the foreign capital that poured into Sulaco after it established itself as a nation has brought with it social unrest. Even though the narrator never specifies where this unrest will lead, in the final part of the book he asserts that a profound transformation has indeed occurred: "Material changes swept along in the train of material interests. And other changes more subtle, outwardly unmarked, affected the minds and hearts of the workers" (504). Although the narrator offers this comment with no further explanation of what these changes are, when considered in the context of the other references to labor, the implication seems to be that the workers are developing class consciousness and that Sulaco is headed toward yet another revolution, one that will transform the social order rather than simply exchange one set of oppressors for another.

As Fleishman suggests, this final revolution will occur in two stages, for the workers' revolution cannot happen until the capitalist system is identified as the adversary and the various social classes and factions unite in order to defeat it (166). The first stage will be initiated by rich liberals, represented by Antonia Avellanos, and the *campesinos*—or rural peoples—represented by Father Corbelàn, who hope to "annex the rest of Costaguana to the order and prosperity of Sulaco" (509). Such an act would be opposed by the "material interests" that dominate Sulaco, as Dr. Monygham points out, since they "will not let you jeopardize their development for a mere idea of pity and justice" (509). Corbelàn, however, is undeterred by the thought of capitalist opposition to the plan: "'Let them beware, then, lest the people, prevented from their aspirations, should rise and claim their share of the wealth and their share of the power,' the popular cardinal-archbishop of Sulaco declared significantly, menacingly" (510). Unlike the privileged Avellanos, who still believes that the development of the mine by foreign investors is crucial to the material prosperity of both Sulaco and Costaguana, Corbelàn already seems to recognize capitalists as potential class enemies, something that the coming war of annexation should make all the more apparent. The coming war will also build solidarity between newly radicalized groups, represented by Avellanos and Corbelàn, and the already-radicalized workers. As Monygham observes, Avellanos and Corbelàn will ally themselves with the workers' organizations, which themselves are made up of both "immigrants and natives," in order to acquire the "necessary force" to annex Costaguana, and he adds that they will acquire popular support "with the new cry of 'the wealth for the people'" (511).

The second stage of this revolution will occur when, having annexed Costaguana, the alliance of workers, *campesinos,* and liberals unite against the "material interests" and finally end capitalist exploitation in Sulaco/Costaguana. Monygham anticipates this as well. When, contemplating the coming war, Emilia Gould asks, "Will there be never any peace? Will there be no rest?" he replies, "There is no peace and no rest in the development of material interests. They have their law, and their justice. But it is founded on expediency, and it is inhuman; it is without rectitude, without the continuity and force that can be found only in a moral principle" (511). Monygham already sees what Corbelàn suspects and Avellanos will learn: the global capitalist system itself exploits the people of Sulaco/Costaguana. He also recognizes that there has been a change of consciousness in Sulaco, predicting that the San Tomé mine, which was once considered a source of prosperity by locals, will soon "provoke resentment, bloodshed, and vengeance, because men have grown different" (511). To illustrate this point, he notes that the miners who, during the previous revolution, "march[ed] upon the town" to save Charles Gould would not do so again, presumably because they no longer look on him as a benefactor.

Transculturation and the Sulacan Revolution

Superficially at least, Conrad's representation of social revolution resembles the Marxist model, as Fleishman suggests (166). Like Marx, Conrad sees social revolution as unfolding in a number of stages. Conrad does not simply impose Marx's model on his imagined South American nation, however. Rather, he presents the social revolution that occurs in Sulaco as a product of its unique history and culture. Sulaco is a *contact zone,* to borrow Mary Louise Pratt's term, a space occupied by *mestizos,* indigenous peoples (including "tame Indians" and "wild" ones), Creoles, "Negroes," English railway engineers, Italians and Basque laborers, *campesinos,* European merchants and company officials, itinerant traders, and political refugees from Costaguana, among others. Together these groups form a society with multiple social and economic classes and conflicting beliefs, values, and interests. The complexity of this society is reflected in the social revolutions that occur in Sulaco when it is a part of Costaguana and the one that is set to occur when it becomes a newly independent nation. Rather than simply employ revolutionary ideologies and practices imported from Europe or, conversely, reject European ideologies in favor of indigenous ones, the people of Sulaco develop new ones through the process known as "transculturation." As Pratt notes, "Ethnographers have used this term to describe how subordinated groups select and invent from materials transmitted to them by a dominant or metropolitan culture. While subjugated peoples cannot readily control what emanates from the dominant culture, they do determine to varying extents what they absorb into their own, and what they use it for" (6). Such a process describes just what happens in Sulaco. Synthesizing the old and the new, the indigenous and the imported, Sulaco develops its own beliefs, values, and practices, incorporating elements of Christian charity, liberalism, pragmatism, folklore, Marxism, antiforeign sentiment, localism, and racism, among other things. Rather than being blind "to other histories, other cultures, other aspirations," as Said asserts (Said 1988, 70), Conrad recognizes that places like Sulaco have been permanently changed by colonization, and then decolonization, and that the postcolonial societies that will eventually emerge will be hybrids of sorts, societies that incorporate both European and indigenous elements but cannot be understood simply as a combination of the two.[19]

The Final Irony: Emilia Gould and the Absurdity of Imperialism

As I suggested earlier, although Conrad was no Marxist, *Nostromo* registers a fundamental shift in Conrad's political thinking as he came to recognize that a new form of economic imperialism was emerging and that new revolutionary ideologies would have to be developed to contest it. Not surprisingly, the change in the content of Conrad's work was accompanied by a change in style. Rather than relying on narrative layering—that is, tales within tales—to offer multiple perspectives on imperialism, Conrad employs an omniscient narrator who, as Keith Carabine notes, "combine[s] an Olympian omniscience which works for detachment and thematic suggestiveness with a rich exploitation of the free indirect style which renders the characters' thoughts in their own idiom, initially invoking the reader's scorn but also arousing sympathy for their desperation and bewilderment" (ix). To an extent, Conrad's use of such a narrator represents a return to the narrative style he employed in *Almayer's Folly.* The narrator of *Nostromo,* however, is relentlessly ironic: unlike the narrator of *Almayer's Folly,* who privileges Nina Almayer over her father by representing her without irony at the end of the novel, the narrator of *Nostromo* spares no one, not even Emilia Gould, a character whom many critics, including Irving Howe and Eloise Hay, regard as the novel's true hero since she is the only central character who is not obviously corrupted by the silver.

Ironically, early on in the novel, the narrator emphasizes Emilia Gould's own sense of irony—that is, her ability to find amusement in the "absurdities that prevail in this world" (378): she agrees "ironically" with a visiting Englishman when he insists that nothing important has happened in Sulaco in a hundred years, for example, and her conversation has "a slight flavour of irony" when she speaks of the silver mine (36, 67). As a European who has come to South America only recently, she finds Costaguana absurd. At the end of the novel, however, after Nostromo has died and Giselle, a woman "who would have followed a thief [Nostromo] to the end of the world," turns to her for comfort, Emilia Gould realizes that she is as absurd as those around her, since she, "the first lady of Sulaco, the wife of the señor administrator of the San Tomé mine," has followed a thief of a different sort to the end of the world (561). Apparently, she has taken Nostromo's dying declaration—that the wealth she and her husband have accumulated comes "from the hands of the poor"—to heart and recognizes that despite their charity toward the poor, she and her husband are complicit in their exploitation (560). The realization that she has devoted herself to a man who, like Nostromo, is a "slave of the treasure," results in "the first and only moment of bitterness in her life": she tells the sobbing Giselle, "Console yourself, child. Very soon he would have forgotten you for his treasure" (561). Although she speaks to Giselle, she is clearly referring to herself as well, for when Giselle whispers, "Señora, he loved me. He loved me," Emilia Gould replies, "I have been loved, too" (561). In the end, it seems, she recognizes that her own "naïve pretences" are no better than those of the Costaguaneros and that she herself is part of an absurd "comedy," someone whose very destiny is determined by material interests (49). Like Nostromo, who had "full self-knowledge" of his condition, Emilia Gould becomes fully aware of her own, knowing that she can do nothing to alter it. Her story thus ends with a final irony, one that suggests that ultimately, even the most privileged have no control over their fate.

The Assault Resumes: Nostromo *as a Direct Attack on Imperialism*

As I suggested in chapter 6, although pervasive irony like that which can be found in *Nostromo* is frequently associated with modernism, it is also characteristic of postcolonial fiction. The type of irony that dominates *Nostromo* is markedly different from the type that Conrad employed in his early short stories when he was trying to build a larger audience, however. In works such as *Heart of Darkness* and *Lord Jim,* Conrad constructed Trojan horses of sorts: double-voiced fictions in which the radical content is concealed within seemingly innocuous tales. But by the time he began *Nostromo* in December 1902, Conrad had established himself as a professional writer. Although his commercial success was still limited, he was widely respected by other writers, had won a couple of literary awards, and was treated with respect by reviewers and publishers (Watts 1989, 87). He had also acquired the services of a highly skilled literary agent, James Pinker, who brought Conrad some measure of financial stability, not only by placing stories for him, but by regularly lending him money.[20] Even though Conrad continued to have serious financial problems, his letters of early 1903 indicate that his newfound professional confidence was peaking just as he began *Nostromo,* largely because of *Youth*'s promising early sales.[21] On January 5, for example, he writes to Pinker about his hopes of following up on "the success of *Youth*":

> For success it is. The West End booksellers are satisfied. I have had reports as to that from several sources. Last Saturday only, a friend going into Bumpus's saw piles of the book on the counter. B[lack]woods wrote to me on N Year's day that it is selling "very well" . . . Naturally we cannot expect a fortune out of *Youth*. Mudie and Smith [a lending library and a chain of bookstores, respectively] have not yet been captured; but a beginning has been made with the "Trade" and I look upon my position as distinc[t]-ly improved. (*Letters* 3:6)

Conrad's newfound confidence coincides exactly with the genesis of *Nostromo,* for later in the very same letter, he tells Pinker about the story for the first time. Other letters he wrote that winter show just how great his expectations of financial success became. On February 16, for example, he writes to John Galsworthy that he thinks *Nostromo* may earn him "up to a thousand pounds, or thereabouts" (*Letters* 3:18), twice what he earned for *Lord Jim* (*Letters* 3:22).[22]

Because his professional situation appeared to be improving, Conrad felt that he could be more direct in his critiques of various forms of subjugation and exploitation, using irony to augment his social criticism rather than to cloak it. Employing irony in such a manner always involves risk, of course, since the irony is often missed or misunderstood. In the case of *Nostromo,* such risks were particularly great, because Conrad's irony often involved subtle juxtapositions and temporal shifts whose implications were not always obvious, particularly on the first reading.[23] As a result, some of the novel's original reviewers considered *Nostromo* a "shapeless" work and even an "artistic failure" (Sherry 1973, 164–65). Such critics tended to regard the novel as "a failed romance about a Genoese sailor . . . who sinks to theft and his own contempt," all but ignoring its political content (Sherry 1973, 164). Critics who regarded the novel as political, however, were more able to appreciate its structural complexity. The reviewer for the *Illustrated London News,* for example, writes:

> The criticism to be leveled against it [*Nostromo*]—that it is formless—is in reality a criticism of its extreme length. It is longer even than it appears, because, to a degree unparalleled in any other novelist we can think of, every word goes to the development of the story and the enlightenment of the appreciative reader. It is not an exaggeration to say that an imperfect understanding of the author's intention may result from a moment's slackness of attention and the failure to read between two (or more) particular lines. (Sherry 1973, 180)

Reading between the lines, of course, involves recognizing irony, something that is easiest when one knows where and when to look for it. It should not be surprising, then, that those who knew Conrad and his work best were able to appreciate the novel's political implications. Even Graham seems to miss the significance of the novel's ironic ending, however, and in his review for the *Speaker,* Garnett goes so far as to express "regret that the last two chapters describing Nostromo's death are included in the novel" (Sherry 1973, 177).[24] What Graham and Garnett are unable to see is that without Nostromo's death and Emilia Gould's response to it, the liberal capitalist views that Emilia Gould represents would remain unchallenged: it is only by having Gould subject herself to her own sense of irony that Conrad is able to convey that Sulaco/Costaguana cannot be saved from without, and that although Gould's altruism might improve circumstances for some, her philanthropy is possible only because of the mass exploitation of Sulaco/Costaguana and its resources. Hope for social justice in Costaguana relies not on the good will of enlightened capitalists but on the destruction of the capitalist system of exploitation. Conrad's novel thus succeeds where Said says it fails. As I noted earlier, although Said concedes that Conrad is critical of imperialism in certain ways, he argues that all Conrad "could see is a world totally dominated by the Atlantic West, in which every opposition to the West only confirms the West's wicked power" (xviii). In *Nostromo,* however, as in "Autocracy and War," Conrad does imagine an end to capitalist domination, suggesting that it will create the means of its own destruction. Whereas in "Autocracy and War," Conrad focuses on transnational competition for resources and markets, in *Nostromo,* he focuses on organized labor, in combination with other radical elements, as a destructive force. In both works, however, he anticipates an end to capitalism and the emergence of a new social order, one that will allow for the possibility at least of social justice.

If Conrad provides little indication of what this postimperial, postcapitalist social order will be like, neither do later postcolonial writers such as Achebe, Soyinka, and Thiong'o. To do so would be to write fantasy or speculative fiction, something that early postcolonial writers seldom did since there was little market for such work. What Conrad did do was help establish the postcolonial novel as a viable genre. Although many of Conrad's original readers found *Almayer's Folly, Lord Jim,* and *Nostromo* difficult, these novels were widely recognized as works of art by publishers, critics, and established writers such as H. G. Wells, George Bernard Shaw, and Henry James. As Alan Sinfield suggests, such recognition gives the work in question cultural authority: "To have your work accepted as art or literature, or to be judged an expert, is to gain voice in a discourse with certain claims to significance" (28). It can also help establish new categories of privileged discourse, new literary genres. Novels like Conrad's that were set in colonies and represented indigenous points of view developed into such a genre, one that encompasses what is now known as the postcolonial novel. Although it would be an overstatement to claim that Conrad invented this genre, he certainly pioneered it in Great Britain, thereby providing a model for future postcolonial writers.

CHAPTER EIGHT

Irony, Duplicity, and the Postcolonial Aesthetic

> The *bricoleur,* says Levi-Strauss, is someone who uses the means at hand, that is, the instruments he finds at his disposal around him, those which are already there, which had not been especially conceived with an eye to the operations for which they are to be used and which one tries by trial and error to adopt them, not hesitating to change them whenever it appears necessary, or try out several at once, even if their form and their origin are heterogenous—and so forth.
>
> JACQUES DERRIDA, *Writing and Difference*

> How does newness come into the world?
> Of what fusions, translations, conjoining is it made?
> How does it survive, extreme and dangerous as it is? What compromises, what deals, what betrayals of its secret nature must it make to stave off the wrecking crew, the exterminating angel, the guillotine?
>
> SALMAN RUSHDIE, *The Satanic Verses*

It may seem ironic for a study that declares itself "decidedly not poststructuralist" to use a passage from *Writing and Difference* for an epigraph in its concluding section. I am not citing the poststructuralist Derrida here, however, but the postcolonial one—the one who recognized the revolutionary potential of "absence" and "play," privileging Nietzschean affirmation over Rousseauistic despair. As a colonial subject working within the French academy to challenge the epistemologies upon which Western power is based, Derrida knew well what it was to be a *bricoleur*—to initiate new discourse through use of the old.[1] Like Conrad, S. K. Ghosh, Solomon Plaatje, Frantz Fanon, Chinua

Achebe, Gayatri Spivak, and so many other colonial subjects, Derrida adopted and adapted existing tools for new, revolutionary uses.

Creating the new out of the old is difficult, of course, not only because it entails doing what, by definition, has never been done before, but because, as Rushdie suggests in *The Satanic Verses,* it involves compromise and even betrayal. This was certainly true for Conrad, a man who accepted the fact that readers "demand from their writers as much subservience as from their footmen" (*Letters* 3:286). To an extent, Conrad was willing to give imperialistic readers what they wanted: exotic tales of adventure and romance. As we have seen, however, he was unwilling to celebrate imperialism or imperialist ideology in his work: on the contrary, Conrad employed the conventions of popular imperialist genres only to subvert them, creating hybrid texts that were unlike anything else being published in Great Britain. In effect, he was writing postcolonial novels well before the genre was established.

Given the fact that the postcolonial did not exist in recognizable form in the 1890s, it should not be surprising that Conrad's work is rarely if ever identified as such today. What is surprising is that Conrad is frequently identified as a "colonial," "colonialist," and even an "imperialist" writer by those who, like Padmini Mongia, concede that Conrad had considerable influence on later postcolonial writers such as Ngugi wa Thiong'o and Tayeb Salih, and Amitav Ghosh.[2] This phenomenon can be explained at least in part by the Trojan horse strategy Conrad adopted. Texts such as *Heart of Darkness* and *Lord Jim* operate on two levels at once: as exotic tales of empire that appeared to affirm imperialist ideology and as subversive tales that challenged its legitimacy. Ironically, like late nineteenth-century imperialist readers, postcolonial critics such as Mongia, Bhabha, and Said respond only to the texts' surface features, missing the radical critique concealed within.[3]

That this radical critique is missed by even the best of critics is at least partly due to Conrad's duplicity. What I want to suggest here is that such duplicity remains part of the postcolonial aesthetic. Early postcolonial writers like Conrad, S. K. Ghosh, and Solomon Plaatje had no choice but to dissemble if they wanted to reach a broad market. Even in the late twentieth century, postcolonial writers had to work with European and

American publishers if they were to reach large international audiences, and therefore, they had to, at least at times, employ misdirection, subterfuge, and deception. The same appears to be true today, as evidenced by the work of Wole Soyinka, Aruhdhati Roy, and Wendy Law-Yone. With this in mind, it is no wonder that irony has become so pervasive in postcolonial fiction.[4] How else could postcolonial writers sell books to metropolitan readers even as they challenge their beliefs and values? In this sense, at least, such writers are "Conrad's descendents," to borrow Peter Nazareth's phrase:[5] like Conrad, they use irony as a "rhetorical strategy for working within existing discourses and contesting them at the same time," as Linda Hutcheon puts it (154). Double-voicedness of this sort is anything but ambivalent, of course, since it has a political function: rather than simply deconstructing "existing orthodoxies," contemporary postcolonial writers such as Soyinka, Roy, and Law-Yone use various forms of irony to subvert such orthodoxies in order to advance alternative "agendas" (Hutcheon 150). For these writers, as for Conrad, irony is not "immoral" or "decadent" but "fortifying," giving it the potential, at least, to "change the reader's political beliefs and actions" (Miller 2005, 5–6).[6] To postcolonial writers, who are by definition political, this potential is essential: irony—that is, double-voiced discourse—allows them to be radical without seeming radical, to say things that otherwise cannot be said. In this sense, at least, double-voiced discourse is more than just part of the postcolonial aesthetic: it makes the postcolonial possible.

Notes

Introduction

1. Nazareth identifies Conrad as a "Third World Writer" in "Out of the Darkness," and he identifies a number of postcolonial writers as Conrad's "descendents" in "Conrad's Descendents."
2. As Boehmer notes, the hyphenated term *post-colonial* is now generally used to indicate the period of decolonization following World War II (3). For a more detailed discussion of the various way the terms *post-colonial* and *postcolonial* have been defined, see Loomba's *Colonialism/Postcolonialism* and Graham Huggan's *The Postcolonial Exotic.* My own understanding of the terms—and the discussion that follows regarding them—is based largely on what I have learned from Loomba and Huggan.
3. By *colonialist writers* I mean writers who were proponents of imperialism, whether or not they lived in colonies. By *colonial,* I mean writers who, as colonial subjects, contested imperialism and imperialist ideology.
4. Boehmer defines *colonial literature* as "writing concerned with colonial perceptions and experiences," noting that it "includes literature written in Britain as well as the rest of the empire during the colonial period" (2). She defines *colonialist literature* as "literature specifically concerned with colonial expansion" that "embodied the imperialists' point of view" (3).
5. Ironically, Conrad's work reached later postcolonial writers only because it was considered part of "the Great Tradition" and therefore considered suitable for colonial schools (Nazareth 1982, 178).
6. Indeed, during World War I, Conrad wrote two political essays on Poland, and, in 1916, he met with George Russell Clerk of the British Foreign Office in an effort to persuade the British to support the reconstitution of the Polish state (Najder 1983, 416). In 1919, he published "The Crime of Partition," an essay that challenged official British policy towards Poland (Najder 1983, 436).
7. In his letter to Cunninghame Graham of October 14, 1899, for example, he refers to the Boer War as "idiotic," asserting that "it is always unwise to begin

a war which to be effective must be a war of extermination" (*Letters* 2:206–7). In the same letter he also expresses skepticism about Kipling's claim that the war was "undertaken for the cause of democracy," writing, "C'est a crever de rire." Conrad was similarly skeptical about Great Britain's claims of altruism during World War I. As Najder notes, "Conrad never joined the chorus of enthusiastic supporters of 'the war in the defense of justice and civilization,' and he carefully avoided jingoistic phraseology" (1983, 414). For more on Conrad and "the Polish Question," see Najder 1983, 415–17, 436–37.

8. Although most critics continue to regard modernists as apolitical, there are exceptions. In *Modernism, Nationalism, and the Novel,* for example, Pericles Lewis argues that a number of early modernists, including Conrad, focus on "national consciousness" as a "means of mediating between the apparently hostile and meaningless social world and the meaningful but powerless consciousness of the individual novelist-hero" (4). See also *Modernism and Empire,* edited by Howard J. Booth and Nigel Rigby.
9. Rather than focus on the cultural context of Conrad's works, Jameson, like many critics, including Said and Ian Watt, instead considers it in an intellectual context, relating Conrad's ideas to those of thinkers such as G. W. F. Hegel and Friedrich Nietzsche.
10. Following common practice, I use the term *colonial subject* to refer to those who have been subjected to and directly conditioned by colonial institutions and the term *subaltern* to refer to those living in colonies who have had only limited or indirect contact with such institutions, fully recognizing that both terms represent fuzzy categories. I use the term *subject peoples* to refer to all those who are subject to colonial authority, whether or not they have had a significant amount of direct contact with colonial institutions.
11. For a discussion of how European "races" were differentiated in the nineteenth century, see Robert J. C. Young's *Colonial Desire,* 55–82. See also Anne McClintock's *Imperial Leather,* 52–53.
12. Conrad's understanding of what it is to be treated by a racial other by Western Europeans is reflected in at least two of his stories: in "Amy Foster," a refugee from Eastern Europe with an "olive complexion" is left to die by his English wife because of his alterity (111), and in "The Black Mate," Winston Bunter faces "ignorant prejudice" because he dyes his hair and looks like a "furriner" (86, 120). In both stories, Europeans are discriminated against by other Europeans because of perceived racial differences.
13. For a discussion of Conrad's feelings of self-consciousness as a "b—y furriner," see Allan H. Simmons's "The Art of Englishness."
14. In his introduction to *"Youth," "Heart of Darkness," "The End of the Tether,"* John Lyon challenges Said's argument in another manner. After noting Said's assertion that Conrad reproduces imperialist ideology even as he criti-

cizes it, Lyon counters that "for Conrad to recognize his non-comprehension of other cultures is for him to have moved beyond the position imputed to him here, to have identified a space beyond Western ideologies which such cultures inhabit. Conrad is thus not merely a symptom of the colonial imagination; he has an active and initiatory role in post-colonial thinking. Indeed, much of the thinking which energizes post-colonial criticism has been anticipated, albeit in embryo, and enacted with wonderful economy by Conrad himself" (xli).

15. Searches of the phrases "postcolonial classroom" and "postcolonial Chaucer" on major search engines such as Google reveal that they are used frequently at academic conferences and in papers.
16. *The Postcolonial Jane Austen,* edited by You-me Park and Rajeswari Sunder Rajan, is another example of how reconsidering canonical texts from a postcolonial perspective can lead to new insights. The essays contained therein do not reconsider Austen as a postcolonial author, of course. Rather, as Rajan indicates in his preface to the volume, "The focus of the collection is on Austen viewed in light of postcolonial theory, as well as, reciprocally, upon postcolonial theory viewed in light of a certain 'Austen'" (xi).
17. See also Vincent Cheng's *Joyce, Race, and Empire,* another seminal study on Joyce that suggests that he was postcolonial.
18. Even those who accept the premises of poststructuralist theory recognize the problematic ways in which deconstructionist postcolonial theory is presented. Parry, for example, notes that "Bhabha's flagrantly ambivalent presentation . . . leaves it vulnerable to innocent misconstruction" (Parry 1995, 42). For a lengthy discussion of the limitations of deconstructionist postcolonial theory, see Aijaz Ahmad's *In Theory.* For a less detailed but more recent assessment, see Nagesh Rao's "Resistance and Representation."
19. In general, I enclose terms such as *half-caste, savage,* and *native* in quotation marks to indicate that I am following Conrad's usage. I do not provide page references for Conrad's use of such terms unless I am focusing on a particular passage.

Chapter 1

1. Conrad himself did not like to be thought of as a freak, as his correspondence makes clear. For example, in 1903 he wrote to Kazimierz Waliszewski, "Et puis, franchement, je n'aime pas à paraître comme une espèce de phénomène des lettres" (*Letters* 3:69). See also *Letters* 3:488.
2. Conrad briefly considered trying to get *Almayer's Folly* published in French in the *Revue des Deux Mondes.* The letters he wrote to Marguerite Poradowska regarding the matter demonstrate just how difficult it would have been to

access the French literary market despite Poradowska's literary connections. He first proposed that she submit it as a translation and then suggested it be proposed as a "collaboration" (*Letters* 1:165, 170). The novel did not appear in French until 1919 (Watt 1994, xxxvi).

3. As White demonstrates, Conrad was very much aware of an author's value as a commodity (242–44). Nonetheless, as I noted previously, he refused to allow himself to be marketed as a literary phenomenon.
4. As the phrase "Russian-occupied Polish Ukraine" suggests, defining Conrad's original national identity in exact terms is exceedingly difficult. When he was born in 1857, there was no Polish state: what was once Poland had been partitioned and annexed by Prussia, Austria-Hungary, and Russia. Moreover, as Avrom Fleishman notes, he was born in a part of Ukraine that itself had been annexed by the kingdom of Poland centuries earlier (3). Fleishman goes on to note that Poles made up only 3 percent of the population of that part of Ukraine and that the region is "not claimed by Poland today" (4). For Conrad's views on Polish history, see his essays on Poland, particularly "The Crime of Partition" (1919).
5. The following account of Conrad's parent's political activities and their consequences is based largely on the work of Najder, particularly *Conrad in Perspective.*
6. This phrase is drawn from proceedings of the Special Military Commission, which sentenced Korzeniowski and Bobrowska to exile, as translated by Najder (1997, 30).
7. In the glossary he provides for Bakhtin's *The Dialogic Imagination,* Michael Holquist identifies "dialogism" as a "mode" in which everything "is understood, as part of a greater whole—there is a constant interaction between meanings, all of which have the potential of conditioning others" (426).
8. See, for example, Conrad's letter to Marguerite Poradowska (*Letters* 1:178, 221, 229).
9. As she explains in a later interview, subalterns may be able to "talk," but it takes both "speaking and hearing" to "complete the speech act" (Spivak 1995, 292). Spivak goes on to argue that the subaltern woman is "doubly-effaced," an assertion that raises a technical problem in her argument, since she defines the silence of subalterns in absolute terms. (She further suggests that "if you are poor, black, and female" in the "first-world," "you get it in three ways" [90].) Spivak seems to be indicating that there are degrees of silence—or at least of silencing—a point that seems to undermine her argument that the subaltern is silent by definition.
10. I use the term *colonial subject* instead of *indigenous elite* to emphasize the process through which certain people are made subjects by a complex of colonial social, political, and economic institutions including language. Fol-

lowing Spivak and others, I use the term *subaltern* to indicate those who have not been subjected to colonial institutions in a systematic manner. There are, of course, degrees of alterity, just as there are degrees of exposure in colonial institutions. As Spivak herself emphasizes, groups like these are "heterogeneous," and their attitudes and relations with one another are marked by "ambiguities and contradictions" (1994, 79–80).

11. In "The Commitment to Theory," Bhahba identifies this "space" as the Third Space of Enunciation (1988, 23).
12. For a brief demonstration of how Bakhtin's theory of linguistic hybridity can be applied to Conrad's texts, see William Atkinson's introduction to *"The Lagoon" and Other Stories.*
13. The Trojan Horse function I describe here is only one of several ways discourse can be constructed so as to challenge an ideology even as it gives it voice. Another example is parody: both are types of double-voiced discourse, or what Bakhtin terms "intentional hybrids" when he discusses them in the context of the novel. For an illuminating discussion of Bakhtin's theory of linguistic hybridity, see Gary Saul Morson and Caryl Emerson's *Mikhail Bakhtin,* especially pages 147–56. For a discussion of how Bakhtinian concepts such as the "dialogic" and "polyphonic" can be applied to Conrad's work, see Mark Wollaeger's *Joseph Conrad and the Fictions of Skepticism,* especially pages 20–24.
14. It is worth noting that Gandhi himself translated the Gujarati word *satyagraha,* or *sadagrahas,* as "passive resistance," since the Gujarati word literally denotes "firmness in a good cause," according to Anthony J. Parel, the editor of the Cambridge edition of Gandhi's *Hind Swaraj and Other Writings* (85n167). Gandhi's idiosyncratic translation of the term suggests that he purposely created an oxymoron to conceal his radical intent from British authorities.
15. In "The Doctrine of the Sword," Gandhi seems almost ambivalent towards revolutionary violence, writing, "Where there is only a choice between cowardice and violence, I would advise violence" (quoted in Chadha 247). Such openly subversive writings led to his arrest in 1922, an event that, ironically, provided an even greater opportunity for him to disseminate his ideas.
16. Those writing in languages other than English could be more openly seditious, a point Mukherjee illustrates by contrasting Bankimchandra Chatterjee's Bangla novels to his only English-language novel, *Rajmohan's Wife.* In the Bangla novels, the English are depicted negatively, while in *Rajmohan's Wife,* "the white man is ascribed a positive function and the justice and efficiency of British rule is unequivocally, if briefly, proclaimed at the end" (2000, 16).
17. In *Ratanbai,* Nikambe tells the story of a young Hindu who struggles to acquire a formal education in colonial India. As Paranjape demonstrates, despite

"kowtowing to colonial power," the novel appears to offer a "nuanced and ambivalent form of resistance" to that power (67).

18. This reading of *The Prince of Destiny* is based largely on "'My Unknown Bride Who Are Thou?'": Insurgency and Miscegenation in S. K. Ghosh's *The Prince of Destiny*," a paper I presented with Kerry Kaneshiro at the Thirty-First Annual Comparative Literature Conference: Love and Politics in Literary Perspective, sponsored by the Department of Comparative World Literature and Classics at California State University, Long Beach, in March 1996.
19. For more on Indo-Anglian novels that seem to affirm unequivocally imperialist ideology, see Mukherjee 2000, 16–17. See also Mukherjee 2003, 95–96.
20. These excerpts from contemporary reviews, as well as the one that follows, are taken from the second edition of *The Prince of Destiny,* which was released in 1910. The fact that it went into a second edition after only one year is, of course, significant: although the novel was not a best seller, it generated a certain amount of interest. There was also at least one colonial edition.
21. For a detailed analysis of *Mhudi,* see "'Never be Led by a Female . . . ,'" by Tom Henthorne and Shannon Young.
22. The information that follows regarding the publication of *Mhudi* is based largely on Brian Willan's *Sol Plaatje.*
23. The ten-year delay in publication undoubtedly affected the novel's reception. Removed from its original sociopolitical context, the novel's radical elements were probably both less apparent and less relevant to what was going on in South Africa at the time.
24. Day's novel *Govinda Samanta* (1874) is a remarkable example of an early Bengali novel written in English that employs a Trojan Horse strategy to challenge British imperialism in India. Tutuola's *The Palm-Wine Drinkard* also succeeds as a Trojan Horse as evidenced by the fact that it was well received by British readers and critics even though its protagonist ultimately rejects colonial society in favor of traditional ways. For a detailed account of the difficulties Tutuola faced in getting his work published, see Berth Lindfors's introduction to the facsimile edition of the original manuscript of *The Wild Hunter in the Bush of the Ghosts.*
25. Although the fact that Conrad was white certainly worked to his advantage, it is worth noting that Edward Garnett, a reader for T. Fisher Unwin's firm, recommended that Conrad's first novel be published even though he assumed that Conrad "had Eastern blood in his veins" (Garnett 1956, 2).
26. See, for example, his letters to Unwin, Hugh Clifford, David Meldrum, and William Blackwood in *Letters,* vols. 1 and 2.
27. In a letter to Karol Zagórski dated March 10, 1896, Conrad reports that he refused the command of a ship and goes on to declare that "the literary profession" was his "sole means of support" (*Letters* 1:266)

28. As Robert Hampson notes, "Achebe's essay has, indeed, been so influential that . . . it has sometimes produced an automatic and unthinking rejection not just of *Heart of Darkness* but of all Conrad's work" (Hampson 2002, 225).
29. In *Rule of Darkness,* Brantlinger discusses in some detail various responses to Achebe's charges of racism. See also Peter Firchow's *Envisioning Africa.*

Chapter 2

1. That the novel violates genre conventions has long been recognized. In his introductory essay to *Conrad's Prefaces,* Garnett, for example, notes that although "Kipling's example paved the way for the 'exotic' Conrad's arrival," the characters of *Almayer's Folly* and *An Outcast of the Islands* must have seemed "beyond the pale" to most English readers (8). See also Dryden 51–52.
2. It is important to note that the concepts *monologic* and *dialogic* do not constitute a binary opposition. Rather, they mark the extremes of a continuum. As Bakhtin indicates, discourse is by definition dialogic; there are, however, degrees of dialogism and monologism (Morson and Emerson 131).
3. For an extended analysis of the conversation Garnett reports, see Firchow 31–37. For discussions of Conrad's changing sensibilities as a result of his experiences in the Congo, see James Clifford's *The Predicament of Culture.* See also Ribeiro de Oliveira 257–58.
4. Regarding his experiences as an Imperial police officer in Burma, Orwell writes, "I gave it up partly because the climate had ruined my health, partly because I already had vague ideas of writing books, but mainly because I could not go on any longer serving an imperialism which I had come to regard as very largely a racket" (quoted in Meyer 68). For detailed accounts of Orwell's change in attitude as a result of his experiences, see Sheldon 79–112.
5. For a detailed discussion of Gandhi's experiences in South Africa and their effects on his consciousness, see Chadha 56–122.
6. It is worth noting that Conrad revisited the Ukraine just before leaving for Africa, particularly since while there, he was forcibly reminded of what it was to be a colonial subject and that it was his duty as a Pole to promote the culture of his birth and act patriotically (Najder 1983, 119–22).
7. The phrase "to his eastern mind" does not appear in the novel's original manuscript. This addition, in concert with other changes Conrad made, tends to highlight Kaspar's race consciousness, while other changes tend to reduce racial stereotyping on the part of the narrator. As an example of the latter,

Conrad twice omits the word *asiatic* as an adjective to describe the behavior of indigenous characters.

8. Kaspar's fantasies that "witnessing" Nina's "triumphs" in Europe will enable him to "grow young again" do not appear in the original draft of chapter 1 (5). By detailing Kaspar's absurd fantasies, Conrad makes Kaspar seem more ridiculous.
9. One could argue, of course, that *Almayer's Folly* would not be "nihilistic" even if Kaspar were the only hero, since rather than be "void" of values, in the course of the story Kaspar demonstrates that he has the values and characteristics of late nineteenth-century European colonists.
10. See also Watt 1979, 38–39; and Jones 86–89.
11. One notable exception is the unsigned review in the *Daily Chronicle* that identifies Nina as the "heroine" (Sherry 1973, 49).
12. A number of critics, including Andrea White and Linda Dryden, compare *Almayer's Folly* to Robert Louis Stevenson's *The Beach of Falesá* (1893), a novella that treats one of its main characters, Uma, a "native" woman, sympathetically. Although Uma is never overtly identified as being of mixed descent, the narrator describes her in stereotypical terms that suggest that she is partially European—"very slender for an island maid, with a long face, a high forehead"—and he mentions that Uma's mother was in a long-term relationship with a white man (192, 212). As Barry Menikoff documents in *Robert Louis Stevenson and "The Beach of Falesá,"* for this and other reasons—including negative representations of Europeans—the novel was "received with suspicion and distaste" (4). It is, of course, possible that Conrad was influenced by Stevenson's novella, which first appeared in *Illustrated London News* in July and August of 1892, nearly two years before he completed *Almayer's Folly* and submitted it to Unwin.
13. That *Almayer's Folly* can be regarded as an adventure novel has been ably demonstrated by White in *Joseph Conrad and the Adventure Tradition.* That it can be read as a romance has been demonstrated in Dryden's equally impressive *Joseph Conrad and the Imperial Romance.*
14. The *Times,* for example, put its review of the novel under the heading "An Oriental Romance" (Watt 1994, xlv). As Watt notes, a number of reviews, including those in the *Guardian, Academy,* and *Daily Chronicle,* also treated the book as a romance (Watt 1994, xlv).
15. As Hampson indicates, alternatively, "it could be argued, in the language of Homi Bhabha, that she [Nina] finds her identity not through finally choosing (or being forced to choose) her mother's world rather than her father's . . . but rather as a constant performance of identity in the interstices between the different codes and traditions in which she is situated through 'the overlap and displacement of domains of difference'" (106–7). See also Sewlall,

who goes even further in applying Bhabha's theory of the Third Space of Enunciation to Conrad's first two novels.

16. Thomas Moser regards Nina and Dain's romance as "the weakest part of *Almayer's Folly*" (52). D. C. R. A. Goonetilleke argues that their romance "is of a conventionally romantic kind" (1990, 19).
17. For an alternative reading of the significance of the novel's "happy end" (259), see Ribeiro de Oliveira (263–71). She argues that, despite her efforts, "Nina cannot totally obliterate her white inheritance" and that ultimately, she transmits "the virus of a hated civilization to infect Dain's comparatively untainted culture" (269). In *Conrad and Empire,* Stephen Ross develops a similar argument (93)
18. For a more detailed account of how Indonesian nationality emerged earlier in the twentieth century, see GoGwilt's *Invention of the West,* particularly pages 83–87.
19. In *Developing Countries in British Fiction,* Goonetilleke argues that none of Conrad's Malay characters "reveal even a semblance" of the "corporate identity" that is a basic characteristic of nationalism. In *Almayer's Folly,* however, it seems clear that at the very least, Conrad represents the emergence of such an identity.
20. Although John Lester argues in "A Fictional Chronology of Conrad's Eastern World" that "since Nina is five at the time of *An Outcast of the Islands* in 1870, the main action of *Almayer's Folly* must occur in 1886" (60), I believe that the novel must be set in the 1870s since the narrator mentions the beginning of the "Acheen War," which started in 1873, at the beginning of chapter 4. See Watt 1994, 255n38.5. For more on Sulu responses to imperialism, see Hampson 2000, 41–43.
21. As E. S. De Klerck notes in *The History of the Netherland East Indies,* control of Aceh became important when, with the opening of the Suez Canal, international shipping lanes shifted, passing through the Straits of Malacca (2:342). Fearing apparently that another European state would acquire control of Aceh, the Dutch invaded the independent state in 1873 (Ulekke 319). The war continued into the twentieth century.
22. The initial draft of the opening chapter suggests that Maroola's battle with the Dutch was conceived only after Conrad returned from the Congo and decided to focus more on anticolonial insurgencies, since in the original version, Maroola's boat is still intact.
23. Even GoGwilt, whose work is invaluable to understanding the formation of Indonesian national consciousness as it is represented in *Almayer's Folly,* seems to overlook Maroola's significance, treating him as a love object of both Nina and Taminah (GoGwilt 1995, 84).
24. For a discussion of Taminah and her agency, see GoGwilt 1995, 83–85.

25. In White's view, Conrad's "ventriloquism resulted more from his growing technical interest in writerly concerns than from any liberal consciousness" (120). The original author's note to *Almayer's Folly,* which was written in 1895 but not published until 1921, suggests otherwise, however. In this note Conrad focuses on similarities between the British and their colonial subjects rather than differences, declaring that "there is a bond between us and that humanity so far away" and adding that he is "content to sympathise with common mortals no matter where they live; in houses or in huts, in the streets under a fog or in the forests behind the dark line of dismal mangroves that fringe the vast solitude of the sea" (3). Clearly, Conrad had the sort of consciousness that was unlikely to be popular with the imperialistic readers of the 1890s. Indeed, as White herself notes, Conrad intended his author's note as a "disclaimer" of sorts: in it, he attempted to distinguish his work from that of imperialist writers such as Frederick Marryat, G. A. Henty, and Rider Haggard (White 118).
26. As I indicated in chapter 1, for the purposes of this study, I use the term *colonial subject* to denote those who are subjected to colonial institutions directly and the term *subaltern* to denote those who are largely unconditioned by such institutions. I use the term *subject peoples* when referring to both groups.
27. For a discussion of *The Ebb-Tide,* see Sandison, especially pages 317–20.
28. As White argues, "His good intentions amount to 'meddling' and ultimately bring disaster down on the heads of the very people he seeks to protect, contributing to the chaos of the local rivalries and intrigues that plague Sambir and the eventual revolution there" (142). See also Nadelhaft 1991, 15–19.
29. For a discussion of European political and colonial rivalries as they are represented in Sambir, see Hampson 2000, 110–11.
30. Other Europeans believed the opposite, of course—that "half-castes" were hopelessly degenerate and essentially useless. John W. Griffith argues that Conrad shared this view, noting that the narrator of *An Outcast of the Islands* uses the term *degenerate* when describing the Da Souza family (141). Griffith's argument is unconvincing, however, since Conrad develops a "half-caste" character, Nina Almayer, as a protagonist and hero in *Almayer's Folly.*
31. In her discussion of both "interbreeding" and what Benedict Anderson described as "mental miscegenation"—that is, efforts to create "Europeanized natives" through education—Ania Loomba suggests that the belief was that colonial subjects could "mimic but never exactly reproduce English values, and that their recognition of the perpetual gap between themselves and the 'real thing' [would] ensure their subjection" (173).
32. A review of *Almayer's Folly* that appeared in a Singapore newspaper, the *Strait Times,* in 1896 seems to confirm this. The anonymous reviewer writes, "The author has drawn with great power and fidelity the miserable results

of a mixed marriage under existing social conditions. . . . The social prejudice against mixed blood, unjust in itself, has been aroused by the narrowing influence of local education and limited interests, and serves to save many foolish lives from mental shipwrecks. Its general utility does not, however, prevent its operating with very cruel harshness against individuals" (quoted in Marle 31). For a discussion of this review and a letter that appeared in the *Strait Times* the next day that vehemently denied that prejudices even existed against people of mixed race, see van Marle's "Jumble of Facts and Fiction."

33. Heliéna Krenn identifies nine instances in which the word *savage* is used to highlight in Aïssa "a total absence of the physical and mental changes that result from exposure to and assimilation of civilization's influences" (64).
34. Like the reference to "sweet words" cited earlier, this passage does not appear in the original manuscript. Such additions tend to amplify Conrad's point about the threat that subalterns pose to the colonial order.
35. For an analysis of Aïssa's function as a "pivot," see Schneider, 49–52. See also Susan Jones's discussion of Aïssa's transcendence of the "role of *femme fatale*" (10).
36. As Nadelhaft (1991) demonstrates, Spivak's studies of subaltern women provide a framework for better understanding the complexities of Conrad's representation of women in *An Outcast of the Islands,* particularly Aïssa. Nadelhaft goes on to analyze Aïssa's encounter with Lingard in detail (32–33). See also Sewlall.
37. The role of British fiction in promulgating imperialist ideology has been widely examined. See, for example, Brantlinger's *Rule of Darkness* and Said's *Culture and Imperialism.*
38. In *Who Paid for Modernism?* Joyce Piell Wexler interrogates the relationship between the complexity of texts and their marketability, demonstrating that a market existed for writers who challenged their readers with difficult texts.
39. In a letter to Garnett, for example, Conrad thanks him for attempting to help him to find a ship (*Letters* 1:262). About a month later, he announced to Garnett that he had begun a third novel, "The Rescuer" (*Letters* 1:268). There is little evidence that Conrad seriously considered going to sea again after this date, except for a brief period in 1898 (Najder 1983, 233).

Chapter 3

1. According to Najder, "In his critical articles, published in various periodicals, [Apollo] Korzenioski, as was customary in post-partition Poland, defended the public and national functions and obligations of literature" (1997, 26).
2. Although Apollo Korzenioski earned money as a land manager, writer, and translator, his wife, Ewa Bobrowska, came from a well-off family, and there-

fore, as Najder notes, he was able "to rely upon the assistance of his wife's relatives" even after his wife died (1997, 35). Following the death of his uncle, Tadeusz Bobrowski, Conrad received no assistance from his own family, and his wife's family did not have the financial resources to provide any support.

3. According to Peter Keating, the number of weeklies and monthlies in Great Britain more than tripled between 1875 and 1895 (34).
4. *The Cornhill* also rejected the story, even though the editor had specifically requested Conrad's work. Garnett's delay in responding to Conrad's queries about the story can probably be attributed to the fact that he was recovering from typhoid at the time.
5. See Garnett's *Letters from Joseph Conrad,* 14.
6. Indeed, one could argue that Conrad was too moral for Christianity, which, he wrote, "has lent itself with amazing facility to cruel distortion" (quoted in Watts 1993, 48).
7. For more on Conrad and religion, see Cedric Watts's *A Preface to Conrad,* 47–51.
8. A letter from Conrad to Garnett of October 16, 1896, suggests that, as Conrad's agent, Unwin received 10 percent of the proceeds from the stories he placed (*Letters* 1:306).
9. As William Nelles notes, Conrad's letters to Cunninghame Graham show that he was very conscious of the "effect of the whole" when grouping short stories together in a volume (65).
10. Even though the details the narrator provides make it clear that Susan falls into the water and then tries to save herself, a number of critics, including Lawrence Graver and Ted Billy, regard her death as a suicide (Graver 9; Billy 169). To do so is to miss the story's point about resistance and responsibility: Susan believes that she is justified in killing her husband and wants to explain that to the authorities, even though she knows that they will not sympathize with her or her actions. Her efforts to explain herself and her actions are futile, however: it is as if nature itself conspires against her, and heaven itself is indifferent to her fate, something that the narrator emphasizes by describing Susan's final cry as seeming "to dart upwards along the perpendicular face of the rock and soar past, straight into the high and impassive heaven" (84). By dramatizing Susan's end in such a manner, Conrad suggests that Susan's struggle against oppression involves resisting not only her brutal husband but also the hierarchal system of authority that begins with God in heaven. Like Charlotte Perkins Gilman in "The Yellow Wall-Paper," a story Conrad may have been familiar with since it was published by Unwin in 1895, Conrad indicts not only individuals but the oppressive patriarchal social order as well.
11. In *Conrad and Women,* Susan Jones connects Levaille's actions to Aïssa's in *An Outcast of the Islands,* arguing that both are part of "a recurring theme . . .

in which women play an important role in the critique of imperialism (both in colonialist and European settings" (11).

12. As Yves Hervoet demonstrates in *The French Face of Joseph Conrad,* in "The Idiots," Conrad seems to have used the stories of Maupassant as a model: "Like Maupassant, who began more than half of his 300 short stories by setting up a frame in the form of a brief discussion or scene to introduce the main tale, Conrad begins with a narrator who describes his encounter with the idiots and explains how he managed to piece together their story. He then becomes an omniscient narrator, preserving with rare intrusions of the Conradian voice, the detached stance of a typical Maupassant narrator. And the story ends in Maupassant fashion with a satirical coda on the themes of hypocrisy, selfishness and corruption in a meeting between Susan's ambitious mother and the intriguing Marquis de Chavanes" (32).
13. For more on how critics relate "An Outpost of Progress" to *Heart of Darkness* see Hilson and Tim, 107; Billy, 63; Maisonnat, 101.
14. For a detailed analysis of the story's narrative technique, see Lothe 1989, 45–56; and Hawthorn 1990, 159–68.
15. The story was originally published under the name "A Victim of Progress" in *Cosmopolis* in 1897. It was renamed "An Outpost of Progress" for *Tales of Unrest* in 1898.
16. For more on this anti-imperialist literary circle, see GoGwilt 2000, 141–56.
17. In "Geography and Some Explorers," Conrad uses the word *arm-chair* as an adjective when describing with disdain those who substitute reading for experience, as in "arm-chair geographers" (8).
18. Erdinast-Vulcan goes on to argue, "'The Lagoon' is a spectacle for the entertainment of the observing (imperial, white, male) reading/writing/narrating subject, who thus secures a stable sense of his own subjectivity against that exotic foil" (58).
19. For more on the relationship between "The Lagoon" and the exotic imperial fiction of Conrad's contemporaries, see Ruppel, "'The Lagoon' and the Popular Exotic Tradition."
20. For example, in *An Outcast of the Islands,* Almayer's books are understood by the people of Sambir as "books of magic—of magic that guides the white men's ships over the seas, that gives them their wicked wisdom and their strength; of magic that makes them great, powerful, and irresistible while they live, and—praise be to Allah!—the victims of Satan, the slaves of Jehannum when they die" (299–300).
21. Robert Hampson uses this passage as a basis for arguing that "the narrative is presented through a Malay perspective," constructing "a non-European reality of ghosts and spirits against which the European is defined" (2000, 119).

22. Guérard and others identify the narrator of "The Lagoon" with Marlow. To an extent, this seems appropriate: like Marlow, the narrator seems engaged with the tale and even offers judgment upon it. Whereas Marlow openly sympathizes with his white protagonists, however—those he considers "one of us"—the narrator of "The Lagoon" is ambivalent toward the unnamed white man.
23. See, for example, Hugh Clifford's *Tales in Brown Humanity* and Kipling's *The Phantom 'Rickshaw and Other Stories.*
24. The fact that Conrad identifies both the white colonist's materialism and Arsat's proprietary obsession with Diamelen as pathological opens up an interesting interpretive possibility since it challenges the critical commonplace that Conrad was deeply misogynistic. Conrad seems to be just as critical of men who treat women as possessions in "The Lagoon" as he is in "The Idiots."
25. Ted Billy also categorizes the white colonist and Kurtz together "as believers in the will to power" (174).
26. For a discussion of how various critics have interpreted "The Lagoon," see Ruppel, "'The Lagoon' and the Popular Exotic Tradition."
27. For the story to be a full "intentional hybrid," both perspectives would have to be active and, in effect, unmask each other (though one might be subtly privileged over the other). In "The Lagoon," however, the imperialist point of view is represented in a "passive" manner and not fully dialogized (Morson and Emerson 150).
28. As Conrad himself says in the author's note to *Tales of Unrest,* "The Lagoon" marked the end of his "first phase" of his career as a writer: "Conceived in the same mood which produced 'Almayer's Folly' and 'An Outcast of the Islands,' it is told in the same breath (with what was left of it, that is, after the end of 'An Outcast'), seen with the same vision, rendered in the same method—if such a method did exist then in my conscious relation to this new adventure of writing for print" (vii).

Chapter 4

1. To put Conrad's earnings into perspective, in 1897 the average yearly income of an adult male in England was 56 pounds (Carabine viii, n5). For more on Conrad's financial situation in 1896–97, see Najder 1983, 201–6.
2. One review, published by *Saturday Review,* recognized the *"volte face"* in Conrad's work and applauded it, writing that it had "begun to fear" that the "single theme" of Conrad's previous works—"the degeneracy of the white man under the influences of the South Sea Islands"—was becoming his "specialty" and that it was good to see him "wisely leaving the degenerate sots of the islands to their unlamented fate" (Sherry 1973, 99).

3. A number of critics, including Brian Schaffer and Jeremy Hawthorn, are troubled by Conrad's representation of Wait because, they argue, he shams illness, thereby reinforcing negative stereotypes about blacks. I would argue, however, that Wait does not sham his illness at all—he is terminally ill, and the severity of his symptoms is evident from his very first appearance in the text. Certainly, Conrad, whose parents both died of tuberculosis, would be unlikely to depict a person in the last stages of the disease as faking illness. To me, Conrad's point seems to be that the prejudiced crew of the *Narcissus* refuses to accept the seriousness of Wait's illness because of the color of his skin.
4. If, as I suggest, Conrad was trying to misdirect his readers, it appears that he succeeded, since many of the novel's original reviewers did not even recognize Wait as a main character despite the fact that the title refers directly to him. The reviewer for *Academy,* for example, writes, "The story is simply that of a voyage from Bombay to London in a sailing-ship, and the incident consists only of the storm and the death of a nigger" (Sherry 1973, 95). None of the other seven reviews collected by Norman Sherry in *Conrad: The Critical Heritage* recognize Wait as the protagonist, and some barely mention him at all.
5. In a newspaper column for the *Pace Press,* Allah M. Merciful writes, "We were assigned to read the book, The Nigger of the Narcissus. I explained to the instructor during and after class that my reaction to the title of the book was offensive. After the day's conference, a personal conflict grew between the instructor and I.

   "I wasn't intelligent enough to simply withdraw from the class and I stopped going because of this principle. Needless to say, I received an 'F' for the World Literature class. I chucked it up as an experience. (This was no blow to my ego because I have received F's before.) This one was different because instead of the 'F' for failure, this 'F' stood for Freedom. If I have to repeat the class, that's fine. Hopefully, it won't contain that bogus 'blacks as niggers' jargon" (8).
6. Graham's article appeared in the *Social-Democrat* four months before *The Nigger of the "Narcissus"* began to appear in the *New Review* in August 1897. As Hawthorn indicates, Conrad reacted to the article approvingly (1990, 84). For a discussion of Graham's essay, see Watts and Davies, 161–63; GoGwilt 2000, 145–46.
7. The difference between them becomes evident in their very first encounter when Donkin says to Wait, "Giv' us a bit of 'baccy, mate," and Wait replies, "Don't be familiar . . . Here's your tobacco" (14). The narrator observes that Wait reacts to Donkin "like a man addressed unexpectedly in a foreign language."
8. It is important to note that Conrad does more than simply displace the term *nigger* onto working-class whites as if to suggest that whites can be "niggers," too. Rather, as I shall demonstrate, Conrad interrogates *nigger* as a conceptual category, exposing its ideological function.

9. Thomas Henry Huxley (1825–1925) was a leading nineteenth-century naturalist. William Booth (1829–1912) was a revivalist preacher and the founder of the Salvation Army. William Barry (1849–1930) was a priest and author of the best-selling novel *The New Antigone* (1887).
10. McClintock notes that the "phrase 'white negroes' appeared in *The Times* as early as 1880" (52).
11. As McClintock observes, racialists also sought to differentiate the Irish and other "races" from themselves through comparative physiognomy. See, for example, Cope, 281–93.
12. As Allan Hunter demonstrates, Conrad appears to have read much of the racialist theory of his time. According to Hunter, for the most part, Conrad rejected racialist theory since he believed "humanity to be a socially and economically guided organism" (2).
13. W. L. Courtney's review for the *Daily Telegraph* is a notable exception. Although Courtney does not recognize Wait as the protagonist, he includes him in a list of characters of whom he writes, "one and all are our familiar friends before the voyage is over. They are not a pleasant lot altogether, yet they are very human—big children in their petulant moods, and heroes in times of crisis" (Sherry 1973, 87).
14. Indeed, in the United States the story was entitled *Children of the Sea* because, as Conrad explained to Hamlin Garland, "America would not buy a book about niggers" (Garland 41).
15. Ironically, this reviewer, who, earlier in the review, refuses to identify the title character by name, ends by referring to Wait as "Jimmy" (90–91). Since "Jimmy" is the name the crew uses for Wait when they are feeling most compassionate towards him, the reviewer's use of it suggests that he or she has been affected by the pathos of the story: on some level the reviewer regards the "nigger" as human even though he or she is disinclined to do so.
16. A letter written to Stephen Crane seems to affirm that the misdirection is intentional. He writes, "I was anxious to know what you would think of the end. If I've hit *you* with the death of Jimmy I don't care if I don't hit another man. I think however artistically the end of the book is somewhat lame. I mean after the death. All that rigmarole [*sic*] about the burial and the ships coming home seems to run away into a rat's tail—thin at the end" (*Letters* 1:409–10).
17. For a detailed analysis of how Conrad manipulates narrative voice in "radical" ways, see Richardson 2005, 216. He demonstrates how the "posthumanist" narrative techniques Conrad develops are employed by a number of postcolonial writers, including Raja Rao, Ngugi wa Thiong'o, and Ayi Kwi Armah, among others, making it part of what I term the *postcolonial aesthetic* (221).
18. For a discussion of this passage, see Parry 1983, 69.

19. Many English, of course, did not deny that Africans had souls; indeed, various missionary societies were formed to save the souls of Africans. As Young demonstrates, the very humanity of Africans was debated throughout the century by the English and others, with polygenesists, for example, arguing that blacks and other nonwhites were created by God as beings distinct from whites.
20. Conrad also uses free indirect discourse and passive formulations to distance himself from subversive elements in the text. Hawthorn (1990) discusses Conrad's use of these devices at some length, arguing that they generate ambiguities that reflect Conrad's own ideological uncertainties. I am arguing that Conrad uses such devices to generate ambiguity for a different reason—to distance himself as an author from the radical content of his work.
21. Henley's conservatism is reflected in his writing of the period. In his introduction to C. de Thierry's *Imperialism,* for example, he wrote: "it would seem that, at last, after years of stupor—years in which the blind were content to be led by the insane—the British Empire is by way of realising the fact that it is the greatest and strongest which the world has ever seen.... We have renewed our old pride in the Flag, our old delight in the thought of a good thing done by a good man of his hands, our old faith in the ambitions and traditions of the race" (quoted in Porter, 36–37).
22. A letter of Conrad's from 1904 confirms that the novel was written with Henley—and therefore a conservative audience—in mind. He writes that the novel "was written 'with an eye one him [Henley]—and yet with no idea whatever that it would ever meet his eye'" (*Letters* 3:115).
23. Guérard, for example, argues that the character-narrator of "Karain" anticipates Marlow, particularly as he is represented in *Lord Jim.* Most of the critics who address the development of Conrad's narrative technique make similar observations.
24. Guérard describes the coin episode as a "trivial anecdote" (91). Graver describes the ending as "Kiplingesque," noting that it is "good-hearted enough to please the average magazine reader" (33). For a fascinating, detailed discussion of Graver's interpretation of "Karain," see Wollaeger, 45–47.
25. That the European, Hollis, uses the word *amuck* while the Malay, Pata Matari, uses the word *amok* suggests that white men, even sympathetic ones like Hollis, can never really understand Malay culture (37).
26. The fact that the sixpence is gilt adds another level of symbolism to the charm since, as David Adams argues, Jubilee sixpences were often gilded so that they could be passed for half-sovereigns (103–4).
27. Adams makes a similar point, noting, "The activities of Karain's three white acquaintances . . . typify the not uncommon imperial practice of pursuing material gain—especially gain from the sale of weaponry—even at the price of instability and 'disaster' for the local populations" (97).

28. According to Billy, "At the end of the story, Conrad transforms the abstract mechanical pulsations of time into an insidious heartbeat that propels and dominates civilized life. It promotes 'progress,' it advances 'culture,' and it 'colonizes the globe'" (127).
29. That it is the narrator who describes the "shabby children" and the "ragged old man with a face of despair" suggests that Jackson has succeeded in inducing the narrator to see London as Jackson sees it, however briefly.
30. Erdinast-Vulcan contrasts what she sees as the "neat enclosure of otherness in 'The Lagoon'" with "the unresolved tension between two perceptual sets or spheres" in "Karain," arguing that in the latter story, Conrad takes his "first steps . . . into the troubled waters of Modernism" (62). I argue, in contrast, that Conrad subverts imperialist ideology in both stories and that the complex narrative technique he employs in the latter story is motivated by his politics rather than any "will to style" (56).
31. Indeed, one could argue, as Watts does, that "the predominant effect of the description of the crowded city is to undercut ironically the narrator's confidence and to support Jackson's doubts. Against the turbulence, overcrowding, noise, ugliness, confusion and squalor associated with the city, Karain's picturesquely tropical world with its archaic values (simple heroism and leadership, passionate actions and betrayals, superstitious credulities) seems 'more real': aesthetically, ontologically, and morally better" (1992, 22). Similarly, Adams discusses the "ironic treatment" of the narrator in the closing section of the story (115). Hampson takes a more neutral position, arguing that in the ending of the story, "Conrad presents radically different realities without attempting any resolution or even hierarchising their differences" (2000, 127).
32. See Erdinast-Vulcan, 62.
33. Just how socially conservative—and enigmatic—*Blackwood's* could be is evidenced by a note William Blackwood wrote to his brother George regarding the Stephen Crane story "The Blue Hotel": "George read this story and ask your aunt Bee to read it and if she thinks it is too strong for Magas then we must I fear decline it" (Blackburn 202). "Aunt Bee" was Elizabeth Blackwood, William Blackwood's sister, who also acted as his housekeeper.
34. For a more detailed account of how Conrad placed "Karain," see Dryden, 110–11.
35. In a letter to Garnett of August 28, 1897, for example, Conrad writes: "All the good moments—the real good ones in my new life I owe to you—and I say it without a pang; which is also something of which you may boast. O! Wiser than the serpents. You sent me to Pawling—You sent me to Black[wood's]—when are You going to send me to heaven?" (*Letters* 1:378).
36. In *The Invention of the West,* GoGwilt argues that Marlow is "hailed . . . by that highly volatile dynamic, described by Homi Bhabha, whereby an indi-

vidual's sense of subjectivity is structured around the effect of racist stereotypes, producing the colonial subject, subjected to colonial control" (GoGwilt 1995, 24).

37. Hawthorn identifies this "native gaze" as a "legitimate interrogation of the European by another culture" (2001, 282). Similarly, Hampson (2000) notes that the scene "briefly registers the fact of Asian agency and contains possibilities of critical self-questioning, both of which remain important features of Conrad's writing of Malaysia" (8).
38. Conrad uses sea imagery in a similar manner to describe the Moslem pilgrims boarding the *Patna* in *Lord Jim:* "They streamed aboard over three gangways, they streamed in with a continuous tramp . . . and when clear of the confining rails spread on all sides over the deck, flowed forward and aft, overflowed down the yawning hatchways, filled the inner recesses of the ship—like water filling a cistern, like water flowing into crevices and crannies, like water rising silently even with the rim" (13).
39. As Hay demonstrates, Conrad's suggestion that Nemesis awaits Europeans in Asia is consistent with the nineteenth-century Polish hope that "'Nemesis' will bring a turn of fortune to the Poles" (1993, 25).

Chapter 5

1. In Bakhtinian terms, *Heart of Darkness* could be described as "passive double-voiced" discourse: "passive" because the liberal perspective on imperialism Marlow represents is never fully dialogized (Morson and Emerson 150–51).
2. William Harper, for example, argued that slavery "has done more to elevate a degraded race in the scale of humanity . . . to enlighten the ignorant . . . than all the missionaries that philanthropy and religion have ever set forth" (116). James Hammond uses similar rhetoric when he suggests that the slaves held in Africa would be better off in America: "Though they might be perpetual bondsmen, still they would emerge from darkness to light—from barbarous into civilization—from idolatry to Christianity—in short from death to life" (171).
3. In *King Leopold's Ghost,* Hochschild draws a similar conclusion, noting that Morel "ignored his own country's use of forced labor—widespread, though far less murderous—in its own African colonies, particularly in the east and south." He continues, "There was nothing inherently wrong with colonialism, he [Morel] felt, if its administration was fair and just. He believed this to be the case in the British colonies in west Africa" (210).
4. For a detailed discussion of how Schreiner attacks British imperialism in *Trooper Peter Halket of Mashonaland,* see Chrisman, 120–62. Schreiner's

book, like Conrad's first two novels and his first volume of short stories, was published by T. Fisher Unwin.

5. Garnett's manifesto for "The Over-Seas Library" was printed on the front inside cover of his *The Ipané,* the first book in the series. For a discussion of the series and its significance, see GoGwilt 2000, 141–41; and Watts and Davies, 141–51. White discusses Conrad's participation in a small "underground movement" at some length, arguing that Conrad and others prepared the way for writers such as E. M. Forster and Graham Greene. She goes on to argue that this movement ultimately "helped to break the silence long imposed on the Other" (195–98).
6. According to Najder (1983), "Conrad's participation in *The Inheritors* consisted almost entirely of advising Ford, or rather inciting him to revise the manuscript, and of negotiating with publishers. Ford was responsible for both the idea and most of the entire text" (259).
7. In *Blackwood's,* the story appeared as "The Heart of Darkness." Conrad renamed it "Heart of Darkness" when he collected it in the volume *Youth* in 1902.
8. In his brief introduction to an edition of *Conradiana* dedicated to "Conrad and the Reader," Richardson observes, "Conrad's fiction . . . often seems to create two or more different and opposed implied readers" (2). He goes on to suggest that in *Heart of Darkness,* it is the "anti-imperialist" reader who is "privileged."
9. Conrad's duplicity surfaces again when, in a letter to Blackwood of February 12, 1899, he tries to convince his publisher to allow him to dedicate *Youth* to Graham. He writes, "I wished for some time to ask you whether you would object to my dedicating the Vol: to R. B. Cunninghame Graham. Strictly speaking it is a matter between the dedicator and the other person, but in this case—considering the imprint of the House and your own convictions I would prefer to defer to your wishes . . . I do not share his political convictions or even all his ideas on art, but we have enough ideas in common to base a strong friendship on" (*Letters* 2:165). As I argue in chapter 7, Conrad's convictions were much closer to Graham's than they were to Blackwood's. Indeed, in his very first letter to Graham, Conrad assures him, "I mean to hold my beliefs," referring to the anti-imperialism he expressed in "An Outpost of Progress" (*Letters* 1:370). For a discussion of this letter of February 12, 1899, see Watts 1969, 136–37.
10. Although Conrad rarely wrote openly of the political intent of his work, an 1898 letter to Graham in which he accuses his friend of preaching to the converted affirms that Conrad believed it important to at least try to influence those with whom one did not agree (*Letters* 2:69). Years later, he wrote the same to H. G. Wells, this time going into more detail: "After all why

should you preach to people already convinced. That sort of thing leads only to a sort of high priesthood in a clique and it should be left to people who seek simply the satisfaction of their vanity. It is just to the unbelievers that *you* should preach; and believe me that no one is too benighted (emotionally or rationally) to be spoken to with some effect by him who *can* speak" (*Letters* 3:63).

11. Responding to a letter from Graham, Conrad writes in a letter of April 17, 1899, "Your letter this morning made me feel much better. Is it possible that you like the thing [*Heart of Darkness*] so much. Well, you say so and I believe you but—do you quite believe it yourself soit dit sans vous offenser. The element of friendship comes in. But still I am willing, even eager, to believe in your scrupulous literary honesty" (*Letters* 2:178–79).
12. William Atkinson demonstrates just how unlikely it was that "the average *Blackwood's* reader" would read the story "against the grain"—that is, "as ultimately subversive of its own reader's discourse" (2004, 375).
13. Even Patrick Brantlinger does this in *Rule of Darkness,* conflating his Conrad and his narrator as "Conrad/Marlow" (268).
14. White describes Marlow as being "not so much Conrad's spokesman" as "a strategic innovation" intended to disrupt "the generic adventure story and its essentially monolithic illusions" (177). While White is certainly correct, it is the frame narrator who represents the more significant strategic innovation since he represents the means through which Conrad dialogizes Marlow's narrative.
15. Byron Caminero-Santangelo explores dialogism in *Heart of Darkness,* demonstrating how "Conrad encourages the reader to interrogate Marlow's narration critically" (111). Caminero-Santangelo does not recognize the narrator's radical function, however, which leads him to regard the story as an intentional hybrid to the extent that it "resists ideological closure" (128). I argue, in contrast, that the radical perspective represented by the anonymous narrator is ultimately privileged, making the story a Trojan horse.
16. The article on Drake to which Hampson refers, "The Case of Mr. Doughty," appeared June 1898, along with an installment of Conrad's story "Youth," and therefore Conrad was almost certainly aware of it. In this article, David Hannay argues that Drake had Tom Doughty executed on false charges at St. Julian's Bay "to establish his own irregular, but indispensable authority" (808).
17. Late nineteenth-century debate on Drake's heroism is reflected in Froude's lectures. He writes: "Vandalism, atrocity, unheard of among civilized nations, dishonour to the Protestant cause, Drake deserving to swing at his own yardarm; so indignant Liberals shrieked, and have not stopped shrieking" (192). Froude goes on to justify Drake's actions, arguing that they were in defense

of England since "for fifteen years the Spaniards had been burning English seamen whenever they could catch them, plotting to kill the Queen and reduce England into vassaldom to the Pope" (192).

18. A note to the article on Franklin in the ninth edition of the *Encyclopedia Britannica* indicates that it was "revised by Miss Cracoft, Sir John Franklin's niece" (722). This fact perhaps explains the article's unqualified praise for Franklin.
19. That he is being obtuse seems to be a possibility, at least if one identifies him with the narrator of "Youth," who, as I argued in chapter 4, misunderstands Marlow's liberal critique of empire as a paean to youth. Comparing the two texts is certainly not unreasonable, since early in *Heart of Darkness* the frame narrator seems to refer to "Youth" when he writes of himself and the others aboard the *Nellie:* "Between us there was, as I have already said somewhere, the bond of the sea" (3). I would argue, though, that in *Heart of Darkness,* Conrad develops the frame narrator in such a different way that, as so often happened in his writing, at some point the story began to change in a direction Conrad himself could not have predicted when he began it. Conrad recognized that this frequently occurred in his writing and seemed to view it as a positive thing, writing in the preface to *The Shorter Tales of Joseph Conrad,* "And things that 'just happen' in one's work seem impressive and valuable because they spring from sources profounder than the logic of a deliberate theory suggested by acquiring learning, let us say, or lessons drawn from analysed practice" (209). For a discussion of Marlow as a "transtextual character," see Greaney, 59.
20. Hampson makes his views on the frame narrator clear in the article already cited, and White describes him as "undiscerning" (181).
21. The line also appears to refer to H. M. Stanley, for, according to Hampson, "When Stanley arrived at Marseilles Railway Station (on 8 January 1878) after completing a journey from Zanzibar to Boma, he was met by emissaries of King Leopold II" (1995, 138n111).
22. That Marlow is responding to the frame narrator's words is made clear early in Marlow's narrative when, referring to the frame narrator's talk of knights-errant, Marlow says, "—You say Knights? Yes; but it is like a running blaze on a plain, like a flash of lightning in the clouds. We live in the flicker—may it last as long as the old earth keeps rolling! But there was darkness here yesterday" (49).
23. As Firchow notes, Marlow's account of the Roman conquest is naïve if not misleading. He writes, "Altogether Marlow's description of what Roman Britain was supposed to have been like seems, once one begins to look at it a little more closely, eccentric and even downright wrongheaded. His bald assertion, for example, that the Romans 'were no colonists' but mere admin-

istrators is at the very best a half truth. As virtually all nineteenth-century historians were agreed (and subsequent ones too, for that matter), the Romans settled or 'colonized' (and in the process thoroughly 'Romanized') that part of Britain that was eventually to become the heart of England, namely the southern and eastern parts" (90). "Wrongheadedness" like that which Firchow describes only affirms the frame narrator's implication that Marlow is unreliable.

24. Marlow's attitude should not be surprising, given the strength of nationalist feeling in the late nineteenth century. In the same edition of the *New Review* that the first installment of *The Nigger of the "Narcissus"* appeared in, for example, C. de Thierry praises the British Empire for being "founded on character" while disparaging the "hopeless incapacity" of the Germans and the spitefulness of the French (159–61). In *Greater Britain,* Charles Dilke celebrates the British Empire and Ango-Saxonism in even more hyperbolic terms, writing, for example, "The countries ruled by a race [the Saxons] whose very scum and outcasts have founded empires in every portion of the globe, even now consist of 9 1/2 millions of square miles, and contain a population of 300 millions of people. Their surface is five times as great as that of the empire of Darius, and four and a half times as large as the Roman Empire at its greatest extent. It is no exaggeration to say that in power the English countries would be more than a match for the remaining nations of the world whom in the intelligence of their people and the extent and wealth of their dominions they already considerably surpass. . . . Italy, Spain, France, Russia become pigmies by the side of such a people" (564–65).
25. For the purposes of this study, I define a *liberal critique* as one that criticizes a system from within, one that attacks elements of a system without challenging the system as a whole. A *radical critique,* in contrast, challenges the system from without; that is, it attacks not only elements of the system but the system as a whole.
26. For a detailed discussion of how a "literary text simultaneously asserts and denies the authority of its own rhetorical mode," see Paul de Man's "Semiology and Rhetoric" (230).
27. Eloise Knapp Hay writes that we are meant to "see through" Marlow in "both senses of the phrase": that is, we see Africa "through" Marlow's eyes and we must see "through" the "Marlovian fog" in order to glimpse the truth. The frame narrator suggests that we "see through" Marlow in a third sense: we must "see through" Marlow's conscious attempt to legitimate imperialism (1963, 133).
28. The frame narrator's suggestion that Marlow is not to be trusted, at least as an interpreter of his own experiences, is reinforced by Marlow's lie to the Intended, the significance of which the frame narrator highlights by inter-

rupting Marlow's narrative just before Marlow refers to it for the first time in chapter 2 so that Marlow's admission begins a new segment of his narrative (115). Towards the end of chapter 3, Marlow recounts the episode in more detail. Rather than tell the Intended the truth about Kurtz's end—that his last words were "The horror! The horror!" (149)—Marlow says, "The last word he pronounced was—your name" (161). The significance of the lie has been widely debated by critics. Thomas Moser, for example suggests that the Intended "does not *deserve* to hear the truth" (81, Moser's italics), and Ian Watt argues that the lie is "an appropriately ironic ending for Marlow's unhappy quest for the truth" (1979, 248). As far as Marlow's credibility is concerned, however, it is the fact of the lie that is important. As Christopher Lane suggests, it "casts doubt on the veracity of all his preceding statements" (403).

29. A number of critics, including Parry and Marianna Torgovnick, have analyzed Conrad's representation of women in relation to imperialism in some detail. In *Joseph Conrad,* Ruth Nadelhaft not only examines gender and empire as they are represented in *Heart of Darkness* but discusses feminist criticism of Conrad's work in general and Parry's and Torgovnick's criticism in particular.
30. Marlow, of course, is a hypocrite himself. Even though he asserts earlier that he "can't bear a lie," that lies have "a taint of death," that they make him "miserable and sick like biting into something rotten would do" (82), his lie to the Intended is one of several in the course of the story that he either tells or benefits from (Bode 29–30; Firchow 163–64). Marlow is thus implicated in the very types of behavior that he, as a liberal critic of imperialism, condemns. Although not overtly malevolent, Marlow is, as he himself recognizes, a liar and hypocrite, just like the "pilgrims" who consider themselves emissaries "of light" even though they have come to the Congo for profit.
31. Catherine Gallagher and Stephen Greenblatt briefly discuss the difficulties of ascertaining a work's ideological effects with any certainty: "An 'ideological effect' is not something a text contains in the same way a well contains water or a battery energy, to be drawn or tapped by any user. It is, rather, something that might occur in reading under certain conditions; when literary critics undertake ideological critique, they judge how texts might have affected hypothetical readers at different times and places, sometimes supplementing their accounts with other kinds of historical evidence" (170).
32. As Robert Haugh notes, most of the story's original reviewers "read it as a critique of Belgian colonialism, an issue that remained alive until Conrad's death and got attention in his obituary notices" (35). Indeed, the reviewer for the *Manchester Guardian* seems to be the only one to miss the critique of imperialism entirely, writing, "It must not be supposed that Mr. Conrad

makes attack upon colonization, expansion, even upon Imperialism. In no one is the essence of the adventurous spirit more instinctive. But cheap ideals, platitudes of civilization are shriveled up in the heat of such experiences" (Sherry 1973, 135).

33. In his later introductory essay to *Conrad's Prefaces to His Works,* Garnett seems to recognize the story's political significance: "*Heart of Darkness,* the second tale in *Youth,* was of European importance. In it Conrad, drawing on his own experiences in the Congo, had put in a long short-story what scores of travellers and investigators affirmed about the enslavement of the Congo peoples by their Belgian masters. But what reports and the evidence of Blue Books cannot do, *Heart of Darkness* did, by catching the infinite shades of deterioration in the white man's morale when he is freed from European restraint and planted down in the tropics to make trade profits out of black subject races" (13).
34. Najder notes that "*Youth* sold slightly better than *Lord Jim:* the first two editions (November 1902 and February 1903) amounted to 4,200 copies" (1983, 286).
35. As Nazareth (1982) indicates in the passage that serves as one of the epigraphs of this chapter, F. R. Leavis played in a critical role in the dehistoricization of *Heart of Darkness.* For a lengthy discussion of Leavis's influence, see Collits 51–66. See also Williams, 145.
36. Achebe's lecture, which he gave at the University of Amherst in February 1975, was later published in the *Massachusetts Review* in 1977. A revised version was published in 1987 and later included in the widely circulated Norton Critical Edition of *Heart of Darkness.*
37. For detailed discussions of changing responses to *Heart of Darkness,* see Peter Firchow's *Envisioning Africa* and Padmini Mongia's "The Rescue."

Chapter 6

1. Although readings of *Lord Jim* as an anti-imperialist text go back at least to Hay's *The Political Novels of Joseph Conrad* (1962), it was not until the 1990s that scholars began to view *Lord Jim* as postcolonial. In 1995, I presented a paper called "The End(s) of Imperialism: Marlow, Jim, and the Postcolonial Conrad" at the special international meeting of the Joseph Conrad Society of America at Kent State University, an expanded version of which appeared in *Conradiana* in 2000. Dryden's *Joseph Conrad and the Imperial Romance* also appeared in 2000, as did Robert Hampson's *Cross-Cultural Encounters in Joseph Conrad's Malay Fiction:* both offer suggestive new readings of *Lord Jim.* More recently, Stephen Ross and Terry Collits have published important studies of Conrad that include chapters on *Lord Jim.* Although Byron

Caminero-Santangelo's *African Fiction and Joseph Conrad* (2005) makes only a passing reference to *Lord Jim,* the study makes important connections between Conrad and later postcolonial writers; Caminero-Santangelo was also a participant in the 1995 Conrad meeting in Kent, Ohio, and contributed significantly to the reassessment of Conrad that took place there.

2. George Orwell treats the importance of appearing fearless in his celebrated essay "Shooting an Elephant," where he writes, "A white man mustn't be frightened in front of 'natives'; and so, in general, he isn't frightened" (2231). A number of critics, including Jameson, Miller, Dryden, and Collits, focus on the social implications of Jim's abandonment of the *Patna.* Jameson, for example, describes Jim's actions as undermining the ability of "a governing class to function and to assert its unity and legitimacy" (264).
3. As Hampson (2000) indicates, Jim's actions in Patusan parallel those of British colonists such as Thomas Raffles and James Brooke, particularly the latter (140). For an account of Brooke's "one-man imperialism," see Hampson 2000, 63–70.
4. In the original manuscript, part of which is housed at the Huntington Library in San Marino, California, Conrad indicates that these "experiments" included importing Chinese laborers to mine ore and organizing a police force.
5. Although Jim does not initiate either relationship, at least according to his own account, both relationships appear to play into his fantasies of being a white lord. In any case, as Hawthorn (1990) suggests, Jim's relationship with Jewel is typical of the imperialist "sexual exploitation of 'native' women" (188).
6. The scene in which Marlow tells Doramin that Jim will never leave Patusan represents a point at which Marlow's interpretation is particularly suspect. Even though Marlow himself recognizes that Doramin "cherished the hope of seeing his son ruler of Patusan," Marlow seems to think that Doramin wants Jim to remain in Patusan permanently (164). Accordingly, when he insists to Doramin that Jim will never leave Patusan, Marlow misses the irony when Doramin responds, "This was good news indeed," and then misinterprets Doramin and his wife's disappointment as disbelief.
7. D. C. R. A. Goonetilleke (1977) asks whether the "Malayans" in *Lord Jim* are nationalists and concludes that they are not. To me, a more interesting question is whether they are becoming nationalists—whether a national consciousness is emerging.
8. In characterizing Jim's death as a "romantic suicide" (192), Dryden misses some of its political implications. Jim may indeed be acting out a romantic fantasy, as Dryden, Ross, and others observe, but he is also asserting superiority as a white man, thereby affirming one of the main tenets of imperialist

ideology. See Ross, 110–13, for a Lacanian reading of Jim's death as a "final" act of "evasion" from the "paternal function" of empire.

9. As Conrad himself indicates in a letter to Edward and Garnett, he constructed the text so as "to obtain a sort of lurid light" out of the "events" he describes, a light that would expose not only the self-serving nature of imperialism but the inevitability of its end (*Letters* 2:302; see also 198).
10. There is, of course, the possibility that Jim's end is based partly on that of Gordon. Gordon's death may well have fascinated Conrad, since Gordon was widely celebrated as a martyr by British imperialists. Indeed, as Mark Girouard notes in *The Return to Camelot,* Gordon's death in 1885 "was a catalyst which did as much as anything to create imperialism as a mass emotion" (229). Girouard further notes that "biographies poured from the press in his praise" (229) and that Gordon's contemporaries likened him to everyone from King Arthur and Lancelot to Thomas More and David Livingstone. Conrad may well have been responding to such hyperbole in *Lord Jim.*
11. As Hampson (2000) notes, the colonialist discourse Marlow's narrative represents is also undercut by the text's representation of other histories and cultures (145).
12. Dryden describes the ending of the novel as "self-conscious melodrama," arguing that Jim takes "pride and evident self-satisfaction" in his "'heroic' death" (192). Jameson also describes the Patusan of the novel in terms of melodrama (216).
13. Hawthorn (1979) interprets the phrase "one of us" in a similar manner, suggesting that it refers to "the solidarity of the colonialists" (42).
14. Hawthorn (1990) makes a similar argument, relating Jim's romantic fantasies to those of Carlier and Kayerts in "An Outpost of Progress" (162).
15. At a couple of points, Marlow does acknowledge Jim's love of written romances but makes little of it (141, 143). To him, Jim is a true romantic rather than a deluded one.
16. Boo Eung Koh argues that Doramin is a "comprador" rather than an "authentic native" (173). For Doramin to be a comprador, however, his power would have to rest not "upon its own strength but . . . upon the imperial power for its existence," as Koh concedes. Doramin, however, is established well before Jim arrives and is in the process of becoming the dominant power in Patusan as more Bugis—such as Tamb' Itam—enter the area. It is also not clear whom Koh considers "authentic" natives. The context suggests that he means the Malays, since he calls the Rajah the rightful ruler. The Malays themselves, however, are invaders, having driven the Dyaks into the interior.
17. McClure offers an alternative reading of Jim's execution, suggesting that Doramin's "exertions" as he rises to shoot Jim have "an emblematic quality": "his uprising, painful, enraged, and only barely successful, may be seen

as epitomizing Conrad's view of colonial rebellions in general" (130). He adds that "Conrad's view is a deeply pessimistic one" and that Doramin is "the vengeful representative of a shattered tradition." While I agree that Doramin's exertions are indeed emblematic, I think they represent revolution rather than rebellion and that Doramin represents a new postcolonial order rather than a "shattered tradition."

18. Although Dryden's interpretation of the novel is generally consistent with my own, she interprets Jim's death and its implications differently: "We are . . . left to conclude that the Patusan of the latter part of the novel, the utopia which Jim regarded as 'the work of his own hands,' will disintegrate into the political chaos of the days before his arrival. With Dain Waris dead, Doramin stricken by grief, and the white Tuan no longer there to protect the people with his mythic reputation, there is nothing to prevent a return to the strife and tyranny that Jim ended" (194).
19. Najder reports that the first impression of 2,100 copies sold out in two months but that the second impression, which numbered only 1,050 copies, lasted four years (1983, 271).
20. In his introduction to the Penguin edition of *Lord Jim* (1986), Cedric Watts neatly summarizes critical response to the novel: "On its appearance in book form, *Lord Jim* was widely and often lengthily reviewed. Some reviews were hostile, but the majority were highly encouraging. Repeatedly Conrad was praised for his vividness, distinctiveness, flair, subtlety; the richness and diversity of characterization were frequently noted. The most controversial area was the narrative technique. Some readers objected that Marlow's narration was implausibly lengthy: he was telling the after-dinner story to his companions for eleven solid hours, grumbled the *Academy.* More important was consideration of the narrative's seeming vagrancy as it moved to and fro in time, collecting first one view of Jim, then another; progressing while apparently digressing. In the *Daily Telegraph,* W. L. Courtney complained that the method of story telling adopted in *Lord Jim,* the constant wandering from the point, the recurrent introductions of incidents, which do not affect the main issue, are distinctly weakening to the general aim of the book. The *Sketch* added: "*Lord Jim* is an impossible book—impossible in style" (118).
21. Modernism, of course, involves much more than difficulty. As Leonard Diepeveen demonstrates in *The Difficulties of Modernism,* however, difficulty was strongly associated with modernism from the very beginning and continues to be so today: "Modernism's difficulty set up the terms and protocols by which readers read and gained access to modernist texts, and it became a litmus test: one could predict both a given reader's response to modernism by his or her reaction to the difficulty, and a writer's place in the canon by the difficulty of his or her work. Modern difficulty was a powerful aesthetic, then.

It continues to be one, for aesthetic difficulty retains its legitimizing force today. Modern difficulty has profoundly shaped the entire twentieth century; one's ability to move in high culture continues to depend, in large part, on how one reacts to difficulty" (xi).

Chapter 7

1. A number of critics note the change in Conrad's narrative style but attribute it to other causes. For example, Michael Greaney follows Albert Guérard in arguing that the shift in Conrad's narrative strategies resulted from his "growing mastery of the language and fiction of his adopted homeland" (115). Greaney goes on to argue that Conrad uses anecdote and other marginalized speech genres to interrogate "the traditional wisdom of oral culture and the impersonalities of modernist *écriture*" (134).
2. Brantlinger asserts that Conrad had "reactionary political attitudes," noting that in *Heart of Darkness,* Conrad "mourns the loss of the true faith in modern times, the closing down of frontiers, the narrowing of the possibilities for adventure, the commercialization of the world and art, the death of chivalry and honor" (274). Although he believes that the "anti-imperialist message" of *Heart of Darkness* is undercut by Conrad's racism, among other things, he still finds in the text a "moral idealism" that exceeds that of any other modernist text.
3. Although Conrad's political attitudes changed considerably between 1885, when he wrote this letter, and 1895, when he published his first novel, his attitude toward popular democracy does not seem to have changed much, at least not by 1904, since in *Nostromo,* he demonstrates how easily it can lead to "Caesarism," or what he also refers to as "imperial democracy" (325).
4. Although Lenin's *Imperialism* is now considered outdated by many Marxist theorists, it had considerable influence on many postcolonial writers, including Peter Nazareth and Ngugi wa Thiong'o. For more on Lenin's influence on postcolonial writers and theorists, see Neil Larsen's "Imperialism, Colonialism, and Postcolonialism."
5. That Conrad and Graham were particularly close while Conrad was writing *Nostromo* is evidenced by the fact that Conrad dedicated "Typhoon" to him, telling Graham in a letter of May 9, 1903, that he considered it "a public declaration of [their] communion." For more on the relationship between Conrad and Graham, see Watts 1969, 3–36; and GoGwilt 2000, 144–55.
6. In a letter written more than three weeks later, Conrad again uses the knitting-machine metaphor, suggesting just how central it was to his thinking at the time. Referring to the ending of "An Outpost of Progress," in which Kayerts hangs himself from a cross with his tongue sticking out, he writes:

"'Put the tongue out' why not? One ought to really. And the machine will run on all the same. The question is, whether the fatigue of the muscular exertion is worth the transient pleasure of indulged scorn. On the other hand one may ask whether scorn, love, or hate are justified in the face of such shadowy illusions. The machine is thinner than air and as evanescent as a flash of lightning" (*Letters* 2:16).

7. Frederick Karl and Laurence Davies translate this passage as follows: "Man is a vicious animal. His viciousness must be organised. Crime is a necessary condition of organised existence. Society is fundamentally criminal—or it would not exist. Selfishness preserves everything—absolutely everything—everything we hate and everything we love" (*Letters* 2:160).
8. Andrea White writes that Conrad's "willingness to view the imperial project in disinterested ways was reflected in the work of a growing number of writers" that, because of "its unpopularity and low visibility . . . constituted something of an underground movement" (195). As GoGwilt (2000) demonstrates, Garnett attempted to organize the movement into something more visible through the Over-Seas Library, a series of books to be published by T. Fisher Unwin's firm that would directly contest imperialist ideology (141–43).
9. Gould's function within capitalism is, of course, very different from Kurtz's. Though they both become acquisition machines, Gould acquires capital, while Kurtz acquires commodities that are converted to capital for the benefit of people of Gould's class.
10. Eloise Knapp Hay (1996) suggests that Emilia Gould is a hero of sorts, arguing that in refusing to let Nostromo tell her where the treasure is hidden, she "takes upon herself a public responsibility" (93). As I shall argue presently, however, in the end Gould proves to be as ineffectual and absurd as all of the other central characters.
11. Terry Collits, too, sees "remarkable affinities" between Conrad's view of history and Marx's, arguing that "*Nostromo*'s world-view is no more deterministic than Marx's" (152).
12. For a discussion of Conrad's attitudes toward history as reflected in *Nostromo,* see Cooper, 147–50.
13. Conrad's belief that history was a function of economics is reflected not only in his letters to Graham but in "Autocracy and War."
14. Avrom Fleishman identifies another way in which not only Nostromo but also Decoud can be identified as a tragic hero, arguing that "the very social rootedness of the individualistic hero contains the contradictions which destroy him" (164).
15. Sid Ray argues that the African woman has set up a "reciprocal relationship with Kurtz": "Only with the help of her people in raiding other villages, for

example, can Kurtz procure ivory when he runs out of supplies to barter with" (151).

16. See, for example, Achebe's *No Longer at Ease,* Soyinka's *The Interpreters,* and Thiong'o's *Petals of Blood.*
17. Whether the novel ends where it began has, of course, been the subject of great debate since the late 1940s. For a discussion of this debate, see Watt 1988, 70–72.
18. Fleishman makes a similar argument, noting that "it is possible to read (though by no means to exhaust) *Nostromo* as a record of the transition from precapitalist to capitalist—and, prospectively, to postcapitalist—society." He does so by analyzing "the main characters in the novel as representatives of . . . [various] social classes" (171).
19. Surprisingly, perhaps, even Collits, who sees *Nostromo* as more "politically advanced" than Conrad's earlier works, does not find in the novel any indication that Conrad "detect[ed] in the world around him the dawn of a new order" (158, 146).
20. For more on Conrad's relationship with Pinker, see Wexler, 41–48.
21. Conrad was not the only one who believed that he had finally established himself professionally, for in a letter to Garnett of October 15, 1904, Cunninghame Graham writes, "Success has not spoiled Conrad" (quoted in Watts 1969, 156).
22. Later that winter, Conrad's confidence began to dim, in part because he was unable to place *Romance,* a novel he wrote together with Ford Madox Ford, as a serial as he had expected to (*Letters* 3:11, 16). By this time, he was fully committed to *Nostromo,* however, a synopsis of which he had already sent to *Harper's* in hopes of getting the novel serialized (*Letters* 3:17).
23. For detailed discussion of the structure of *Nostromo* and Conrad's use of irony in it, see Watts 1993, 144–58; and Lothe 1989, 175–225.
24. As Watts notes, Graham's opinion on the ending of *Nostromo* was very similar to Garnett's. In a letter to Garnett of October 31, 1904, Graham writes: "Certainly the last chapters are a mistake . . . To me, the interest is in the affairs of Costaguana, & the monologue of the inimitable Captain Mitchell would have been a fit ending" (quoted in Watts 1969, 159).

Chapter 8

1. Derrida was a Sephardic Jew raised in Algeria. He came to France when he was nineteen. For more on how Derrida can be understood as a colonial subject, see Gayatri Spivak's translator's preface to *Of Grammatology.*
2. Mongia (2005) identifies Conrad as a "colonial" writer. Following Asako Nakai, she argues that rather than write like Conrad, later postcolonial writers

"write back" to him, "using aspects of his fiction to tell alternative stories of the people and places with which Conrad familiarized a British reading public" (88).

3. See Mongia 2005, Bhabha 1994, and Said 1993 for more on these critics' respective takes on Conrad and his work.
4. For a brilliant if idiosyncratic study of postcolonial irony, see W. H. New's *Grandchild of Empire.*
5. In his recent study of Conrad's influence on African fiction, Caminero-Santangelo argues that writers such as Chinua Achebe, Ngugi wa Thiong'o, and Tayeb Salih, among others, are Conrad's descendants in a different sense. Rather than "write back" to Conrad as most postcolonial critics claim, these novelists, Caminero-Santangelo demonstrates, incorporate "Conradian elements" into their narratives so as "to intervene in specific repressive (often neocolonial) situations in late twentieth century postcolonial Africa and how these elements were transformed in the process" (4).
6. Miller outlines irony's performative functions in his foreword to *Conrad in the Twenty-First Century.* See also Laurence Davies's outstanding essay on Conrad's use of irony in the same volume. Miller himself builds on Davies's argument in his foreword.

Works Cited

Achebe, Chinua. "An Image of Africa: Racism in Conrad's *Heart of Darkness.*" *Heart of Darkness.* 3rd ed. Ed. Robert Kimbrough. New York: W. W. Norton, 1996. 251–62.

Adams, David. *Colonial Odysseys: Empire and Epic in the Modernist Novel.* Ithaca: Cornell University Press, 2003.

Ahmad, Aijaz. *In Theory: Classes, Nations, Literatures.* London: Verso, 1994.

Ashcroft, Bill, Gareth Griffiths, and Helen Tiffin. *The Empire Writes Back: Theory and Practice in Post-Colonial Literatures.* New York: Routledge, 1989.

Atkinson, William. "Bound in Blackwood's: 'The Heart of Darkness' in its Immediate Context." *Twentieth-Century Literature* 50.4 (2004): 368–93.

———. Introduction. *The Lagoon and Other Stories.* Oxford: Oxford University Press, 1997. vii–xxiii.

Baines, Jocelyn. *Joseph Conrad: A Critical Biography.* New York: McGraw-Hill, 1960.

Bakhtin, M. M. *The Dialogic Imagination.* Ed. Michael Holquist. Trans. Caryl Emerson and Michael Holquist. Austin: University of Texas Press, 1981.

Batchelor, John. *Lord Jim.* London: Unwin Hyman, 1988.

Beckson, Karl. *Arthur Symons: A Life.* Oxford: Clarendon Press, 1987.

Berton, Pierre. *The Arctic Grail: The Quest for the North West Passage and the North Pole.* New York: Lyon, 2000.

Bhabha, Homi K. "The Commitment to Theory." *New Formations* 5 (1988): 5–23.

———. *The Location of Culture.* New York: Routledge, 1994.

Billy, Ted. *A Wilderness of Words: Closure and Disclosure in Conrad's Short Fiction.* Lubbock: Texas Tech University Press, 1997.

Blackburn, William, ed. *Joseph Conrad: Letters to William Blackwood and David S. Meldrum.* Durham: Duke University Press, 1958.

Bode, Rita. "'They . . . Should Be Out of It': The Women of *Heart of Darkness.*" *Conradiana* 26.1 (1994): 20–34.

Boehmer, Elleke. *Colonial and Postcolonial Literature: Migrant Metaphors.* New York: Oxford University Press, 1995.

Booth, Howard, and Nigel Rigby. *Modernism and Empire.* Manchester: Manchester University Press, 2000.

Bradbury, Malcolm, and James McFarlane, ed. *Modernism: A Guide to European Literature, 1890–1930.* New York: Penguin, 1991.

Brantlinger, Patrick. *Rule of Darkness: British Literature and Imperialism, 1830–1914.* Ithaca: Cornell University Press, 1988.

Burt, Daniel. *The Literary 100: A Ranking of the Most Influential Novelists, Playwrights, and Poets of All-Time.* New York: Checkmark, 2001.

Caminero-Santangelo, Byron. *African Fiction and Joseph Conrad: Reading Postcolonial Textuality.* Albany: State University of New York Press, 2005.

Carabine, Keith. Introduction. *Joseph Conrad: Selected Short Stories.* Ware: Wordsworth, 1997. vii–xxvii.

Chadha, Yogesh. *Gandhi: A Life.* New York: John Wiley & Sons, 1997.

Chakrabarty, Dipesh. *Provincializing Europe: Postcolonial Thought and Historical Difference.* Princeton: Princeton University Press, 2000.

Chamberlain, Joseph. "The True Conception of Empire." *Mr. Chamberlain's Speeches.* Ed. Charles W. Boyd. Boston: Houghton Mifflin, 1914. 1–6.

Cheng, Vincent J. *Joyce, Race, and Empire.* Cambridge: Cambridge University Press, 1995.

Chow, Rey. "Where Have All the Natives Gone?" *Contemporary Postcolonial Theory: A Reader.* Ed. Padmini Mongia. New York: Hodder Arnold, 1996. 122–46.

Chrisman, Laura. *Reading the Imperial Romance: British Imperialism and South African Resistance in Haggard, Schreiner, and Plaatje.* Oxford: Clarendon Press, 2000.

Clifford, James. *The Predicament of Culture: Twentieth-Century Ethnology, Literature, and Art.* Cambridge: Harvard University Press, 1988.

Collits, Terry. *Postcolonial Conrad: Paradoxes of Empire.* New York: Routledge, 2005.

Conrad, Joseph. *Almayer's Folly: A Story of an Eastern River.* Ed. Floyd Eugene Eddleman and David Leon Higdon. Cambridge: Cambridge University Press, 1994.

———. "Amy Foster." *Typhoon and Other Stories.* New York: Doubleday, Page, 1924. 105–42.

———. "Autocracy and War." *Notes on Life and Letters.* New York: Doubleday, Page, 1924. 83–114.

———. "The Black Mate." *Tales of Hearsay.* New York. Doubleday, Page, 1925. 85–120.

———. "Books." *Notes on Life and Letters.* New York: Doubleday, Page, 1924. 3–10.

———. *The Collected Letters of Joseph Conrad.* Vol. 1. Ed. Frederick Karl and Laurence Davies. Cambridge: Cambridge University Press, 1983.

———. *The Collected Letters of Joseph Conrad.* Vol. 2. Ed. Frederick Karl and Laurence Davies. Cambridge: Cambridge University Press, 1986.

———. *The Collected Letters of Joseph Conrad.* Vol. 3. Ed. Frederick Karl and Laurence Davies. Cambridge: Cambridge University Press, 1988.

———. *The Collected Letters of Joseph Conrad.* Vol. 4. Ed. Frederick Karl and Laurence Davies. Cambridge: Cambridge University Press, 1990.

———. "The Crime of Partition." *Notes on Life and Letters.* New York: Doubleday, Page, 1924. 115–40.

———. "Geography and Some Explorers." *Last Essays.* London: J. M. Dent & Sons, 1926. 1–31.

———. "Heart of Darkness." *"Youth" and Two Other Stories.* New York: Doubleday, Page, 1924. 45–162.

———. "The Idiots." *Tales of Unrest.* New York: Doubleday, Page, 1924. 56–85.

———. "Karain: A Memory." *Tales of Unrest.* New York: Doubleday, Page, 1924. 3–55.

———. "The Lagoon." *Tales of Unrest.* New York: Doubleday, Page, 1924. 187–204.

———. *Lord Jim.* Ed. Thomas C. Moser. 2nd ed. New York: W. W. Norton, 1996.

———. *The Nigger of the "Narcissus."* Ed. Robert Kimbrough. New York: W. W. Norton, 1979.

———. *Nostromo: A Tale of the Seaboard.* New York: Doubleday, Page, 1924.

———. *An Outcast of the Islands.* New York: Doubleday, Page, 1924.

———. "An Outpost of Progress." *Tales of Unrest.* New York: Doubleday, Page, 1924. 86–117.

———. Preface to *The Nigger of the "Narcissus."* Ed. Robert Kimbrough. New York: W. W. Norton, 1979. 145–48.

———. Preface to *The Shorter Tales of Joseph Conrad. Last Essays.* London: J. M. Dent & Sons, 1926. 205–16.

———. "Youth: A Narrative." *"Youth" and Two Other Stories.* New York: Doubleday, Page, 1924. 3–42.

Cooper, John X. "Nostromo." *A Joseph Conrad Companion.* Ed. Leonard Orr and Ted Billy. Westport: Greenwood, 1999. 125–63.

Cope, E. D. *The Origin of the Fittest: Essays on Evolution.* New York. Appleton, 1887.

Cudjoe, Selwyn R. "A. R. F. Webber: West Indian Nationalist and the First Novelist of Trinidad and Tobago." *Those That Be in Bondage: A Tale of Indian Indentures and Sunlit Western Waters.* Wellesley: Calaloux Publications, 1988.

Davies, Laurence. "'The Thing Which Was Not' and That Thing That Is Also: Conrad's Ironic Foreshadowing." *Conrad in the Twenty-First Century: Contemporary Approaches and Perspectives.* Ed. Carola M. Kaplan, Peter Lancelot Mallios, and Andrea White. New York: Routledge, 2005.

De Alva, Jorge. "The Postcolonization of the (Latin) American Experience: A Reconsideration of 'Colonialism,' 'Postcolonialism,' and 'Mestizaje.'" *After Colonialism: Imperial Histories and Postcolonial Displacements.* Ed. Gyan Prakash. Princeton: Princeton University Press, 1995. 241–75.

DeKlerck, E. S. *History of the Netherland East Indies.* Vol. 2. W. L. & J. Brusse: Rotterdam, 1938.

De Man, Paul. "Semiology and Rhetoric." *Critical Theory since 1965.* Ed. Hazard Adams and Leroy Searle. Tallahassee: Florida State University Press. 222–30.

Derrida, Jacques. *Writing and Difference.* Trans. Alan Bass. Chicago: University of Chicago Press, 1978.

De Thierry, C. "Colonial Empires." *The New Review* (June 1897): 151–62.

Diepeveen, Leonard. *The Difficulties of Modernism.* New York: Routledge, 2003.

Dilke, Charles. *Greater Britain.* London: Macmillan, 1869.

Dryden, Linda. *Joseph Conrad and the Imperial Romance.* New York: St. Martin's, 2001.

Duffy, Enda. *The Subaltern Ulysses.* Minneapolis: University of Minnesota Press, 1994.

Eagleton, Terry. *Criticism and Ideology: A Study of Marxist Literary Theory.* London: Verso, 1978.

Erdinast-Vulcan, Daphna. *The Strange Short Fiction of Joseph Conrad: Writing, Culture, and Subjectivity.* New York: Oxford University Press, 1999.

Emerson, Barbara. *Leopold II of the Belgians: King of Colonialism.* New York: St. Martin's, 1979.

Fanon, Franz. *Black Skin, White Masks.* Trans. Charles Lam Markmann. London: Pluto, 1986.

Fernando, Lloyd. "Conrad's Eastern Expatriates: A New Version of His Outcasts." *Joseph Conrad: Third World Perspectives.* Ed. Robert Hamner. Washington, D.C.: Three Continents Press, 1990. 59–78.

Firchow, Peter Edgerly. *Envisioning Africa: Racism and Imperialism in Conrad's "Heart of Darkness."* Lexington: University of Kentucky Press, 2000.

Fleishman, Avrom. *Conrad's Politics: Community and Anarchy in the Fiction of Joseph Conrad.* Baltimore: Johns Hopkins University Press, 1967.

Ford, Ford Madox. *Joseph Conrad: A Personal Remembrance.* New York: Ecco Press, 1989.

Fothergill, Anthony. "The Poetics of Particulars: Pronouns, Punctuation, and Ideology in *Heart of Darkness.*" *Conrad's Literary Career.* Ed. Keith Carabine, Owen Knowles, and Wieslaw Krajka. Boulder: Eastern European Monographs, 1992. 57–73.

"Franklin, Sir John." *Encyclopedia Britannica.* 9th ed. 1890.

Fraser, Gail. *Interweaving Patterns in the Works of Joseph Conrad.* Ann Arbor: UMI Research Press, 1988.

———. "The Short Fiction." *The Cambridge Companion to Joseph Conrad.* Ed. John H. Stape. Cambridge: Cambridge University Press, 1996. 25–44.

Friedman, Alan Warren. "Conrad's Picaresque Narrator." *Marlow.* Ed. Harold Bloom. New York: Chelsea, 1992. 61–79.

Froude, James Anthony. *English Seamen in the Sixteenth Century.* London: Longmans, Green, 1917.

Gallagher, Catherine, and Stephen Greenblatt. *Practicing New Historicism.* Chicago: University of Chicago Press, 2001.

Gandhi, M. K. *Hind Swaraj and Other Writings.* Ed. Anthony J. Parel. Cambridge: Cambridge University Press, 1997.

Garland, Hamlin. "We Visit Joseph Conrad." *Joseph Conrad: Interviews and Recollections.* Ed. Martin Ray. Iowa City: University of Iowa Press, 1990. 490–95.

Garnett, Edward. "Introductory Essay." *Conrad's Prefaces to His Works.* 1937. Ed. Edward Garnett. New York: Haskell House, 1971. 3–34.

———. *Letters from Joseph Conrad.* 1928. Ed. Edward Garnett. Indianapolis: Charter, 1956.

Ghosh, Sarath Kumar. *The Prince of Destiny or the New Krishna.* London: Rebman, 1909.

Girouard, Mark. *The Return to Camelot.* New Haven: Yale University Press, 1981.

GoGwilt, Christopher. *Broadcasting News from Nowhere: The Fiction of Geopolitics.* Stanford: Stanford University Press, 2000.

———. "Conrad's Alien Genealogies: Joseph Conrad's 'Karain: A Memory,' Pramoedya Ananta Toer, and Postcolonial Perspectives." *Western Humanities Review* 52.2 (1998): 99–109

———. *The Invention of the West: Joseph Conrad and the Double-Mapping of Europe and Empire.* Stanford: Stanford University Press, 1995.

———. "Pramoedya's Fiction and History: An Interview with Indonesian Novelist Pramoedya Ananta Toer." *Yale Journal of Criticism* 9.1 (1996): 147–64.

Goonetilleke, D. C. R. A. *Developing Countries in British Fiction.* London: Macmillan, 1977.

———. *Joseph Conrad: Beyond Culture and Background.* New York: St. Martin's Press, 1990.

Gordon, John. *Joseph Conrad: The Making of the Novelist.* 1940. New York: Russell & Russell, 1963.

Graver, Lawrence. *Conrad's Short Fiction.* Berkeley: University of California Press, 1969.

Greaney, Michael. *Conrad, Language, and Narrative.* Cambridge: Cambridge University Press, 2002.

Griffith, John W. *Joseph Conrad and the Anthropological Dilemma: "Bewildered Traveller."* Oxford: Clarendon Press, 1995.

Guérard, Albert J. *Conrad the Novelist.* Cambridge: Harvard University Press, 1958.

Hammond, James Henry. "Letter to an English Abolitionist." *The Ideology of Slavery: Proslavery Thought in the Antebellum South, 1830–1860.* Ed. Drew Gilpin Faust. Baton Rouge: Louisiana State University Press, 1981. 168–205.

Hamner, Robert. "The Enigma of Arrival in 'An Outpost of Progress.'" *Conradiana* 33.3 (2001): 171–87.

Hampson, Robert. *Cross-Cultural Encounters in Joseph Conrad's Malay Fiction.* Houndmills: Palgrave, 2000.

———. Introduction. *Heart of Darkness.* Ed. Robert Hampson. New York: Penguin, 1995. ix–xliv.

———. *Joseph Conrad: Betrayal and Identity.* New York: St. Martin's, 1992.

———. "'An Outpost of Progress': The Case of Henry Price." *Conrad in Africa: New Essays on "Heart of Darkness."* Ed. Attie de Lange and Gail Fincham with Wieslaw Krajka. Boulder: Social Science Monographs, 2002. 211–30.

Hannay, David. "The Case of Mr. Doughty." *Blackwood's Edinburgh Magazine,* June 1898, 796–808.

Harper, William. "Memoirs on Slavery." *The Ideology of Slavery: Proslavery Thought in the Antebellum South, 1830–1860.* Ed. Drew Gilpin Faust. Baton Rouge: Louisiana State University Press, 1981. 78–135.

Harpham, Geoffrey Halt. *One of Us: The Mastery of Joseph Conrad.* Chicago: University of Chicago Press, 1996.

Harris, Wilson. "The Frontier on Which 'Heart of Darkness' Stands." *Research on African Literature* 12 (1981): 86–92.

Harrison, Nicholas. *Postcolonial Criticism: History, Theory, and the Work of Fiction.* London: Blackwell, 2003.

Hart, Michael. "The Subaltern Ulysses." *Modernism/Modernity* 2.3 (1995): 182–83.

Haugh, Robert. *Joseph Conrad: Discovery in Design.* Norman: University of Oklahoma Press, 1957.

Hawkins, Hunt. "Conrad and the Psychology of Colonialism." *Conrad Revisited: Essays for the Eighties.* Ed. Ross Murfin. Tuscaloosa: University of Alabama Press, 1985. 71–87.

Hawthorn, Jeremy. *Joseph Conrad: Language and Fictional Self-Consciousness.* Lincoln: University of Nebraska Press, 1979.

———. *Joseph Conrad: Narrative Technique and Ideological Commitment.* New York: Edward Arnold, 1990.

———. "Power and Perception in Joseph Conrad's Political Fiction: The Gaze and the Other." *Conrad at the Millennium: Modernism, Postmodernism, and Postcolonialism.* Ed. Gail Fincham and Attie de Lange with Wieslaw Krajka. Boulder: Social Science Monographs, 2001. 279–308.

Hay, Eloise Knapp. "Cities like Whited Sepulchres." *Conrad's Cities: Essays for Hans van Marle.* Ed. Gene M. Moore. Atlanta: Rodopi, 1992. 125–37.

———. *"Nostromo." The Cambridge Companion to Joseph Conrad.* Ed. J. H. Stape. New York: Cambridge University Press, 1996. 81–99.

———. *The Political Novels of Joseph Conrad: A Critical Study.* Chicago: University of Chicago Press, 1963.

———. "Reconstructing 'East' and 'West' in Conrad's Eyes." *Contexts for Conrad.* Ed. Keith Carabine, Owen Knowles, and Wieslaw Krajka. Boulder: Eastern European Monographs, 1993. 21–40.

Hennessy, Maurice. *The Congo: A Brief History.* New York: Praeger, 1961.

Hervoet, Yves. *The French Face of Joseph Conrad.* Cambridge: Cambridge University Press, 1990.

Hilson, J. C., and D. Tim. "Conrad's 'An Outpost of Progress' or, the Evil Spirit of Civilization." *Joseph Conrad: Third World Perspectives.* Ed. Robert Hamner. Washington, D.C.: Three Continents Press, 1990. 107–16.

Hochschild, Adam. *King Leopold's Ghost: A Story of Greed, Terror, and Heroism in Colonial Africa.* Boston: Houghton Mifflin, 1998.

Holquist, Michael. Glossary to *The Dialogic Imagination,* by M. M. Bakhtin. Ed. Michael Holquist. Austin: University of Texas Press, 1981.

Homer. *The Odyssey.* Trans. Robert Fitzgerald. New York: Farrar, Straus and Giroux, 1998.

Huggan, Graham. *The Postcolonial Exotic: Marketing the Margins.* New York: Routledge, 2001.

Hulme, Peter. "Including America." *Ariel* 26.1 (1995): 117–23.

Hunter, Allan. *Joseph Conrad and the Ethics of Darwinism.* Kent: Crom Helm, 1983.

Hutcheon, Linda. "'Circling the Downspout of Empire': Post-Colonialism and Postmodernism." *Ariel* 20.4 (1989): 149–75.

Jameson, Fredric. *The Political Unconscious: Narrative as a Socially Symbolic Act.* Ithaca: Cornell University Press, 1981.

Johnson, Bruce. "Conrad's 'Karain' and *Lord Jim.*" *Lord Jim.* 1st ed. Ed. Thomas Moser. New York: W. W. Norton, 1996. 462–70.

Jones, Susan. *Conrad and Women.* Oxford: Clarendon Press, 1999.

Keating, Peter. *The Haunted Study.* London: Secker and Warburg, 1989.

Kingsley, Mary. *West African Studies.* New York: Barnes & Noble, 1964.

Kipling, Rudyard. "The Man Who Would Be King." *The Phantom 'Rickshaw and Other Stories. Kipling's Works.* Vol. 2. New York: P. F. Collier and Son, 1920. 107–71.

Koh, Boo Eung. "Contradictions in Colonial History in *Lord Jim.*" *Conradiana* 28.3 (1996): 163–78.

Krenn, Heliéna. *Conrad's Lingard Trilogy: Empire, Race, and Women in the Malay Novels.* New York: Garland, 1990.

Krupabai, Satthianadhan. *Kamala: The Story of a Hindu Child-Wife.* Ed. Chandani Lokugé. New York: Oxford University Press, 1998.

Lane, Christopher. "Almayer's Defeat: The Trauma of Colonialism in Conrad's Early Work." *Novel: A Forum for Fiction* 32.3 (1999): 401–23.

Larsen, Neil. "Imperialism, Colonialism, Postcolonialism." *A Companion to Postcolonial Studies.* Ed. Henry Schwarz and Sangeeta Ray. London: Blackwell, 2000. 23–52.

Leavis, F. R. *The Great Tradition.* 1948. New York: New York University Press, 1964.

Lester, John. "A Fictional Chronology of Conrad's Eastern World." *Conradiana* 15.1 (1993): 65–71.

Lewis, Pericles. *Modernism, Nationalism, and the Novel.* Cambridge: Cambridge University Press, 2000.

Lindfors, Bernth. Introduction. *The Wild Hunter in the Bush of the Ghosts.* Ed. Bernth Lindfors. Washington, D.C.: Three Continents Press, 1982. xi–xviii.

Lokugé, Chandani. Introduction. *Kamala: The Story of a Hindu Child-Wife.* Oxford: Oxford University Press, 2004. 1–18.

Loomba, Ania. *Colonialism/Postcolonialism.* New York: Routledge, 1998.

Lothe, Jakob. "Conradian Narrative." *The Cambridge Companion to Joseph Conrad.* Ed. J. H. Stape. Cambridge: Cambridge University Press, 1996. 160–78.

———. *Conrad's Narrative Method.* Oxford: Clarendon Press, 1989.

Louis, William, and Jean Stengers. *E. D. Morel's "History of the Congo Reform Movement."* Oxford: Clarendon Press, 1968.

Lutoslawski, Wincenty. "A Visit to Conrad in 1897." *Joseph Conrad: Interviews and Recollections.* Ed. Martin Ray. Iowa City: University of Iowa Press, 1990. 89–94.

Lyon, John. Introduction. *"Youth," "Heart of Darkness," "The End of the Tether."* Ed. John Lyon. New York: Penguin, 1995. vii–xlv.

Maisonnat, Claude. "Alterity and Suicide in 'An Outpost of Progress.'" *Conradiana* 28.2 (1996): 101–14.

Marle, Hans van. "Jumble of Facts and Fiction: The First Singapore Reactions to *Almayer's Folly.*" *Joseph Conrad: Third World Perspectives.* Ed. Robert Hamner. Washington D.C.: Three Continents Press, 1990. 29–35.

McClintock, Anne. *Imperial Leather: Race, Gender and Sexuality in the Colonial Contest.* New York: Routledge, 1995.

McClure, John. *Kipling and Conrad: The Colonial Fiction.* Cambridge: Harvard University Press, 1981.

McLauchlan, Juliet. "Almayer and Willems—'How Not to Be.'" *Joseph Conrad: Third World Perspectives.* Ed. Robert Hamner. Washington, D.C.: Three Continents Press, 1990. 79–106.

Menikoff, Barry. *Robert Louis Stevenson and "The Beach of Falesá": A Study in Victorian Publishing.* Stanford: Stanford University Press, 1984.

Merciful, Allah M. "holla back." *Pace Press,* November 2, 2000, 8.

Meyer, Jeffrey. *Orwell: Wintry Conscience of a Generation.* New York: W. W. Norton, 2000.

Miller, J. Hillis. *Fiction and Repetition: Seven English Novels.* Cambridge: Harvard University Press, 1982.

———. Foreword. *Conrad in the Twenty-First Century: Contemporary Approaches and Perspectives.* Ed. Carola M. Kaplan, Peter Lancelot Mallios, and Andrea White. New York: Routledge, 2005. 1–14.

———. "*Lord Jim:* Repetition and Subversion of Organic Form." *Lord Jim.* 2nd ed. Ed. Thomas Moser. New York: W. W. Norton, 1996. 439–53.

Mongia, Padmini. "Between Men: Conrad in the Fiction of Two Contemporary Indian Writers." *Conrad in the Twenty-First Century: Contemporary Approaches and Perspectives.* Ed. Carola M. Kaplan, Peter Lancelot Mallios, and Andrea White. New York: Routledge, 2005. 85–99.

———. "The Rescue: Conrad, Achebe, and the Critics." *Conradiana* 33.2 (2001): 53–63.

Moore, Gene M. "Conrad's Influence." *The Cambridge Companion to Joseph Conrad.* Ed. J. H. Stape. Cambridge: Cambridge University Press, 1996. 223–41.

Morel, Edmund. *King Leopold's Rule in Africa.* Westport: Negro Universities Press, 1904.

Morson, Gary Saul, and Caryl Emerson. *Mikhail Bakhtin: Creation of a Prosaics.* Stanford: Stanford University Press, 1990.

Moser, Thomas. *Joseph Conrad: Achievement and Decline.* Cambridge: Harvard University Press, 1957.

Mukherjee, Meenakshi. "The Beginnings of the Indian Novel." *A History of Indian Literature in English.* Ed. Arvind Krishna Mehrotra. New York: Columbia University Press, 2003. 92–102.

———. *The Perishable Empire: Essays on Indian Writing in English.* Oxford: Oxford University Press, 2000.

Nadelhaft, Ruth. Introduction. *Nostromo.* Ed. Ruth Nadelhaft. Orchard Park: Broadview, 1997. 7–29.

———. *Joseph Conrad.* Atlantic Highlands: Humanities Press International, 1991.

Najder, Zdzislaw. *Conrad in Perspective: Essays on Art and Fidelity.* Cambridge: Cambridge University Press, 1997.

———. *Conrad's Polish Background.* Oxford: Oxford University Press, 1964.

———. "Introduction to 'The Congo Diary' and the 'Up-river Book.'" *Heart of Darkness.* Ed. Thomas C. Moser. 2nd ed. New York: W. W. Norton, 1988. 155–59.

———. *Joseph Conrad: A Chronicle.* New Brunswick: Rutgers University Press, 1983.

Nazareth, Peter. "Conrad's Descendents." *Conradiana* 22.2 (1990): 101–9.

———. "Out of the Darkness: Conrad and Other Third World Writers." *Conradiana* 14.3 (1982): 173–87.

Nelles, William. "'Youth,' *Heart of Darkness,* and *Lord Jim:* Reading Conrad's Trilogy." *Conradiana* 35.1–2 (2003): 63–73.

New, W. H. *Grandchild of Empire: About Irony, Mainly in the Commonwealth.* Vancouver: Ronsdale, 2003.

Newbold, Henry John. "Conrad and the Royal Bounty Fund." *Joseph Conrad: Interviews and Recollections.* Ed. Martin Ray. Iowa City: University of Iowa Press, 1990.

Nikambe, Shevantibai. *Ratanbai: A High-Caste Child-Wife.* Oxford: Oxford University Press, 2004.

Orwell, George. "Shooting an Elephant." *Norton Anthology of English Literature.* Vol. 2. 6th ed. Ed. M. H. Abrams. New York: W. W. Norton, 1993. 2228–33.

The Oxford Companion to English Literature. Ed. Margaret Drabble. Oxford: Oxford University Press, 1998.

Paranjape, Makarand. Afterword. *Rantanbai: A High-Caste Child-Wife.* Ed. Chandani Lokugé. Oxford: Oxford University Press, 2004. xi–xli.

Parry, Benita. *Conrad and Imperialism.* London: Macmillan, 1983.

———. "Problems in Current Theories of Colonial Discourse. *The Postcolonial Studies Reader.* Ed. Bill Ashcroft, Gareth Griffiths, and Helen Tiffin. New York: Routledge, 1995. 36–44.

Porter, Bernard. *Critics of Empire: British Racial Attitudes to Colonialism in Africa, 1895–1914.* New York: St. Martin's, 1968.

Pratt, Mary Louise. *Imperial Eyes: Travel Writing and Transculturation.* New York: Routledge, 1992.

Pugh, Edwin. "Joseph Conrad as I Knew Him." *Joseph Conrad: Interviews and Recollections.* Ed. Martin Ray. Iowa City: University of Iowa Press, 1990. 96–99.

Rajan, Rajeswari Sunder. Preface. *The Postcolonial Jane Austen.* Ed. You-me Park and Rajeswari Sunder Rajan. New York: Routledge, 2004. xi–xiii.

Rao, Nagesh. "Resistance and Representation: Postcolonial Fictions of Nations in Crisis." *Postcolonial Text* 1.1 (2004), http:journals.sfu.ca/pocol/index.php/pct/issue/7.

Ray, Sid. "Marlow(e)'s Africa: Postcolonial Queenship in Conrad's *Heart of Darkness* and Marlowe's *Dido, Queen of Carthage.*" *Conradiana* 38.2 (2006): 143–61

Redmond, Eugene B. "Racism, or Realism? Literary Apartheid, or Poetic License? Conrad's Burden in *The Nigger of the 'Narcissus.'*" *The Nigger of the "Narcissus."* Ed. Robert Kimbrough. New York: W. W. Norton, 1979. 358–68.

Reilly, Jim. *Shadowtime: History and Representation in Hardy, Conrad, and George Eliot.* New York: Routledge, 1993.

Ribeiro de Oliveira, Solange. "The Woman in White and the Man in Motley: Aspects of Hybridism in Conrad's *Almayer's Folly* and "Heart of Darkness." *Joseph Conrad: East European, Polish and Worldwide.* Ed. Wieslaw Krajka. Boulder: Eastern European Monographs, 1999. 257–75.

Richardson, Brian. "Conrad and Posthumanist Narration: Fabricating Class and Consciousness Onboard the *Narcissus.*" *Conrad in the Twenty-First Century: Contemporary Approaches and Perspectives.* Ed. Carola M. Kaplan, Peter Lancelot Mallios, and Andrea White. New York: Routledge, 2005.

———. "Introduction: Conrad and the Reader." *Conradiana* 35.1–2 (2003): 1–5.

Roberts, Andrew Michael, ed. *Joseph Conrad.* London: Longman, 1998.

Ross, Stephen. *Conrad and Empire.* Columbia: University of Missouri Press, 2004.

Ruppel, Richard. "'The Lagoon' and the Popular Exotic Tradition." *Contexts for Conrad.* Ed. Keith Carabine, Owen Knowles, and Wieslaw Krajka. Boulder: Eastern European Monographs, 1993. 177–88.

Rushdie, Salman. *The Satanic Verses.* New York: Henry Holt, 1988.

Said, Edward. *Culture and Imperialism.* New York: Knopf, 1993.

———. "Through Gringo Eyes: With Conrad in Latin America." *Harper's Magazine,* February 1988, 70–72.

Sandison, Alan. *Robert Louis Stevenson and the Appearance of Modernism: A Future Feeling.* New York: St. Martin's, 1996.

Schaffer, Brian. "Joseph Conrad's *The Nigger of the 'Narcissus.'*" *A Joseph Conrad Companion.* Ed. Leonard Orr and Ted Billy. Portsmouth, N.H.: Greenwood Press, 1999. 49–64.

Schneider, Lissa. *Conrad's Narratives of Difference: Not Exactly Tales for Boys.* New York: Routledge, 2003.

Schwarz, Daniel R. *Conrad: "Almayer's Folly" to "Under Western Eyes."* Ithaca: Cornell University Press, 1980.

Sewlall, Harry. "The Postcolonial Space in Joseph Conrad: A Consideration of Two Early Novels." *Journal of Literary Studies* 19.1 (2003): 33–52.

Sharpe, Jenny. "Figures of Colonial Resistance." *Modern Fiction Studies* 35.1 (1989): 137–55.

Sheldon, Michael. *Orwell: The Authorized Biography.* New York: HarperCollins, 1991.

Sherry, Norman. *Conrad: The Critical Heritage.* London: Routledge & Kegan Paul, 1973.

———. *Conrad's Eastern World.* Cambridge: Cambridge University Press, 1966.

Simmons, Allan H. "The Art of Englishness: Identity and Representation in Conrad's Early Career." *The Conradian* 29.1 (2004): 1–26.

———. "'Conflicting Impulses': Focalization and the Presentation of Culture in 'Almayer's Folly.'" *Conradiana* 29.3 (1997): 163–73.

Sinfield, Alan. *Literature, Politics, and Culture in Postwar Britain.* Berkeley: University of California Press, 1985.

Spivak, Gayatri Chakravorty. "Can the Subaltern Speak?" *Colonial Discourse and Post-Colonial Theory: A Reader.* Ed. Patrick Williams and Laura Chrisman. New York: Columbia University Press, 1994. 66–111.

———. *The Spivak Reader.* Ed. Donna Landry and Gerald Maclean. New York: Routledge, 1995.

Stevenson, Robert Louis. "The Beach of Falesá." *Fictions of Empire.* Ed. John Kucich. Ann Arbor: University of Michigan Press, 2003. 187–245.

Strachey, Lytton. *Eminent Victorians.* New York: Random House, 1918.

Thiong'o, Ngugi wa. 1997. *Writers in Politics: A Re-Engagement with Issues of Literature and Society.* London: Heinemann, 1997.

Torgovnick, Marianna. *Gone Primitive: Savage Intellects, Modern Lives.* Chicago: University of Chicago Press, 1990.

Trollope, Anthony. *The West Indies and the Spanish Main.* 1859. London: Cass, 1968.

Ulekke, Bernard. *Nusantara, A History of the Philippines.* Chicago: Quadrangle Books, 1960.

Virgil. *The Aeneid.* Trans. Robert Fitzgerald. New York: Vintage, 1990.

Vreeland, Nena, Geoffrey Hurwitz, Peter Just, Philip Moeller, and R. S. Shinn. *Area Handbook for the Philippines.* Washington: U.S. Government Printing Office, 1976.

Wallenstein, Jimmy. "*Heart of Darkness:* The Smoke-and-Mirrors Defense." *Conradiana* 29.3 (1997): 205–21.

Watt, Ian. *Conrad in the Nineteenth Century.* Berkeley: University of California Press, 1979.

———. Introduction. *Almayer's Folly: A Story of an Eastern River.* Ed. Floyd Eugene Eddleman and David Leon Higdon. Cambridge: Cambridge University Press, 1994. xxi–lxiv.

———. *Joseph Conrad: Nostromo.* Cambridge: Cambridge University Press, 1988.

Watts, Cedric. "Conrad and the Myth of the Monstrous Town." *Conrad's Cities: Essays for Hans van Marle.* Ed. Gene M. Moore. Atlanta: Rodopi, 1992. 17–30.

———. Introduction. *Lord Jim.* New York: Penguin, 1986. 11–30.

———. *Joseph Conrad: A Literary Life.* New York: St. Martin's, 1989.

———. *Joseph Conrad's Letters to R. B. Cunninghame Graham.* London: Cambridge University Press, 1969.

———. *A Preface to Conrad.* New York: Longman, 1993.

Watts, Cedric, and Laurence Davies. *Cunninghame Graham: A Critical Biography.* Cambridge: Cambridge University Press, 1979.

Webber, A. R. F. *Those That Be in Bondage: A Tale of Indian Indentures in Sunlit Western Waters.* Wellesley: Calaloux Publications, 1988.

Wells, H. G. "Wat Shall We Do with Thesa Things?" *Joseph Conrad: Interviews and Recollections.* Ed. Martin Ray. Iowa City: University of Iowa Press, 1990. 109–12.

Wexler, Joyce Piell. *Who Paid for Modernism? Art, Money, and the Fiction of Conrad, Joyce, and Lawrence.* Fayetteville: University of Arkansas Press, 1997.

White, Andrea. *Joseph Conrad and the Adventure Tradition: Constructing and Deconstructing the Imperial Subject.* Cambridge: Cambridge University Press, 1993.

Willan, Brian. *Sol Plaatje: South African Nationalist, 1876–1932.* Berkeley: University of California Press, 1984.

Williams, Raymond. *The English Novel from Dickens to Lawrence.* Oxford: Oxford University Press, 1970.

Wollaeger, Mark A. *Joseph Conrad and the Fictions of Skepticism.* Stanford: Stanford University Press, 1990.

Young, Robert J. C. *Colonial Desire: Hybridity in Theory, Culture and Race.* New York: Routledge, 1995.

Young, Shannon, and Tom Henthorne. "'Never Be Led by a Female': Masculinity and Power in Plaatje's *Mhudi.*" *Journal of Commonwealth and Postcolonial Studies.* 8.1–2 (2001): 163–83.

Index